D0245681

— THE —
PARANORMAL
SOURCE BOOK

-8. JUL 10

15 8

WITHDRAWN FROM STOCK

0749914114 3 132 5B

THE PARANORMAL SOURCE BOOK

The Comprehensive Guide to Strange Phenomena Worldwide

JENNY RANDLES

LEICESTERSHIRE LIBRARIES AND INFORMATION SERVICE
REFERENCE & INFORMATION LIBRARY HUMANITIES

PIATKUS

© 1996 Jenny Ruddles
First published in 1996 by
Judy Piatkus (Publishers) Ltd
5 Windmill Street, London W1P 1HF

First paperback edition 1996

The moral right of the author has been asserted

A catalogue for this book is available from the British Library

ISBN 0−7499−1640−0 hbk
ISBN 0−7499−1411−4 pbk

Edited by Esther Jagger
Designed by Paul Saunders

Data capture and manipulation by
Phoenix Photosetting, Chatham, Kent
Printed and bound in Great Britain by
Bookcraft Ltd, Midsomer Norton, Somerset

LEICESTERSHIRE LIBRARIES AND INFORMATION SERVICE	
0749914114 3 132	
J M L S	27/11/96
133	£9.99

CONTENTS

PICTURE CREDITS

Permission to use copyright material is gratefully acknowledged to the following:

Line artworks:
page 41: Editions Michel Chomarat, Lyon, France; *page 57*: Paul Saunders; *page 83*: Fortean Picture Library; *page 93*: Mary Evans Picture Library.

Black and white photographic pages:
page 1: (top) Mary Evans Picture Library; (bottom) Jenny Randles; *page 2*: (top) Jenny Randles; (bottom) Fortean Picture Library; *page 3*: (both) Fortean Picture Library; *page 4*: (top) Fortean Picture Library; (bottom) Mary Evans Picture Library; *page 5*: Mary Evans Picture Library; *page 6*: English Heritage/Dover Castle; *page 7*: Scope Features; *page 8*: (top) Jenny Randles; (bottom) Mirror Syndication International.

Whilst every effort has been made to trace all copyright holders, the publishers apologise to any holders not acknowledged.

INTRODUCTION

What is the paranormal?

To many people this question may seem self-evident. They think of ghosts and psychic phenomena, or visualise weird lights floating through the sky. Indeed, the world is filled with mystery and wonder and all of us seem fascinated and not a little frightened by that fact.

However, the paranormal is also a vast area of human knowledge, ranging from things that lie on the borderline of acceptance by modern science to phenomena that most stalwarts of academia would term nonsense – not always without good cause. The subject spans the entire history of the human race from the days when our ancestors scratched symbols on to the walls of caves in southern Europe and stared awestruck at twinkling stars, pondering the meaning of life, the inevitability of death or the seemingly eternal nature of the universe.

Although we have come a long way in the past few million years, humans are still climbing slowly up the ladder of understanding. For each fantastic discovery that we make, new questions arise to challenge our intellect. In a sense this is why the paranormal is so exciting, because it reaches beyond what is known and into the huge expanse of the unknown. It examines theories and ideas that are not yet fact – and which may indeed never become fact. For every paranormal phenomenon that gets accepted into the world of knowledge there are a dozen others that remain, and perhaps will always remain, in the realms of mumbo-jumbo.

Of course, nobody makes progress of any kind without making mistakes, and it is perfectly legitimate to ask strange questions about our bizarre experiences. Even if the answers that we propose are not always correct, we can often learn more from what we do wrong than from getting it right first time around. So, yes, the world of the supernatural will lead us up more than a few blind alleys, but every now and then it will also illuminate some startling new aspect of a cosmos that is filled with mystery – something that can only ever be unlocked by those who dare to seek out and to wonder.

One of the reasons why scientists are in general so wary of those who pursue strange phenomena is that the pursuers rarely appreciate the limitations of truth. But that caveat applies on either side of this age-old argument. Truth is, indeed, a relative thing. If a biologist says that all life is extinguished when an organism stops exhibiting brainwave activity, then that is a truth – in a biological sense. But does it necessarily negate the opinion of the Spiritualist who may recognise biological science but perceive another kind of life beyond the physical which is not quite so closely connected to time and energy? On the other hand, those who delve into the paranormal have a tendency, as the Reverend Charles Dodgson (alias fantasy writer Lewis Carroll) knew only too well, to believe in a dozen impossible things before breakfast-time.

Just because some claims about the paranormal have a basis in truth does not mean that everything written about UFOs, ghosts or reincarnation must be correct. Far from it – most things will be unprovable and even irresponsible and, just as scientists and agnostics need to learn to apply more broad-minded thinking to the incredulity that surrounds them, so do paranormal adherents need to know when to stop assuming that the mundane and the normal can never apply to a weird story. There can be – and often are – simpler explanations for why something strange has been reported.

Five centuries ago medicine was little different from what today we might call witchcraft, using herbal remedies and barbaric treatments because it was believed that such things worked. Today we know that sometimes these cures were based on knowledge way ahead of themselves and were actually beneficial. A tea made from knitbone comfrey or a similar substance may contain natural chemicals that hundreds of years ago no one could identify or analyse or re-create artificially. Yet even then the sceptics of the day challenged such cures as ridiculous. (Of course, on occasions these sceptics were absolutely right, and some medical practices are best left well in the past!) Today this same process occurs in a different guise. Aspirin, for a long time used just as an analgesic, to relieve pain, also has helpful properties in the limitation of heart disease. It is our twentieth-century equivalent of knitbone – achieving a purpose that nobody understood for a time, but succeeding none the less.

Some of what today we term 'the paranormal' will one day be accepted as completely normal. We will teach it to our children in school and forget that it was ever in doubt or regarded as the province of social outcasts. A century ago not even the wisest scientist on earth knew about nuclear energy, and yet all life on earth depended upon it. This process is, after all, what fuels the sun. That sun had shone for several billion years irrespective of how little we knew about its make-up. Indeed, many things which to us now seem second nature, and various complex processes that we harness or duplicate in laboratories, would have seemed like little more than magic had you tried to explain them to the greatest minds of the Victorian age.

When Benjamin Franklin played with a kite in a thunderstorm he may not have realised the full dangers of what he was doing, but he was pioneering the taming of electricity several generations later. What was then a fad which aroused suspicion in the minds of many scientists is now the basis of much of our technological world. Incredible things are possible today only because a few heretics were willing to face ridicule and stand by their seemingly absurd ideas. It will probably be so with some aspects of the paranormal. We may not grasp today what we can do with the knowledge that could emerge when we unravel why some people spontaneously combust – if, indeed, they ever really do. But such a recognition of new scientific information could revolutionise all our lives in completely unexpected ways. Equally, we might prefer UFOs to be the product of friendly aliens riding in to rescue our misguided planet; but if, instead, they reflect natural energies within the atmosphere waiting to be tapped, who knows whether that outcome may not prove far more important than would a fleeting visit from ET.

This is what my book sets out to chart. I hope to help you steer a course between the myths and the mysteries, the facts and the fantasies, and to enable you to assess in realistic terms what there is about the paranormal that is worth getting excited about. Whether you are a witness who has seen something remarkable and wonders what to do with that disturbing reality, a researcher who wishes to delve deeper into a particular element of the supernatural, or simply someone in need of source material to probe topics out of interest or necessity – it is my hope that this will be the book to set you on your way.

Some things I can safely predict for those who use it as a stepping stone into the supernatural. If you thought that the world was well mapped out and had lost much of its mystery in our rational age, think again. If you believed that the paranormal was merely the province of deluded minds engaged in wishful thinking, you will be proved wrong. And if you want a passport into a magical, mysterious, challenging realm without the need for expensive air fares, or even a university degree to understand what it all means, that opportunity is at your fingertips right now.

For the paranormal is indeed the greatest undiscovered country on earth – a true lost world amidst twentieth-century technology and human self-confidence. You are about to enter some very wild frontier country. Be sure to hold on to your hat.

HOW TO USE THIS BOOK

Topics are presented in alphabetical order and cover many of the most interesting phenomena that span the boundaries of the known and the unknown. First, as you might expect, come a definition and brief history of the subject under consideration. These are followed by two further articles. The first, aimed at witnesses who might have experienced something of this sort, offers helpful ideas on how to cope with the phenomenon in question and what to do next. The second article is directed more at researchers who might wish to pursue the topic further, and offers guidelines on the best approach. A comprehensive look at worldwide research associations in these fields includes appropriate contact details and an annotated bibliography to allow you to study each subject further. These factually based sections are accompanied in each case by an up-to-date status report which aims to provide the very latest and best evidence, from case histories to research projects, all of which sets the phenomenon in its modern context and tells you what is happening at the cutting edge of this field.

Although this book sets out to be as comprehensive as possible, it would not be tenable to include all the associations within each field of research. Such a list would fill several volumes and be very tedious to read, and would quickly become out-of-date. In any event, the calibre of research into the paranormal varies enormously and it would be irresponsible of me to promote every organisation simply on the grounds that it exists. I have therefore taken the following course.

Within each subject under review I include the primary organisations on a worldwide basis. The choice is mine and the fault for omissions (of which there will be some) is also mine.

Some topics are, of course, more popular than others, and this is reflected in the number of groups – sometimes hundreds, located in most major cities of the world. In such cases the reference list of organisations given in the book is inevitably selective, and I know that I have omitted some worthy groups simply for reasons of space. If you feel that your group is doing fine work in any of the areas described and you believe that you should have been included, please let me know. I will do my best to consider your recommendation for the next edition. The same applies to publications and reference books. I would be delighted to consider suggestions about titles that I may have missed out.

Please remember that there is a great deal of interaction between the topics covered, and if a group or publication is listed under one heading there is every chance that its work will also be relevant to others. I have aimed to design the index to help with cross-referencing. It should enable you to check out a number of related topics and possibly find an organisation or magazine that is more convenient for you and may prove helpful in your particular area of interest. Bear in mind that magazines may also serve as investigation outlets.

Finally, if you report your experiences to me at the address given below I will forward them, on your request, to a responsible and relevant organisation that covers your area. If you enclose a stamped self-addressed envelope (UK) or an international reply coupon (elsewhere) I will send you details of newly founded or more local organisations that may allow you to pursue an interest further. Meanwhile, whatever mystery you choose to probe – good hunting!

Jenny Randles
c/o 11 Pike Court
Fleetwood
Lancashire
FY7 8QF
UK

ALIEN ABDUCTIONS

DEFINITION

Sometimes known as spacenappings, or more commonly just as abductions, these are claims of being kidnapped by alien entities, who usually take their human captives into a strange place described as being full of magical light. This is often interpreted by the percipient as a room inside a UFO or unidentified flying object. The abduction almost always takes place against the will of the victim, who is usually female and rarely older than thirty-five. The most common scenarios for the onset of an abduction are when the witness is in bed in the early hours of the morning or in some other quiet environment, such as driving alone late at night.

Whilst multiple abductions are known, usually involving several members of one family or a small group of friends, the majority occur to individuals. Almost 80 per cent of known cases come from the USA, although there are strong pockets of activity in Britain and South America and growing numbers in eastern Europe and Australasia. There are hardly any cases known from China, Japan, India or elsewhere in the Far East.

Around half the victims have required special treatment, such as regressive hypnosis, attempting to piece together a more coherent memory from the fragmented images held within the conscious recall of the witness. However, most witnesses have some recollection – if only that a period of time has vanished from their life following a UFO encounter, or as images from strange dreams in which frightening figures appear.

Alien abductions appear to have post-dated the start of the UFO mystery by at least a decade. Before 1957 no sure cases were reported at the time they occurred, although some were claimed retrospectively which were not remembered by abductees until more recent investigation was carried out. Three-quarters of all known abductions have occurred since 1980, and researchers agree that there is now an epidemic of increasing proportions. However, they disagree on whether this represents a real increase in the number of cases or merely a rise in the discovery of reports that were previously too well repressed by the conscious mind for them to be retrievable.

An opinion poll undertaken by the Roper organisation in the USA in 1992 suggested that several million abductees may exist in that country, at a time when under 1000 had been recorded by research groups. Most investigators suspect that fewer than one in ten cases – perhaps as few as one in a hundred – are ever made public by their victims, who, contrary to popular misconception, are very rarely intererested in fame and fortune or talking openly about their encounter. Indeed, they frequently feel they are the victims of abuse, and post-abduction psychological profiles have shown strong similarities with those taken from victims of rape.

HISTORICAL REVIEW

Some researchers, such as Jacques Vallée and Hilary Evans, have drawn parallels between abduction stories and similar accounts based on mythological concepts like fairy lore and demonology. In these latter cases witnesses said they had been taken by strange entities into a realm where time and space were very different, after which they were returned to their normal environment. People who saw the victims during these encounters often reported that they were in a trance-like state or were possessed.

It is a matter of conjecture whether these similarities imply that modern-type abductions have occurred for centuries and were previously misperceived as demonic in nature – or, indeed, whether a form of psychological experience has always occurred which has simply altered in context according to changing cultural beliefs. The same symptoms reported in 1596 would probably be given a wholly different evaluation by both witness and researcher from those of a case taking place in the space-orientated days of 1996. On the other hand, the similarities may be more apparent than real, and true alien abductions might not have begun until what seems to be the first recorded instance, in 1957.

Sexual relationships

In October that year a Brazilian farmhand called Antonio Villas Boas (see photograph opposite page 26) was captured, whilst working late at night on his tractor, by smallish humanoids and was then seduced by a red-headed female who yelped like a dog. Since that time abduction accounts have persistently focused on sexual reproduction. This may cement a relationship with other historical precedents such as the incubus, an invisible demon lover said to possess its victims in the dead of night (see the supposedly true-life horror movie *The Entity* or the *Star Trek: The Next Generation* episode 'The Child', in which councillor Deanna Troi conceives an alien baby in these circumstances).

In the Villas Boas case the female entity claimed that she was attempting to become inseminated by the human. In what proved to be the second case of alien abduction, reported before the Villas Boas story was published but after it had been investigated by a Brazilian doctor, the theme continued. In September 1961 a married couple from New England, Betty and Barney Hill, were driving home through the White Mountains from a holiday in Canada when they saw a strange object in the sky. Only after they got home did they realise that more than an hour was missing from their recall. However, it was psychiatric treatment given for persistent nightmares of pasty faces with cat-like eyes, and the consequent tension that these caused, that led to revelations about an abduction. When Dr Benjamin Simon of Boston regressed both witnesses over several months, a memory emerged in which Barney claimed that sperm samples had been taken and Betty described a probe of her sexual organs by small entities who had telepathically advised that this was a 'pregnancy test'.

A growing phenomenon

Cases soon began to trickle in from all over the world, including one from Venezuela in 1965 in which a gynaecologist was contacted by tall beings who claimed they were attempting to establish a genetic programme to breed an alien–human hybrid. Many of the stories, which were told completely independently of one another, slotted together in an eerie fashion. However, the vast majority were being reported in the USA, where regression hypnosis was occasionally employed along the lines adopted by Simon as a means of attempting to unravel the missing memories of a UFO encounter.

Psychologist Dr Leo Sprinkle was the first to set up a systematic programme, after being called in by a government-funded UFO research team then at the University of Colorado. He regressed state trooper Herb Schirmer, who in December 1967 had encountered a UFO beside a country road in Ashland, Nebraska. The entities had claimed they were engaged in evaluating some kind of breeding process, but Schirmer was merely given information to retain in his subconscious mind for future reference and anticipated further contacts with the entities – a curious scenario that was becoming commonplace.

Awareness gradually spread, first in the American UFO community and then to the rest of the world. Britain recorded its first abduction cases between 1974 and 1977, and various European countries also did so at about this time. Australia was slower to respond, but by the mid-eighties, when researchers were looking for such stories with gusto, they were definitely in evidence. Many felt that these tales had always been present, but were not being uncovered owing to reluctance outside the USA to utilise controversial techniques such as hypnosis. Indeed, in 1988 British researchers even imposed a moratorium on its use.

Books and movies

In Steven Spielberg's 1977 movie *Close Encounters of the Third Kind* he worked closely with UFOlogists to create a realistic story-line based on actual cases. The abduction theme was included, albeit in far more dramatic fashion than in real life, when the young child Barry was snatched into a giant craft surrounded by broiling clouds. Sexual elements were not included, as they were generally unrecognised even by those UFOlogists who took abduction research seriously.

Spielberg's title was based on a UFO classification scheme that pioneer researcher Dr J. Allen Hynek had developed: the third kind of encounter was one involving the sighting of alien entities. After the film's success a sequel was planned, set during the on-board abduction phase; Hynek, as Spielberg's consultant, discussed it with UFO researchers. The idea that it might be called *Close Encounters of the Fourth Kind* emerged from amendments and additions to the Hynek system discussed with him by Jenny Randles and others. Although the movie has not yet been made, that term – or CE IV as it is often called – is now in widespread use amongst UFOlogists to describe an alien abduction.

In 1982 a New York artist, Budd Hopkins, became one of the first researchers to write a book exclusively on abductions. *Missing Time* described half a dozen cases that he had studied, many with the aid of psychiatrist Dr Aphrodite Clamar. His theme was that there could be hundreds of hidden abductees who had no idea about their true status because their memory of events was repressed. The book ignited a little more interest in the UFO world, but scarcely any in the world at large.

Then, at Christmas 1985, a successful horror novelist called Whitley Strieber was given a present, apparently as a family joke since he had no interest in the subject. It was a copy of a book by Peter Warrington and me called *Science and the UFOs*, based on an article on Hopkins's embryonic work that we had written in *New Scientist* magazine. Strieber realised that scattered nightmare images lurking in his mind could represent a memory of an actual abduction experience. He met Budd

Hopkins, began therapy and unravelled a complex web of missing memories. These were published in 1987 in his powerful autobiography, *Communion*, subsequently a movie. The book was advertised with posters of the strange little triangular-faced aliens that Strieber had recalled, and its extraordinary success ensured that nobody could be unaware of alien abduction. Indeed, tens of thousands of people now tried to link odd memories from their past with the possibility that they had been spacenapped. UFOlogists were soon besieged.

Budd Hopkins found fame in the wake of Strieber's success. His second book, *Intruders*, about the invasion of an Indiana family by spacenapping aliens, appeared in 1987 and led to a 1992 TV mini-series. Although heavily fictionalised, it owed something to the reality that Hopkins and others were recording. This was followed in 1993 by *Fire in the Sky*, a movie that dramatised a true-life abduction from Arizona in 1975, concentrating less on the minutiae of the abduction itself than on the social drama that surrounded it. But perhaps the best fictional rendition of abduction came in the 1992 *Star Trek: The Next Generation* episode 'Night Terrors', which successfully places the phenomenon in a future setting.

The scientific perspective

In June 1992 an in-camera scientific symposium was staged at the Massachusetts Institute of Technology. The week-long debate was organised by an MIT physicist and Dr John Mack, a highly respected psychologist from Harvard Medical School. About a hundred researchers came together to present reports on key cases and original experiments, many of which had been carried out just for the symposium. The proceedings aimed to be a milestone in abduction research, and when published in early 1995 they revolutionised serious scientific research into the alien abduction mystery. Dr Mack laid his reputation on the line in 1994 with the release of his own case history notebook, called simply *Abduction*. Given his high profile it was very influential and attracted serious attention such as a November 1994 BBC *Horizon* documentary which sought medical explanations of the phenomenon in the brain's temporal lobe.

In less than a decade the field had moved on from a minor aspect of UFOlogy to a topic of lively debate among scientists – even if mostly from a sceptical perspective. At least, nowadays, few people doubt that alien abductions do occur – the only questions are how we should interpret their meaning and whether to seek their nature within outer or inner space.

EXPERIENCING ABDUCTIONS

An alien abduction is one of the most traumatic paranormal experiences. It generally happens out of the blue and the victim wishes it had not occurred. As repercussions on witnesses are often similar to those suffered by rape victims they may feel repressed and isolated, looking for someone to blame, even themselves, and feeling tainted by the episode. The situation is made worse because relatively few people can accept the reality of abduction cases, let alone empathise with the victim. Therefore, it is common to push the memory deep inside, not even to share it with close family members, and to suffer nightmares, tension and years of anguish as a result.

However, there are several things to bear in mind. First, there is no evidence that, even if aliens are behind the abductions, they are hostile towards us. The experience may have seemed unpleasant, but this is often a result of the extreme fear felt by the witness, not of the encounter itself. Similarly, if the solution is found in terms of psychology or physiology, there is no reason to suspect delusional or even physical illness. Nearly all studies have suggested that CE IV witnesses are of above average intelligence, visually creative, generally healthy and in most cases completely rational and sincere.

Many fears focus on other members of the family. Women may be afraid that their children will become targets, for example. However, it is important not to convey such anxieties, acute though they may be, since they can have a detrimental effect on the family.

Self-help and hypnotic regression

It is a very good idea to share the experience as soon as possible. This may be with one's closest friend, husband or partner, and can significantly reduce the tension that will otherwise darken the aftermath of an abduction. Seeking out a responsible researcher to listen to the story is useful. Check out the books and organisations listed here, but establish beforehand that confidentiality will be guaranteed and that the researcher's priority is the witness and not the case. Ask if they have a code of practice, as do some groups such as BUFORA in Britain or the Australian Center for UFO Studies.

Certain groups, particularly in the USA, either operate with, or can put witnesses in contact with, a self-help meeting which allows them to talk with other spacenapping victims. It may prove beneficial to share experiences with others who have undergone similar traumas. In addition Ann Druffel, via MUFON in the USA, has defined a number of techniques to try to ward off subsequent abductions should a witness fear that they might occur. These involve exercises in mental self control which can block out what is either contact with an alien intelligence or intrusion from one's own subconscious. Whilst the success of these techniques is a matter of debate, some people may wish to try them. You can now even take out insurance against being abducted – some researchers, however, feel this is a gimmick and are cautious. Some of the American-based insurers argue that such policies offer genuine peace of mind to spacenap victims, though quite how it is established that someone really has been abducted seems unclear.

Many people with scattered memories, dream images or chunks of missing time read popular books about abductions and seek out regression hypnosis as the key. Before doing so they should read in the specialist medical literature about the limitations and pitfalls of hypnosis, paying attention to problems such as *false memory syndrome* (see index for this and other undefined terms). Hypnosis is not a magic wand; whilst it can retrieve memories it is just as likely to provoke fantasies, and a witness may not be able to tell one from the other. If witnesses can live with this uncertainty they may still wish to be regressed to the missing time, but it should always be in the full knowledge that they may end up more – not less – confused. Although many UFO groups will direct abductees to hypnotists, they may not have medical training. It is up to the witness whether to pursue research with a person who cannot provide proper credentials, but the previously mentioned code of practice – which all too few UFO groups have yet adopted – insists upon medically qualified persons being present to protect the abductee's welfare. I would advise nothing less.

Above all, it should be recognised that positive spin-offs often come from claimed abductions. Witnesses not uncommonly find their artistic prowess enhanced. An extremely good way to overcome the trauma is to use it to pour out your feelings in painting or writing, for example. Many abductees have found this the best, easiest (and cheapest) therapy of all.

RESEARCHING ABDUCTIONS

These days it is far from uncommon for a witness to approach a researcher, suggesting that she or he might have been abducted. It is important for the researcher to establish up front why the witness believes this, and what books she might have read or TV dramas she may have watched. These are frequently the spur that drives witnesses to the UFOlogist and leads to the desire to unravel missing time, usually via hypnosis sessions.

It can be very tempting to plunge headlong into such work. Abductions are, after all, the most amazing stories. They are certain to gain researchers kudos with their colleagues, may even lead to lucrative book or film deals and, more altruistically, seem to be keys that unlock the deeper mysteries of the UFO phenomenon.

However, it is essential to remember that, as a researcher, you are dealing with a human being first and a strange case second. To researchers, retrieving 'facts' via hypnosis to add to their knowledge or prove a theory such as alien contact may seem all-important. To the witness it represents the opening of a box that can never be shut again. Yet out of this box may come disturbing images that the mind has locked away for genuine psychological reasons. Leaving someone high and dry, to live the rest of their life coping with all this, is not what researchers should be doing.

In any case, if a witness is led into this minefield without adequate safeguards such as medical support, it is only a matter of time before the researcher is called to task. In recent years the USA has seen the discovery of false memory syndrome, in which hypnosis is blamed (rightly or wrongly) for generating, rather than retrieving, a memory of, for instance, non-existent child abuse against a named individual. Understandably in such circumstances much bitterness, even lawsuits, can result – and it may occur one day in the abduction field. As a researcher you owe it to yourself as much as to the witness to ensure she receives proper medical attention or, if this is unavailable, not to play about with her state of mind in the first place by using unfettered hypnotic regression.

Moreover, whilst hypnosis can add to our knowledge, provided all the reservations about it are borne in mind, it is not the only – indeed, perhaps not even the best – method of working on abductions. Experiments with creative visualisation suggest that this can be just as effective. In these instances the witness is asked physically to retrace the steps of her abduction and describe what she feels. She also takes note of subsequent dreams that may prove relevant. As a third method she may be asked to use latent creative abilities to paint, sketch or write about her experience. It is surprising how often this can be just as illuminating as a dozen hypnosis sessions.

ABDUCTIONS TODAY

—

This is one of the most rapidly expanding phenomena in the paranormal spectrum. Gradually it is gaining a degree of scientific respect, although we are still some way from understanding its nature. Whilst abduction is usually perceived as a straight choice between some kind of hallucination and a literal interpretation as physical kidnapping by aliens, the truth is more complex. Media stories over-emphasise the alien spacenap theory as if it were proven fact, since this idea is utterly dominant in the USA, but it has much less support elsewhere.

The MIT symposium in June 1992 was the first indication that science could respond positively to the topic. In 1993 even *New Scientist* magazine commented objectively, when its 6 November issue featured data that a team from the psychology department at Carleton University in Ottawa, Canada, had released (initially through the responsible outlet of *Abnormal Psychology*). These were test results conducted on samples of the population, UFO witnesses and close encounter victims; the latter were discovered to be 'no less intelligent, no more fantasy prone and no more likely to suffer from mental disorders' than anyone else.

Although this may have seemed a dramatic revelation to many people, it only bore out what abduction researchers had claimed from years of first-hand experience. Indeed, experiments had already established similar patterns, for instance when a group of abductees were secretly sent to a vocational psychologist for screening for a supposed top job. Profiles of the group gave no hint that there was anything odd about these people. Then the unsuspecting doctor was told that the group all claimed spacenappings; but, even after re-evaluating her data, she could only repeat her diagnosis that they were psychologically normal.

Greys and Nordics

A good deal of factual data about abductions has resulted from various studies. Dr Thomas Bullard, a folklorist from the University of Indiana, has compiled major databases on over eight hundred deeply researched cases worldwide. In France, Denys Breysse has for several years pooled computer statistics for what he calls Project Bécassine. I have made a detailed study of all known British abduction reports, and compared the results with sub-sets of European and American data. These are just some of the many experiments currently being carried out.

From such recent research we have learnt that there are two essential types of entity which are (both alone and, not infrequently, together) reported in over ninety-two per cent of cases. These are given the generic names of *greys* (on account of their greyish skin pigmentation; they are also much smaller than normal human height, with large egg-shaped heads and huge eyes) and *Nordics* (because these taller-than-average-human-height entities look basically Scandinavian, with blond hair, blue eyes and clear pale skins, although they have cat-like or oriental eyes). So clear-cut are these two divisions that they challenge psychologically based theories, which should anticipate a rich variety of human imagination populating any expected fantasies with a great diversity of aliens.

Other pointers emerging from this work include the knowledge that abductions are merely part of a sequence of lifelong paranormal experiences which involve the witness, but for which the often repeated abductions tend to become over-emphasised as a result of current cultural bias. Equally, abductees have above-average early-life recall, not uncommonly possess eidetic (that is, near-photographic) memories and are certainly excellent at using visual creativity within the mind. These discoveries may prove that there are important factors within the human brain that either predispose the person to undergo an abduction or facilitate some kind of external contact, rather like mediums may be said to 'tune in' to another intelligence that is attempting to communicate with them.

Abduction and near death experiences

Dr Kenneth Ring, a psychologist at the University of Connecticut, has made a study comparing abductees with people who have had an NDE (near death experience; see page 152). He has found strong evidence that similar points are being uncovered by both sets of witnesses, suggesting that these two seemingly disparate phenomena may be linked. Dr Ring has shunned the idea that we need to choose between whether abductions occur 'in the mind' or 'in the real world' (which is very difficult, as half the evidence supports one conclusion and the rest the other!). Instead, he proposes what he calls an *imaginal* realm with characteristics of both.

This is not unlike my own concept, developed from more case-orientated field research. It terms all these phenomena *waking lucid dreams*. By this I mean drawing a parallel with a *lucid dream* proper (see page 69), where the conscious mind manipulates dream-created imagery and becomes aware of the fact that a dream is occurring. The result is stunning vividness, and the reverse process could be possible. Here the subconscious mind would be capable of manipulating seeming real-world imagery in order to generate equally vivid and apparently real experiences. Just like the lucid dream these would occur in this intermediate hinterland of a quasi-consciousness.

Independent observers

A number of interactive experiments are now underway to test the reality basis of abductions. One is a search for third party observers, who, like passers-by in the street spotting a bank robbery taking place, can observe, without getting involved, the spacenapping of a complete stranger. Only one well-attested case was known until recently. It occurred in Manhattan, New York, in November 1989, and was investigated by Budd Hopkins. Several independent witnesses claim to have seen a woman levitate out of her high-rise apartment in the company of *greys*, then placed inside a UFO which flew underneath the river! When these people came forward the woman had already contacted Hopkins and been hypnotised to reveal an identical story from her own perspective, plus a memory of an on-board medical examination.

Superficially this case looks very powerful. However, it has been the subject of considerable criticism from within the UFO field because few researchers are willing to pin their reputations on wholehearted support of a rather atypical case – although that may be changing in the light of very recent events described below.

Certainly in at least six other instances from all over the world independent observers have seen abductees at the time when these people subsequently reported that they had been inside a UFO and undergoing a spacenapping. However, all the independent observers state categorically that the victim had physically travelled nowhere. They were in altered states of consciousness and assumed to be variously drunk, deeply asleep or in a catatonic trance. This strongly infers that, whatever the origin of the abduction experience, it happens in an altered state of consciousness.

Experiments by Lorne Goldfader and a team of psychologists, sociologists and anthropologists at the UFO Research Institute of Canada are presently attempting to place deeply repressed post-hypnotic commands into abductees and to have them recall these during subsequent abductions. Long-term studies are underway to discover how these commands affect the content of later conscious and hypnotically retrieved abduction claims by the same witnesses.

Abduction research is also becoming intrigued by cases such as one that occurred in Manchester, England, in November 1993. A woman videotaped a light in the sky and the local UFO group, NARO, investigated. They concluded, after objective research, that this was most likely to have been an overflying weather balloon that the witness had misinterpreted. Yet, apparently without being aware of this investigation, another team of local UFOlogists later met the witness and had her hypnotically regressed. From this, according to initial reports, an embyonic abduction story began to emerge – the woman recalled images of being taken from her home to some unknown place.

The debate over this case is in its early stages, but it begs significant questions given the basic credibility of all parties. Of course, the NARO interpretation could have been wrong and the light in the sky may have been something much stranger than its members had supposed. Yet if it was just a balloon after all, and a subsequent memory at least consistent with an abduction could begin to emerge from hypnosis experiments into an honest mistake, that would challenge the type of 'memory' that has emerged from many other equally sincere abduction experiences.

Yet it is the spontaneous cases with some conscious memory behind them that continue to flow in which form the greatest problem for all who seek to evaluate this puzzling phenomenon. For example, a businessman returning home from a meeting in the early hours stopped his car to relieve himself by the road near Leek in Staffordshire. In the fields he saw strange lights that rushed towards him. His next memory was of hiding behind a tree and scurrying away in a dazed state, to discover that he was almost naked and his clothes were piled neatly by his car. As he put on his trousers he found that they were emitting static electricity in the form of sparks, as if charged by some mysterious process.

The Oz factor

In another case, a woman and her boyfriend were driving along a lonely Suffolk road to visit friends when weird blue lights appeared in the sky and the car engine failed. When they got out to investigate the problem the whole area became eerily quiet, with not even birds twittering. This is a common symptom of the onset of such encounters, known by researchers as the *Oz factor*. Then the lights flew towards them, the woman felt an impulse to approach and was struck by a beam of light. Her next memory is of standing next to her boyfriend. Only later did they discover that three hours had somehow vanished from their recall.

Much later, desperate to plug the gap that was plaguing her life and making her a near-recluse, she underwent regression hypnosis. But she awoke screaming from this process after reliving a scene of being medically probed by grey-skinned creatures with huge black eyes that

LEICESTERSHIRE LIBRARIES AND INFORMATION SERVICE
REFERENCE & INFORMATION LIBRARY HUMANITIES

had told her they wanted her to bear an alien child. The woman still carries physical scars and another terrible legacy. According to medical opinion, despite being only twenty-one years old when the encounter occurred and considered in perfect health up to that point, she is now apparently unable to have children.

New cases such as these fill the records every year and imply that there is something more than a simple illusion lurking behind this mysterious phenomenon.

The latest evidence

As I write in 1995 attention is focusing on a new case from Australia which looks very promising and may yet prove to be a fully endorsable independent observation of another person's abduction. Bill Chalker, an industrial chemist, and noted UFO researcher John Auchettl were amongst the principal investigators.

The events took place in the early hours of 8 August 1993, when a young woman was driving with her husband between Monbulk and Fountain Gate near Belgrave in the Dandenongs, a mountain range in Victoria state. They observed something strange in the sky, stopped to watch, then drove on. Another car was seen on the road nearby and its occupants had apparently also witnessed the occurrence, although the woman and her husband were simply passing through the area and had no idea who these fellow travellers might have been.

The woman's full memory of events began to come back a few weeks after the experience. She had a series of terrifying nightmares involving a tall figure bending over, and experienced sucking sensations drawing something from her body and various other events linking these dreams with forgotten events that had occurred after they stopped to look at the UFO. The woman was also taken to hospital suffering from unexplained menstrual bleeding and odd triangular marks around her abdomen. The doctors said her condition resembled a spontaneous abortion, but were baffled when she insisted that she had not been pregnant.

Investigation throughout 1994 revealed that the woman's husband had always had a clear memory of seeing the tall being inside the UFO as he watched from outside. The woman's testimony of on-board examinations grew more complex and did not depend upon hypnosis, which was only tried once – well into the investigation – and was soon abandoned as not being of any value. A history of weird psychic events, such as poltergeist activity, was also noted.

Eventually, after some effort, the other car was traced by investigators. It had contained a man, a woman and a girlfriend of theirs, who were completely unaware that anyone else had witnessed the UFO, as the first couple had not gone public with their story. The three new witnesses had also seen the tall entity, but had never reported it. Hypnotic regression on these witnesses is beginning to unravel interlocking memories that may tie in with the first couple's completely independent story.

It is too early to say how important this case will prove, but Bill Chalker wisely says of it: 'The victims of these experiences must not be unrealistically encouraged by advocates of alien presence, nor, at the other extreme, should they be ridiculed by the sceptical amongst us. They should be helped to confront the reality of their experiences, whether or not it is eventually found to be prosaic, profound or extraordinary.'

SOURCES

ORGANISATIONS

The following organisations are experienced at handling abduction claims and have medically qualified personnel on call to assist with any witnesses. Those marked with an asterisk adopt the code of practice defined by UFO investigators; others may have their own guidelines.

*UFO Research/Center for UFO Studies (UFORA/ACUFOS)
UFORA, PO Box 1894, Adelaide, SA 5001, Australia.
ACUFOS, PO Box W42, West Pennant Hills, NSW 2125, Australia.

*British UFO Research Association (BUFORA)   *Suite 1, 2C Leyton Road, Harpenden, Herts, AL5 2TL, UK.*

Northern Anomalies Research Association (NARO)   *2 Grosvenor Road, Congleton, Cheshire, CW12 4PG, UK.*

UFO Research Institute of Canada (UFORIC)   *Suite 25, 1665 Robson Street, Vancouver, BC, V6G 3C2, Canada.*

Project Bécassine   *9 Avenue St Exupéry, 92160 Antony, France.*

Dr J. Allen Hynek Center for UFO Studies (CUFOS)   *2457 West Peterson Avenue, Chicago, IL 60659, USA.*

INDIVIDUAL SUPPORT FOR WITNESSES

UFO Witness Group   *64 Nightingale Lane, Hornsey, London N8 7QX, UK.*

Intruders' Foundation   *PO Box 30233, New York, NY 10011, USA.*

For advice on how to resist abductions contact *Ann Druffel, c/o* **MUFON** (Mutual UFO Network, the USA's largest membership group investigating UFOs), *103 Oldtowne Road, Seguin, TX 78155, USA.*

PERIODICALS

Ongoing debate can be found in the following publications:

International UFO Reporter *(CUFOS address)* and **MUFON Journal** *(MUFON address)* feature frequent case histories and debates, mostly about and between American researchers and their work but also involving other countries, particularly Britain and Australia.

For British cases and debate on less extra-terrestrially orientated theories, a good source is the quarterly journal **New UFOlogist** *293 Devonshire Road, Blackpool, Lancashire FY2 0TW.*

The most specific abduction publication is the **BAE (Bulletin of Anomalous Experience)** *711 South Hanover St, Baltimore, MD 21230–3832, USA.* This is edited by psychologist Dr David Gotlib and is a superb source of discussion, debate, and digests of relevant mainstream psychology and psychiatric literature. It is returning after a one-year sabbatical during 1995 whilst Dr Gotlib moved to the USA, but back issues are also worthy of detailed study.

BOOKS

The following books will provide a good grounding in the subject:

Abduction by Dr John Mack (Simon & Schuster, New York and London, 1994) is the only one so far from a psychiatrist (attached to the Harvard Medical School). It is a bit raw at the edges, but good.

UFO Abductions: A Dangerous Game by Philip Klass (Prometheus, Buffalo, NY, 1988) is an antidote to the above – an aviation journalist's sceptical look that argues against any strange reality to these cases.

The following three titles are general overviews. Hopkins's is the first general book on the subject. My own is the first international review, with cultural patterns exposed, while Jacob has written the most recent survey of American cases.

Missing Time by Budd Hopkins (Merak, New York, 1982).

Abduction by Jenny Randles (Robert Hale, 1988, and Headline, 1989; published in the USA as **Alien Abductions** by Global Communications, New York, 1990).

Secret Life by Dr David Jacobs (Simon & Schuster, New York; Fourth Estate, 1992; republished in the UK as **Alien Encounters** by Virgin, 1994).

The following, all worth attention, are respectively the first published study of an abduction; the world's best-selling title on the subject, evocatively told first-hand by its witness; and perhaps the most detailed discussion of one case, which was later turned into a (loosely related) TV mini-series.

The Interrupted Journey (the Betty and Barney Hill case) by John Fuller (first published by Dial Press in 1966 in the USA, but reissued and updated in 1982 by Souvenir Press).

Communion by Whitley Strieber (William Morrow, New York, 1987, with subsequent editions in most major countries of the world).

Intruders (the Kathy Davies abduction) by Budd Hopkins (Random House, New York, 1987).

These theoretical studies are, respectively, an attempted psychological solution; the most detailed review of visions; a book on the imaginal theory; and one discussing the kind of witnesses who experience abductions with suggestion as to why this witness selection may occur.

UFOs: The Image Hypothesis by Keith Basterfield (Reed, Australia, 1980).

Visions; Apparitions; Alien Visitors by Hilary Evans (Aquarian Press, 1984).

The Omega Project by Dr Kenneth Ring (William Morrow, New York, 1992).

Star Children by Jenny Randles (Robert Hale, 1994, and Sterling, New York, 1995).

The proceedings of the MIT Symposium, and a book by a journalist who attended and also interviewed participants, are now available. Both are indispensable reference sources.

Alien Discussions edited by Pritchard, Mack, Kasey and Yapp (North Cambridge Press, USA, 1995).

Close Encounters of the Fourth Kind by C. D. Bryan (Weidenfeld and Nicolson, 1995).

ANGELS

DEFINITION

Most mythological and religious philosophies know the concept of angels, seemingly first derived from *angaros*, the Persian term for messenger. They are said to be beings which inhabit the afterlife, nirvana or an intermediate hinterworld – to which all humans must ultimately aspire – but which, unlike most of the dead, enjoy certain special privileges: they are allowed to visit the earth and to take on a visible state. According to religious doctrine there are many types of angels, arranged in a hierarchy. These include the cherubim – or childlike beings – and the highest order, the seraphim. It is widely argued, contrary to popular interpretation, that angels were never human beings but are a distinct, more evolved form of life that co-exists on earth with us. Angels are traditionally said to be human in form, or, more correctly, amorphous in shape and adaptable to whatever form the person who meets them wishes to see; their winged nature is a corruption introduced by Renaissance artists to accommodate their apparent ability to fly. The purpose of angels is almost exclusively to assist human beings in living better lives; although evil angels (which may well overlap with demons) are a necessary counterbalance in many beliefs.

HISTORICAL REVIEW

Angels are probably the best-known type of supernatural entity apart from ghosts, and one of the paranormal phenomena accepted even by the Christian Church. Indeed, the story of the birth of Jesus has its starting point in a visitation by an angel, who – as many are said to – possessed the gift of prophecy (here of the coming birth) due to superior heavenly understanding.

The same principles apply also in other cultures, and another very well-known being derives from a similar basis. This is the genie, as found in fairy stories, pantomimes and Walt Disney movies. The term 'genie', a being who is able to grant wishes to aid mortals, derives from the Middle Eastern tradition of a supernatural entity called a *djinn* – in effect the older brother of the Christian angel.

Scholars of the paranormal often argue that to find such a belief so widespread throughout humanity may well indicate its dimly perceived but yet factual reality. But of course this truth may be more psychological than real – the angel being the manifestation of a root human desire, which, since it is universal, has found an outlet in a wide range of cultures and philosophies.

On the other hand, the view that angels may reflect some kind of reality beyond the psychological has had something of a resurgence in the 1990s, with an epidemic of supposedly real angelic visions taking place. Some of these are of the traditional type that has always occurred – for instance, the apparitions at what are now celebrated Catholic holy sites, such as Fatima in Portugal in 1917. These derive from alleged visionary meetings with prophetic angels (usually interpreted by the witnesses, who are commonly young children, as the Virgin Mary), at which messages are given to advise the world of its wrongdoing and doom-laden predictions are offered. The most modern example is at Medjugorge in former Yugoslavia, where prophecies of war and claims about a visible sign that would be seen by the whole world and guide the human race into a new era of peace began in the mid-eighties. These have continued to occur even during the recent civil war.

When the former Soviet-ruled countries of eastern Europe were freed from Communist repression in the early 1990s there was also a dramatic rise in claimed angelic visions on a one-to-one basis, and without widescale prophecies attached to them. In its most remarkable form, stories emerged persistently from Russia that the crew of an orbiting space mission had to be brought down to earth ahead of schedule because they claimed to see an angelic form outside the windows of their module!

Spiritualism, the religion which believes in life after death and our ability to communicate with this realm via mediums, also adheres to the concept of wise souls returning to earth – either temporarily or (in some beliefs) more permanently. Some cases of what might traditionally be thought of as angels are now reported at Spiritualist meetings. The angel rather than being perceived as a heavenly figure of supernatural origin, is interpreted by the witness as a human spirit returning from the afterlife.

However, the biggest upsurge in angelic encounters seems to be in one-off experiences, in which individuals believe that they have been rescued from some fate by the manifestation of an angel. These experiences often do not seem to depend upon one's prior belief system and have been well studied in recent times – although mostly by researchers with a religious background that enables them readily to accept the reality of angels.

There have always been such reports, of course, and it is widely believed by many people, more or less fervently, that we all have a 'guardian angel' watching over our lives; these days it is often assumed to be a dead loved one guiding us from the afterlife. But, perhaps more curiously, there is also a pattern of such things emerging within the alien abduction data (see page 6). A surprising proportion of spacenap victims seem to believe that their lives were rescued at an earlier age by the appearance of a ministering stranger, who might well be traditionally interpreted as an angel but whom, unsurprisingly, many of these witnesses perceive instead as an extra-terrestrial overseer.

Whatever the case, the idea that help from the supernatural realms can manifest directly into a person's life is more prevalent today than it has been for several centuries. It has spawned a number of best-selling books and was influential in the hugely successful movie *Ghost*, in which the character played by Patrick Swayze attempts to change life for the better even after his death.

The unprecedented popularity and escalating frequency of occurrence of these stories suggests that further objective research into angelic visions is now required.

EXPERIENCING ANGELS

It is extremely rare for anyone to have an angelic experience more than once during their lifetime. Whilst many people may say that they often feel the presence of a 'guide', direct intervention normally occurs only at a moment of extreme crisis – and such moments are, thankfully, rare.

Moreover, it is uncommon for the angelic vision to be terrifying. More likely it will be viewed with a sense of wonder, one which changes a person's viewpoint for the better and often instills awareness of life after death and a greater belief in God. Whilst I would not wish to question any of these benefits, nor anyone's interpretation of an experience as personal, I think it wise to offer a little caution.

When an angelic vision occurs – at a very vulnerable point in somebody's life – they may regard the vision as a dead loved one come back to warn them, or at least feel grateful to have escaped disaster. As a result, if researchers appear to diminish the experience this is the last response that is required in such a situation. However, this vulnerability is in itself a reason why care needs to be taken. It will be extremely tempting to evaluate any powerful vision as reality, but that is to forget that all reality is forged by the human mind – honed and shaped as images inside our consciousness – and that visionary experiences that would not be shared by others if they were present can appear as dramatic as what we would all call complete reality.

The view of the sceptics

The sceptical interpretation of an angel is that it is a form of 'crisis apparition' – an invention of the mind to ease a person through a traumatic moment, when the dramatic impact of such a vision is needed to create a life-saving change in behaviour. A case in point here would be that of noted entertainer Tommy Steele, who as a youth ran away to sea, contracted meningitis and was rushed back to a London hospital. In a near paralysed state, slipping towards death, Tommy claims that he was rescued by a young boy's laughter and a brightly coloured ball that was thrown over the screens on to his bed. Tommy stretched out to toss the ball back to the unseen child and the process went on for an hour or two, until the doctors returned and were amazed at Tommy's sudden recovery of physical strength. Of course when the screens were removed there was no young boy in the ward – there never had been. But was it an angelic intervention that rescued Tommy from death, or was it simply an apparition conjured up by his heavily sedated mind in an effort to push him into the actions that would help him overcome his physical trauma?

We cannot be sure if the sceptics are ever right about angelic visions, but, if what you will read in the rest of this book is to be believed, the human mind has an incredible untapped potential and phenomena such as ESP are certainly possible. So seemingly prophetic messages passed on by angels need not necessarily originate from such a source – they may be received by our own inner self and ascribed to another intelligence simply as a way of resolving what seems to be fantastic. After all, if a voice talks to your mind and tells you to get off a railway track, which you promptly do without thinking, and thus escape an unheard freight train and certain death (a real case recently reported from Chicago), it is easy to understand why we might assume that someone outside of us must have communicated, instead of accepting that the voice was coming from within ourselves.

I would advise you to consider the alternatives, without believing them to be more or less acceptable than a literal interpretation. In truth, nobody yet knows what may really be going on.

RESEARCHING ANGELS

At present the field is wide open for those who wish to research angelic visions, because as yet little objective work is being carried out beyond the religious and Spiritualist communities. I do not wish to imply that such people cannot be objective, but both have a degree of vested interest in proving the reality of angels, and as a result sceptics inevitably belittle their evidence. True objective research simply looks at the data without presupposing any solution, and follows wherever it leads.

However, there is clearly a great deal of data to be uncovered if you are willing to be systematic in your search. When Hope Price, the wife of a British clergyman, decided to place requests for modern-day angelic visions in sources such as local newspapers she was swamped with replies from over 1500 witnesses. If you are prepared to handle this amount of data you will need to plan how to categorise your evidence, and will also probably need a computer to record it all!

Bearing in mind the points I raised in the previous section, it is important to investigate each case as thoroughly as possible. In particular, don't just record what the witness believes has happened to them, but discover what you can about their prior religious and philosophical beliefs, and the emotional and physical circumstances of their life at the time of the experience (questions as diverse as whether they were happily married or suffered from a headache afterwards could prove relevant); then assess in what ways the phenomenon has changed their belief system or lifestyle.

Because we are at a very early stage of serious research into angelic visions it is not easy to predict what evidence will ultimately prove important. Time and experience will determine such things. However, it will be worthwhile seeking out any cases where the episode has some kind of tangible support – in other words, is not solely dependent upon the testimony of one person. If it is to be established that angels exist beyond the mind of the person who reports them, this kind of independent corroboration is essential. It should be one of the first things that objective researchers seek out – but you may find it difficult to come by.

ANGELS TODAY

One of the most remarkable recent cases of angelic visitation was reported by Kate Bridger, and happened when she was on her way to work by bus in Chatham, Kent, one day in 1991. Suddenly the driver was seen to struggle with the vehicle as they descended a hill. She heard him cry out that the brakes had failed as they headed straight towards a brick wall.

Disaster was inevitable – or, rather, it should have been. Then Kate saw

RIGHT
Antonio Villas Boas being examined
after his alleged abduction by aliens
(see page 7).

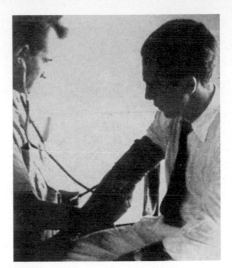

BELOW
The Roswell UFO wreckage on
display by USAF – who say it is a
weather balloon (see page 225).

Possible ball lightning photographed in 1978 by Werner Burger at Sankt Gallenkirch, Vorarlberg, Austria.

The 'Philip' research group from Toronto, Canada pictured during a session in which they tried to make an entity, named Philip, manifest (see pages 165–6).

half a dozen forms floating outside the window. They had blond hair and beautiful white faces, and wore long robes. She immediately identified them as angels, although others might have called them aliens.

Kate watched as they stood in front of the vehicle, sandwiched between the bus and the wall, and vanishing as it screeched to a halt with only inches to spare. Everyone on board had been saved from serious injury or death by this supernatural intervention, although she was the only witness to the means of their salvation. The driver later admitted that when the bus was returned to the garage the mechanics were mystified. The brakes had completely seized up and nobody could explain how the bus could have managed to stop on that hill.

Rescue from death by smiling, blond-haired white-skinned entities is a common part of alien contact lore. Indeed, the description offered in angelic episodes of this kind is very similar to what is termed the *Nordic* type of alien entity (see page 14). However, there are also many cases where the method of rescue is much more baffling, but inevitably becomes ascribed to angelic powers.

A typical, if extraordinary, case was reported to me by Jessica Bellman from Los Angeles, who was driving with her mother on the multi-lane freeway near Hollywood. It was rush hour and every lane contained a solid wall of traffic bumper to bumper, yet moving deceptively fast.

Suddenly a huge van ahead of them lost control and slewed across the road. Being in the slow lane, it was somehow able to swerve off the highway and screech to a halt, avoiding catastrophe. But Jessica was not so lucky. She had only a split second to react and instinctively hit the brakes, sending their car into a massive spin. She was sent careering across three lanes of fast-moving traffic. Utter carnage was inevitable.

Then the miracle happened. Time stretched out and slowed down, and all the sounds around them disappeared. It was as if Jessica, her mother and the car were inside a deep well and every contact with the bustling real-world environment had been removed. This is, in fact, a very common feature of many paranormal phenomena, and is called the *Oz factor*.

Jessica recalls praying for help – the sort of prayer that only imminent death draws forth. She recalls seeing her mother's eyes glazed with terror. Then describes seeing two men in a car in close focus, laughing and joking and completely ignorant of the fact that Jessica's car was slicing through them as if its body were made of fog. There was a bump, and Jessica's car was at a halt.

Certain they were dead, Jessica looked about to see the lines of traffic passing by. She and her mother were completely all right, and the car was not even scratched. Somehow, in a way that neither woman can explain, they had been saved from death by a miracle that had seemingly transported them straight through solid metal.

It is evidence such as this which forms the starting point of today's quest to understand angels. You can see why it is a dramatic new field of exploration.

SOURCES

ORGANISATIONS

As yet there are no organisations specifically devoted to investigating angelic visions. However, there are researchers who collate individual cases. A responsible paranormal research outlet such as *ASSAP* in the UK or *Strange* in the USA would be keen to help.

ASSAP   *31 Goodhew Road, Croydon, Surrey, CR0 6QZ, UK.*

Strange   *PO Box 2246, Rockville, MD 20852, USA.*

PERIODICALS

There are a couple of magazines which publish data; the American one is exclusively devoted to the topic. Kevin McClure edits the British publication and, whilst it ranges over a wider series of associated phenomena, he has a personal passion for angelic visions having written two books on the subject (see below). His authority is without question.

Angels and Fairies   *PO Box 762, Ashland, OR 97520, USA* is billed as the 'Middle Kingdom quarterly of real accounts'.

Promises and Disappointments   *42 Victoria Road, Mount Charles, St Austell, Cornwall, PL25 4QD, UK.*

BOOKS

Of the growing number of books available, I list below some of the more illuminating ones. Those by Kevin McClure offer good objective data, into religious visions in general and one case in particular (the First World War episode of the Bowmen of Mons). Hilary Evans provides an excellent general survey and looks at the data from a psychological viewpoint. Sophy Burnham's first book is widely credited with reawakening modern interest, and her second presents a collection of new stories collated from readers' letters (as does Hope Price's). Keith Thompson offers a much more avant-garde look at other intelligences, including the UFO context.

The Evidence for Visions of the Virgin by Kevin McClure (Aquarian Press, 1984).

Gods; Spirits; Cosmic Guardians by Hilary Evans (Aquarian Press, 1987).

A Book of Angels by Sophy Burnham (Ballantine, New York, 1990).

Angel Letters by Sophy Burnham (Ballantine, New York, 1991).

Visions of Bowmen and Angels: Mons 1914 by Kevin McClure (via **Promises and Disappointments**, address above, 1993).

Angels and Aliens by Keith Thompson (Random House, New York, 1993).

Angels: True Stories of How They Touch Our Lives by Hope Price (Psychic Press, 1993).

BALL LIGHTNING

DEFINITION

Ball lightning is a rare atmospheric phenomenon of as yet unknown origin. It has never been successfully produced on a reliable basis by artificial means. As its name suggests, it commonly appears in the form of a ball of energy, typically just a few inches but sometimes several feet in diameter. However, tubular and other shapes have also been described. It is frequently blue, white or orange in colour, and vivid internal details have been reported by close observers. Despite the use of the word 'lightning' and the fact that it often forms during thunderstorms, these are by no means a prerequisite and there have been many instances of ball lightning appearing during the complete absence of a storm or ordinary lightning. Another of its frightening characteristics is to manifest inside sealed rooms – even aircraft cabins; the phenomenon can enter through windows, down chimneys, via cupboard doors and out of TV screens. It can drift around in the air harmlessly, buzzing and generating electrical charges, or it may explode with terrific violence, evaporating liquids in an instant, welding metal together and melting glass. It has even been suggested that it may induce radiation sickness in people who come too close.

Until about 1970 it was regarded by most scientists as merely an illusion. Paranormal researchers cite it as a classic example of a phenomenon that has crossed over from former pseudo-science into a modicum of respectability. They see it as a possible indicator of what could one day happen to other even more contentious mysteries.

HISTORICAL REVIEW

Good accounts of ball lightning can be found in records dating back several centuries, and old woodcuts visualising its appearance also exist. A French meteorologist made the first study, of thirty cases, in 1853. Older terms included *fireballs* and *thunderbolts* and a good deal of superstition attached to sightings, largely due to its mysterious, dangerous and unpredictable nature.

During the nineteenth century some scientists felt that unusual meteorites were being misidentified as ball lightning, and a subsequent idea was that ordinary lightning discharges were creating optical distortion due to the intense brilliance of the flash impinging on the witness's retina. Spots before the eyes were, in effect, being seen to float about and create the false impression of ball lightning.

A number of meteorologists and physicists attempted to legitimise the field after the Second World War, but the lack of any workable scientific explanation gave them little success in persuading their colleagues to join them. Meanwhile sightings continued to be reported, but remained in a shadowland between complete rejection and scientific credibility.

But things began to change when noted physicist Dr Roger Jennison was one of the passengers on an Eastern Airlines jet flying over New York during the early 1960s – a small example of ball lightning floated down the aisle and disappeared through the sealed fuselage. Dozens of people saw it and could attest that it was no illusion. From then onward it became acceptable to discuss the matter in prestigious journals such as *Nature*.

However, the critics were not completely silenced. As recently as 1972 in his influential *The Lightning Book*, MIT physicist Peter Viemeister called it 'most controversial' and added that 'some scientists do not believe that [it] exists'. However, several well-referenced case histories have since eroded much of the residual scepticism and a number of laboratories have attempted to design experiments to duplicate the phenomenon by artificial means. As this is tied into a basic understanding of how ball lightning might form – which is as yet far from clear – experiments have been generally less than successful, leading to a resurgence of scepticism in some quarters.

Mystery into paradox

One of the problems is that theories have rarely been supported by a consistent chain of evidence. A case in which ball lightning instantly turned a known volume of water in a barrel into steam enabled the energy level to be calculated. But then in further cases such huge energy levels – had they been present – would have resulted in major physical effects on the environment, but evidently did not. The term 'paradoxical energy levels' has been applied to this mystery within a mystery.

Nobody knows why ball lightning sometimes behaves with apparent aggression, generating major physical destruction, while at other times it can merely be a pretty atmospheric effect without any harmful consequences. In one case from Florida a tiny ball completely melted a fly swatter that the innocent victim, reposing on a verandah, had instinctively waved in its direction. But in another case, discussed in depth in *Nature* in April 1976, a woman cooking in the English West Midlands had a tiny piece of blue ball lightning pass right through her midriff, yet the only unpleasant effects were those of eddy currents and electrical heating being induced into her wedding ring, which burnt the finger and caused it to swell.

A connection with UFOs?

Serious attempts have been made to find an atomic-based solution to these shifting energy levels. However, this implies that witnesses who get too close ought to suffer from some degree of radiation sickness, and there is no clear evidence within the records of that taking place.

Several physicists interested in ball lightning began to suspect that they might not have access to all the available data. Mark Stenhoff, who had investigated the West Midlands incident, became interested in UFO sightings while working with BUFORA in the UK, and Professor Paul Davies, then of Cambridge but later of the University of Adelaide, was even willing to discuss the idea of a connection between UFOs and ball lightning. He coined the term 'transient aerial phenomenon' to cover both ball lightning and UFOs, and suggested that real progress would follow if the 'aura of mystery and superstition surrounding unusual aerial events were dispelled'. He wrote of this in both *Nature* and *New Scientist*.

Indeed, UFO research had already looked at the possibility that ball lightning might be the cause of some puzzling cases. It was speculated as the cause of a series of events that occurred near Levelland, Texas, in November 1957 when various cars and trucks found their engines and lights failing in the presence of a large glowing mass that drifted about over a two-hour period. However, there was no thunderstorm in Levelland that night and both repeated or very long duration ball lightning apparitions of this type, as well as vehicle interference of this magnitude, are unknown in the historical records of the phenomenon.

Nevertheless, a few UFOlogists still postulated a link with ball lightning in some cases, and this theory has continued to be well regarded. It is now considered possible that extreme forms of ball lightning (especially those that generate the more serious physical effects) are much less likely to be interpreted by the witness as an atmospheric event and, particularly in today's cultural climate, are instead viewed as UFOs. As a result they are reported outside the scientific community. Because most UFOlogists think of UFOs in exotic, even alien, terms they rarely contemplate the ball lightning explanation for such cases. Similarly, because the vast majority of scientists do not take UFO data seriously they reject examples of extreme ball lightning as nonsense and probably never know that such exciting evidence exists and may support their research.

Thankfully, scientific symposia now meet to discuss the latest evidence, and it is heartening to see some UFO researchers – albeit of the more sceptical variety – participating. Indeed, physicist and meteorologist Dr Terence Meaden, best known for his controversial association with crop circles, has used his respectability to secure and research cases of vehicle interference associated with both UFOs and atmospheric electricity, strongly implying that there is a connection.

We know that hundreds – perhaps thousands – of ball lightning events are being reported every year, although the ones which offer physical evidence are much rarer than that. The greatest search has been for visual evidence. There are surprisingly few reliable still photographs and no well-regarded moving images that indisputably depict ball lightning. This situation is understandable given the transient nature of the phenomenon: it rarely lasts more than a few seconds, and witnesses are usually too terrifed to think of taking a photograph! However, until there is a strong database of this kind of evidence, ball lightning will no doubt continue to sit on the limits of scientific controversy.

EXPERIENCING BALL LIGHTNING

The chances of encountering a ball lightning event at close quarters are fairly remote, unless you live in an area with frequent thunderstorms. Equally, since most people wisely stay indoors during a violent storm, the most likely occasion for ball lightning to appear is either when it 'attacks' within your home or one of the rarer instances when it forms in the absence of storm activity.

If you happen to see such an event it is likely to be a very brief and stunning experience. The chances that you may have a loaded camera (or better still a video camera) ready to use are fairly slim, but if you do and you can regain your composure fast enough to film the object, please do so. This could provide precious scientific evidence.

Failing that, ensure that you bring the event to the attention of anybody else who may be present. Immediately after the incident has ended each witness should be asked to sketch and write a signed account of what they personally experienced. As far as possible this should be done without any discussion. That can come after the reports have been completed.

During the incident itself there is little reason to be terrified. Whilst considerable energy is probably involved in the phenomenon, its ability to cause serious injury or death is contentious and it is known that in most cases you are likely to escape virtually unharmed. Even so the ball lightning must be treated with respect and under no circumstances should you attempt to touch it, even if it does float enticingly close by.

Ball lightning is attracted to electrical wiring, and metal objects – particularly circular ones such as rings and belts – can have energy induced into them, creating heat which will be the primary cause of any resulting injury. So during a storm try to steer clear of electrical wiring in a room, and take off potentially dangerous garments or jewellery. There are interesting examples of ball lightning drifting around rooms and causing fluorescent light tubes to glow even when switched off, notably as it passes underneath. But do not touch power switches during a ball lightning event – if the ball does discharge violently at the conclusion of its lifetime it is invariably the cause of a power surge that earths through these circuits.

If you are on the telephone when ball lightning forms (never a wise move during a thunderstorm) drop the receiver immediately. There are well-attested cases of serious injury even from poorly conducting plastic telephones when the ball has earthed through the wiring.

Overall, enjoy the experience in the few seconds that it lasts and take in as much detail as you can. You will have had the fortune to witness one of the rarest, least-known and most baffling natural phenomena in this modern age, and countless scientists would dearly love to have swapped places with you.

RESEARCHING BALL LIGHTNING

This is a phenomenon that is really best left to the scientific community to study, not only because it is very complex but also because it is a dangerous energy form that it is not wise to pursue without proper caution. Some researchers seek elusive photographic evidence by going out and filming with their camcorders during violent storms, but they would be foolhardy not to remain within their cars. The metal body acts as an insulating medium and the rubber tyres help as well. Indeed, the inside of a car is one of the safest places to be during an electrical storm.

Nevertheless, despite several years of such research the dearth of photographic evidence shows that this is a very difficult task to undertake. This is because you cannot take a photograph of standard lightning at the exact instant that it occurs. You have to set up the camera on a tripod, open the shutter and wait for the lightning flash, hoping that it will be in the direction in which the camera is pointing. So you would be very fortunate indeed to capture a transient and completely unpredictable free floating ball lightning event in the right place at the right time.

What amateurs can do, however, is collect data from old records, such as local newspaper archives from the last century, as well as follow up on events that may get reported in the media today. You will soon learn to recognise the potential of a ball lightning event, even though cases may often be misreported and exaggerated in the context of a 'spaceship'. Certainly any ball of light witnessed during a thunderstorm should be regarded as a suspect, however the witness, media or UFO buffs prefer to describe it.

A fruitful area of research for those with electrical engineering know-how, is that of the car stop or vehicle interference event – such as those described at Levelland, Texas. A full assessment of the damage and any causes of electrical impedance to the circuits of a vehicle after a mysterious stoppage (whether or not ball lightning was seen or a storm was underway) is well worth undertaking. These are little-studied but potentially invaluable areas of research.

Finally, it is important to report your findings to a responsible physics or meteorological publication. *The Journal of Meteorology* (see Sources) will almost certainly be open-minded enough to express an interest.

BALL LIGHTNING TODAY

For the past few years a symposium of ball lightning researchers has met regularly, and this is the yardstick by which progress is measured. Most of the meetings are held in eastern Europe, in countries such as Russia or Hungary, because that is where most research into the phenomenon is undertaken; although China and Japan make strong inputs and Britain is coming up fast on the rails. Indeed, it hosted the symposium at Oxford in 1992 under the guidance of meteorologists Mark Stenhoff, Adrian James and Dr Derek Elsom.

At this event the old guard sceptics were in evidence when science writer Steuart Campbell, who once proposed ball lightning as a solution to many UFO sightings and has recently published a book debunking

UFOs, put forward his 'null hypothesis' that ball lightning – like UFOs – could be nothing more than a collection of misperceived incidents.

From the opposite viewpoint a splendid presentation by Dr Eric Wooding, a physicist from the University of London, set out criteria to follow in an attempt to obtain strong physical evidence. He came up with the disturbing calculation that a camera left to record during all thunderstorms in its vicinity might be expected to pick up a ball lightning image once every thousand years. This means that a widespread global network would be required to maximise the potential of any data gained.

At the time of writing the most recent gathering was held in Salzburg, Austria, in September 1993. Here representatives from ten countries – more than ever before – were once again a mix of amateur sleuths and high-brow scientists, although the latter were now more prominent. Indeed, much of the discussion was heavily rooted in mathematical physics.

In April 1993 three researchers from the Academy of Sciences in Moscow compiled from their computer database a very useful statistical analysis of over 1800 ball lightning reports. This has produced the best guidelines yet on what the phenomenon looks like and how it behaves.

Two-thirds of the examples were between four and twenty inches in diameter, with only 2 per cent greater than about two feet in size. All except about 8 per cent were visible for under 100 seconds and two-thirds again lasted under twenty seconds. By far the best months for ball lightning observation were July and August, coinciding with peak thunderstorm activity in Europe. The biggest time-of-day peak was early afternoon, with a secondary rise in the early evening. As for colours, over 28 per cent were white, with yellow and red close behind and orange, blue and violet following. Green was much the most rarely reported.

A good example of what anyone can do to further ball lightning research was published in May 1993 by Robin Harper in *The Journal of Meteorology*, where he discussed his on-site study of an episode at Llwyngwril, Gwynedd, in rural Wales. It occurred at 5.05 p.m. on 30 August 1992 and badly damaged a bungalow, whose occupants were fortuitously at church. They heard a massive explosion, which was later demonstrated to be ball lightning earthing through their house wiring and blasting a trench in the ground outside. An eye witness who was looking out of his window at a sudden hailstorm chanced to witness the one violent lightning discharge – there was no other storm. It seems to have created what he describes as a sphere about three feet in diameter, blue in the centre and yellow at the edges. It rotated at speed in a clockwise direction and remained hovering in mid-air until it disappeared two or three seconds later.

An expert witness

However, perhaps the best evidence to have come to light was as a direct result of the Salzburg conference. Dr Alex Keul of the local university investigated and, given its unique combination of circumstances, it promises to be of much importance.

The witness was Christian Witz, chief of the Sankt Polten weather observatory in Lower Austria. On the night of 4 July 1989 severe storms had swept the area; while off duty he was indulging in his passion for photography, using time lapse techniques to film lightning bolts as they earthed all around him. At 9 p.m. a huge ground strike appeared a few hundred feet away and Witz was attracted towards it. He then saw a spiral movement near where it had just discharged and witnessed a fuzzy white ball of light, blinding white and the angular size of the full moon. It was about ten feet above ground level and drifted slowly towards the earth over a seven-second period, before extinguishing like a candle flame being snuffed out.

That a professional meteorologist should see ball lightning is rare enough. That he should have his camera shutter open and pointing in approximately the right direction was better still. It transpired that the lightning strike itself was out of the fixed frame of reference of the camera, but the ball lightning event was beautifully captured in colour in the lower left corner of his 100 ASA exposure. In addition to the eye witness account from a professional and this dramatic photograph, full weather data from the nearby observatory is also available for the time of occurrence. It makes this case of immeasurable value to researchers trying to figure out how ball lightning forms.

The UFO dilemma

Another step forward came from Dr Terence Meaden, who published an investigation of a strange incident on 20 July 1992 when a Citroën car at Valognes near Cherbourg in France suffered classic vehicle interference. Its engine failed and it coasted to a halt, but since this incident took place or a summer afternoon the vehicle lights were not on. However, from past experience it is very probable that these too would have failed.

Dr Meaden's on-site investigation found that the car had remained in this paralysed state for several seconds while the driver attempted unsuccessfully to restart it. At the time, although it was raining heavily and there was distant lightning, there was no local storm. However, both of the car's occupants were soon shaken by a dramatic explosion and a simultaneous huge flash of light. Whilst no evidence of it could be found at the site, the phenomenon was taken by the two men to be an extremely close and violent lightning strike. After recovering their composure they got out and checked the wiring, but found no faults. When they got back into the Citroën it started first time.

It appears that massive ionisation in the local atmosphere up to half a minute prior to the lightning strike had induced the car stop event. Had the object witnessed not resembled an ordinary lightning discharge – indeed, had it been a drifting ball of light as in other reports in this section – it is virtually certain that it would have been interpreted as another UFO encounter. Indeed, over a thousand cases are on record of so-called car stops attributed by a witness or investigator to a UFO. It has been argued that no known natural electrical phenomenon could create the physical factors necessary to trigger a car stop, but the French case may well suggest otherwise.

The dilemma that UFOlogists face is illustrated by another case, news of which I received as I was writing this section. Typical of so many others, it was reported to me by a baffled woman via the Jodrell Bank astronomy centre. She did so in the context of a UFO, although later she called back to say that a colleague at work had suggested it was 'a lightning bolt' – an option which I had, naturally, already considered.

She was walking her dog in fields near Bradford, West Yorkshire at about 7 p.m. on the blustery night of 26 January 1995. A severe weather depression was passing over the country, resulting in major snowstorms and devastating floods in northern Europe over the next few days. However, there was no thunderstorm activity that night. The woman observed and heard an aircraft struggling against the weather, bound to or from Leeds/Bradford airport. But immediately behind it was a curious ball of light, bluish white in colour, only a foot or two in diameter and flaring like magnesium. It seemed to be attracted to the fuselage of the aircraft and was, as she put it, 'chasing the plane'. It continued even when the jet changed course. However, after a minute or so the ball of light 'broke free' and shot away at an angle before disappearing.

Such cases may have a prosaic explanation, but a large number of near identical nature are on record. There is at least a possibility that these are close cousins of ball lightning as opposed to examples of visitations from very little green men.

SOURCES

ORGANISATIONS

The following bodies actively collect reports of ball lightning. All are staffed by professional meteorologists and physicists.

TORRO (Ball Lightning Division)   *PO Box 164, Richmond, Surrey, TW10 7RR, UK.*

Alex Keul   *PO Box 151, A-5024 Salzburg, Austria.*

Information Centre on Ball Lightning   *Institute for High Temperature, Izhrskaya 13/19, Moscow 127412, Russia.*

PERIODICALS

The best regular source of ball lightning investigations is found in:

The Journal of Meteorology   *54 Frome Road, Bradford-on-Avon, Wiltshire, BA15 1LD, UK.*

BOOKS

Titles on ball lightning are not thick on the ground and are often difficult for readers who are not trained physicists. The proceedings of the 1992 and 1993 conferences, as discussed in the text, are available from the *TORRO (UK)* and Austrian addresses above. The classic scientific book is considered to be:

Ball Lightning and Bead Lightning by J. D. Barry (Plenum Press, New York, 1980).

COSMIC MESSAGES

DEFINITION

This phenomenon concerns the claimed receipt of messages from some other realm, seeking to guide the earth towards a better future. It is also often known as *channelling* and has some similarities with mediumship, although it is much less concerned with recently deceased people passing on personal communications. Some of the cosmic messengers are said to be wise individuals who have passed on, perhaps centuries ago, and are now living in some nirvanic afterlife in an elevated status. Others claim to be spiritual entities who no longer need to dwell on earth. In further cases extra-terrestrial origins are also professed.

The messages are received in a variety of ways, but most commonly by telepathy directly into the mind of the recipient (or channeller). Also frequently utilised is *automatic writing*, where a person enters a state of reverie and allows their hand to write on paper (or these days type on to a computer screen) information which is not controlled by their own conscious mind (see top photograph opposite page 58). The free flow of data is supposed to originate from the communicating cosmic source, and the messages are given great respect by supporters of the movement.

Most rare of all methods are what might be considered the channelling equivalents of the direct voice mediums, in which a cosmic spirit allegedly seizes a person's vocal cords and speaks directly – often to assembled gathering of supporters. The purpose is still to pass on relevant messages.

By far the majority of the messages received are very general and spiritual or peaceful in nature, but there has been a steady increase in the numbers relating to ecological matters. Prophecy about the fate of the earth in the very near future is a common trend.

A considerable sub-culture has grown up around much of this material, and it has a strong power base within the fringes of today's paranormal community. However, many paranormal researchers shun the data, considering it rather insubstantial in tone and openly suspecting that a lot of it may originate from the subconscious mind of the channeller herself (they are often, but by no means always, female). Chanellers usually adhere closely to the *new age* movement, as opposed to the traditional ranks of the paranormal, and are found particularly amongst young people and in areas where this form of mysticism has become dominant – for example the Californian coast and parts of south central England that are closely attuned to the lure of crop circles.

HISTORICAL REVIEW

There have always been channels for cosmic messages. The Bible, for example, is full of them and the religious prophets are very close equivalents of modern channellers. They warn and eulogise, often in poetic language, but the substance behind their words requires faith and a sprinkling of translation techniques for their audience to understand fully what is being described.

As shown by the impact that the words of the prophets still exert, channelling has always wielded a powerful influence on humanity. During the sixteenth century the French medical doctor and astrologer

A page from Nostradamus's 1566 Almanac giving his predictions for February

Michel de Notredame, better known today as Nostradamus, was a celebrated channeller of messages and visions in which he believed the entire future history of the world was mapped out. His so-called quatrains, four-verse writings printed in groups of a hundred called centuries, remain, with the Bible, the only book never to have been out of print. Even today, despite their archaic style and at best contentious success rate, rarely a year goes by without the publication of several new books attempting to unravel their meaning.

In the Victorian Age, even whilst Spiritualism was becoming very popular with the masses, there were examples of what can only be described as channellers. (The important different was that whilst Spiritualism contacted human beings who were supposedly in the after-life, channellers have set their sights at a higher cosmic level – communing with other planets and trans-dimensional beings who may not have been human at all.) Hilary Evans has researched cases of women who believed they were being contacted by entities from the planet Mars during the 1880s and psychologists such as Dr Carl Jung recorded a number of similar cases around this time.

The first contactees

It was during the early 1950s that the subject first appeared in its more modern form, although submerged in the UFO sub-culture. So-called *contactees* professed that they had been in communication with wise alien beings. These contacts were occasionally claimed as direct meetings, but more often took place through telepathy and other methods. The entities gave strange names, such as Maximus or Aura Rhanes, and their messages were very much the same as those received today – preaching about our need to mend our wicked ways if the earth hoped to join a cosmic federation. There were, however, more references to nuclear holocausts than one would find today.

Although UFOlogists frowned on the contactees and, to this day, write them off as an unfortunate sidetrack which damaged their fight for scientific respectability, the movement flourished throughout the fifties and several best-selling books appeared. Among them were those by American café owner George Adamski, whose contacts were with friendly and handsome Venusians. Adamski went on to have a decade of success, during which he was reputed to have been granted audiences with royalty and even the Pope. His supporters still belong to a society that honours his name and the peace messages more than thirty years after his death.

Other contactees created cults – gatherings of acolytes who came together to try to convert the world to the ways expressed in these cosmic messages. Some created communes, most of which thrived in America and rarely spread to other countries. They staged conventions which attracted thousands of believers, and one of the contactees even ran for the US Presidency in 1960 – until he withdrew on the urgings of his cosmic mentors and supported John F. Kennedy instead.

Today only a few of the cults survive; although one, which has openly shunned that term as derisive and considers itself a serious organisation, is perhaps more visible than ever. The Aetherius Society was formed after a London taxi driver, George King, was contacted in 1954 and told that he was the chosen earthly representative in a sort of galactic parliament. He has since devoted his life to channelling messages, the tapes of which are widely distributed. These come from assorted spiritual entities, of which the one named Actherius is a key example. George (later to become 'Sir' and 'Archbishop', although his knighthood was not conveyed upon him by the Queen) soon moved to California, but his organisation still has thousands of members worldwide who frequently appear in the media to proclaim their undeniably honourable intentions. The Aetherians claim to use 'prayer power' channelled from their cosmic masters to prevent war and suffering, and are undoubtedly sincere in this intention. Focal points of these energy cells apparently include Los Angeles and, in the UK, Barnsley.

Whilst some aspects of contacteeism kept ticking over during the sixties and seventies it was the approach of the millennium that seems to have led to a true revival. The new age movement considers the year 2000 to be a watershed in human history, and many prophetic visions about pole shifts and cosmic upheavals are being received. The new contactees, renamed channellers, were given a great boost by actress Shirley MacLaine who has conducted a personal odyssey into this world. She has related her experiences in a series of immensely successful autobiographies, the first of which was made into a TV mini-series, starring herself, entitled *Out on a Limb*. Britain too has seen a revival of interest following the claims of former soccer player, TV presenter and ecological spokesman David Icke, who has established himself as something of a guru with his revelatory books.

The field of cosmic messages is now as popular as it has ever been, and as the turn of the century approaches most commentators expect it to increase in prominence. What will happen after that depends to some considerable degree on how many of the prophecies actually come to pass. But on previous experience the failure of even very specific predictions is not, by itself, usually enough to destroy the attraction of a movement. A large section of humanity today clearly relates to channelling on a fundamental spiritual level. This may be all that matters.

EXPERIENCING COSMIC MESSAGES

You are most unlikely to receive some kind of channelling suddenly, out of the blue. There always seems to be a preparatory stage, during which a person becomes aware of odd things happening in their lives: poltergeist activity, powerful dream images and out-of-body sensations are particularly common.

Most channellers are born, not bred. They tend to grow up knowing that something is special about them, and aware that they are picking up messages from sources that others simply cannot tune into. In many respects the channeller is Western society's equivalent of the shaman, or medicine man, who in tribal societies has a pivotal and revered role because he senses things that others do not.

Indeed, there are good grounds for thinking that whether a person becomes a channeller or a Spiritualist medium may to some extent depend upon their belief system or the environment which surrounds them. This may even extend to include alien abductees, as there is some overlap between the content of many of these latter-day encounters and the messages from channellers.

This is not to say that any one of these interpretations is more valid than others. What appears to be occurring is that the message is entering the conscious mind of the witness from some source; sceptics say this source is internal, in other words the subconscious mind, while others feel it is something beyond ourselves. Whatever its true origin, the source *appears* alien and unknown. It may, or may not, have a clearly defined origin, but it will often lack a clear sense of where it comes from. Therefore the source of the message has to be elected by its recipient, and it could well be that personal circumstance plays some part in choosing whether this is to be a deceased relative, a spiritual master or an alien race.

The fact that these sources all overlap, even in cases where some choice of origin is apparent, tends to support this claim. Mediums, for instance, have reported alien messages. Channellers have communed with both cosmic and deceased human entities. The boundaries between these things are at best inconclusive.

What this means for someone who should happen to receive a message (and it will not be a one-off communication, but an ongoing sequence of events) is that there will be a great temptation to ascribe blame – to assign the contact to someone or something other than one-self. However, it may be best to suspend all judgement and just let the messages flow and take you where they lead.

Few people have ever reported being disturbed by the experience of channelling. They generally find it spiritually rewarding; although many participants say that it can be unexpectedly draining in a physical sense. A good rest immediately afterwards is strongly recommended.

Use a tape recorder rather than paper to relate the messages that come into your mind. This allows more freedom, can be done easily in a darkened room without distracting stimuli, and lets the right-hand side of the brain (which appears to be involved in the receipt of these messages) have control without the need for left brain motor skills, such as writing, to get in the way. Playback of such a tape afterwards may prove very illuminating.

RESEARCHING COSMIC MESSAGES

There are some significant problems when it comes to research into this field, which may explain why so little of it has been done in comparison with the amount of actual experience. Perhaps the biggest difficulty is that few channellers really want to be researched. Unlike witnesses to simple paranormal events such as UFOs or ghosts, they exhibit no desire to find out what is going on – they already know. Nor is there a fear factor that might drive them to a researcher for protection or rescue. They do not even need a confidant with whom to share their story, as one of the features of the channelling experience is a common desire to shout about it from the rooftops. Even when these difficulties can be overcome – for instance from a cooperative channeller who may be intrigued by the mechanics of what is going on, or from a person who has not become ensnared by one particular theory about the phenom-enon – the problems are not yet over. For then you have to face up to the daunting banality of many of the messages.

There are rarely specific facts that can be checked out – instead, countless philosophical musings that are impossible to attribute. The basic ethos of what channellers report is something that is praiseworthy and healthy. But one cannot ever hope to prove that, if a being says that the earth needs to change its ways or the planet will be destroyed, this is a genuine warning from an outside source or just an expression of a fear that we all share deep down. And if a being says he comes from a world around the distant star Zeta Reticuli and tells you all about his life, you have little hope of ever finding out if this is pure imagination or devastatingly accurate.

Perhaps the only kind of research that is possible is to collate messages and look for changing patterns or to cross-match specific predictions against actual events. One can also attempt to do some kind of psychological study on the channellers themselves to seek out any patterns that might exist. However, that is difficult to do without creating the impression that one is questioning their sanity or honesty, even if one is actually accepting both of these things.

At present channelling seems destined to remain one of the most fascinating modern mysteries, about which very little can be done.

COSMIC MESSAGES TODAY

In a fascinating experiment conducted in 1993 the journal *Mind, Body and Soul* posed identical questions to new age channeller David Icke and the outspoken paranormal sceptic the Reverend Kevin Logan. Many of their answers were closely similar. For instance, when asked if they perceived God as an outside force or something inside every human being, each replied 'Both.' Icke stressed his theme that at the level of consciousness everything is eternal and immeasurable, while the Reverend Logan emphasised that to view God as just a force is unhelpful and inadequate. However, major differences were apparent as well. Indeed, David Icke seems to regard what he is doing almost as a crusade against conventional religion, which he appears to feel is part of a conspiracy to prevent people from learning the truth. The Reverend Logan sees it almost in reverse, with the truth of Christian religion diffused by the attention being paid to the supernatural. None the less, the overall impression that emerges is that both new age mysticism and conventional religion may be talking about much the same thing but using different words to appeal to differing groups of people.

The parallels between channelling and other phenomena are also well illustrated by recent cases which emerge from very different perspectives and yet reach out towards very similar goals. David Icke, in an interview with Jonathan Stilwell published in *Psychic News* of 16 July 1994, talked about his channelled prophecies, which he first picked up from others but then '… basically I realised that I was largely doing the channelling myself'. These tell of massive earthquakes and volcanic eruptions which, as he wrote in 1992, would be 'well underway by

1993/4'. He was asked if this was not a failed prediction, but concluded that the timescale referred to was in fact 'the 1990s onward'. As for channelling abilities he feels that, whilst another entity may work with him during the process, it is mostly tuning into his own higher levels of consciousness. The names and physical attributes of the channelled sources, he suspects, are there to impose the sort of labels that the human mind requires, but grow less important the more advanced one becomes.

Almost the same sentiments can be found coming from certain contactees and abductees in UFO lore. They provide alien names and planets of origin that seem straight out of a comic book, and their predictions about the fate of the earth are being pushed back with assurances that it will still 'happen very soon'. Both stress the need for spiritual awakening to save the earth.

Spiritualism

Within Spiritualism a similar trend is emerging. It began in the early 1980s when communications were recorded by direct voice means (a form of channelling). Amongst the contributors was the recently murdered rock star John Lennon, who reputedly told of a 'white brotherhood' in the afterlife. This group of discarnate beings were using their various gifts – in his case music – to try to influence the peoples of earth towards a spiritual revolution. Various advanced 'souls' are believed to participate from their supposedly advanced state of being. Many were spiritual leaders on earth. Others have a powerful influence over the masses because of their popularity when alive.

Lennon, or to be precise the voice professing to be Lennon, channelled through medium Bill Tenuto in New York, promised that great changes would see a rise in democracy in eastern Europe and sweeping transformations towards peace all over the world. This seemed unlikely then, but as the prophecies became more intense the old order began to fall. Communism was defeated and freedom spread to eastern Europe more quickly than many would have dared hope. This was followed by positive progress towards peace in Ireland, with the IRA (short-lived) ceasefire announced in 1994. Whilst there are many things that still need changing to make the world a better place, it is possible to imagine this 'white brotherhood' on the peaceful offensive, engineering some sort of spiritual breakthrough.

It is not only rock musicians who allegedly channel their talents. Famed classical composers such as Liszt have sent 'new' works from the afterlife via self admitted musical illiterates. Artists, such as Picasso, also channelled new work in remarkably fast time through the hands of psychic Matthew Manning. Other noted artists have appeared in this way through various other earthly sources (see photograph opposite page 58). More directly related to channelling were the claims of Spiritualist Ann Walker, who told in the summer of 1994 how Albert Einstein, the great scientist (and another claimed member of the 'white brother-hood'), was communicating the dire ecological changes that the earth faced. It seems that we only have until the year 2011 to put things right, or else the planet will face catastrophe at the hands of the channellers' favourite foes of earthquakes, volcanoes, flooding, cometary collisions and the like. Einstein, it seems, has dictated a major dossier, which maps out what will happen if we do not act as stated, which the medium is to hand to government leaders all over the world. She claims that the ordinary people of the planet have to create an outcry and make the politicians act.

UFOs

The field of UFOlogy, too, has seen an upsurge in channelled messages. For the past few years documents purporting to be warnings from a communicating alien source – the *Ashtar* – have been circulated around researchers, urging them to act. These are difficult to distinguish from the philosophical messages of straightforward channellers or 'white brotherhood' contacts via a medium.

In 1994 two new blitzes began. A body calling itself *Elite* began to distribute anonymous letters, supposedly channelled via sources named as Destiny and Deliverance. Whilst the Elite files (which dozens of people were sent over a six-month period) feature many standard UFO terms they also included the usual threats and prophecy about what will happen if we do not pay heed. They also claimed that Elite 'finds it easy to communicate at an inter-dimensional level' with those people (the channellers) who 'show signs of being the descendants of earlier civilisations'.

The other series of messages, which was aware of Elite and referred to it rather critically, came from something called *The Voice*. Whilst super-ficially similar, it was more open in presentation, giving an address to contact and the name of its channel. He was Barry King, a well-known UFO researcher during the 1970s who had investigated several major cases, including Britain's first abduction at Aveley, Essex, in October 1974. He himself is a kind of modern-day contactee.

The Voice represented King's return to visibility after many years in the shadows and uses phraseology familiar from elsewhere, such as our 'being at the crossroads'. However, it has a new twist with its claim that individuals are being programmed at a subconscious level in a massive global conspiracy to control the way the spiritual truth emerges. These people, usually unsuspecting and unsuspected, are released back into the world like a plague of zombies.

At first glance this seems wildly atypical, yet within six months of The Voice starting to express such sentiments David Icke, the conventional channeller, had published a book which he had obviously written before the appearance of the Voice messages. Icke spoke about human beings acting as robots and a major worldwide conspiracy to control how the truth was emerging.

Julie's story

As you can see, these seemingly disparate phenomena share much at a deeper level. And they are on the increase. Typical of the communications I receive from people who do not go on world tours to promote their channelling was an epic account from Julie, who comes from rural Victoria in Australia. Her story of becoming a channel is familiar.

She has a background in art, which suggests that she fits the pattern outlined by researchers into alien abductees (see page 15). No data yet exists on channellers. Julie describes her visual creativity being so strong that, as a child, 'I got to watch video films before they were invented.' At times her visits to strange worlds to play with what we might call aliens became so intense that she struggled to reinstate her bedroom in her field of vision and thus 'get home'.

In her teenage years Julie found that amidst these controlled visions were apparent images of real future events. This was the dawning of her awareness of psychic abilities; although when she started to talk about seeing a devastated earth in the future she was sent to Melbourne to see a psychiatrist. This man told her family that Julie was simply highly intelligent and visually creative and there was nothing wrong with her. Not everyone in Julie's position has been lucky enough to meet such an enlightened doctor, especially in the early 1960s when this occurred.

In April 1969, married and with her husband working nights, she was visited in her bedroom by a tall, beautiful entity who touched her forehead, calmed her fears and gave her a profound sense of purpose and depth to life. Many people in Julie's situation have interpreted such a vision as a ghost, angel or alien, and their lives and belief systems have developed accordingly. She began a kind of religious and spiritual quest as a result.

Over the years and through many adventures Julie honed her abilities via a series of out-of-body visions, during which she even thinks she visited distant star systems. Her mentor told her that he was teaching her about the 'ultimate mind' or 'god force'. At first she thought this was a 'mind game' played via her visualisation abilities. But her 'cosmic teacher' set her right by proving that he could interfere with her real world environment, changing clocks, stopping watches, switching on radio sets and causing electrical circuits to crackle whenever she went near them.

Eventually Julie focused more on channelling messages, which are not intended to be global but aimed more at herself and her friends. These told how everyone lived many lives, on earth and other worlds, and all had a 'cosmic family' which was as important as – if not more important than – their temporary genetic family on earth; how 'consciousness holds the cosmos together'; how 'good and evil are man-made concepts' – and much else.

Is this channelling true reality or a psychic one (if there is a distinction)? It is interesting on a symbolic level that when she enquired why all the names of the channels she had encountered began with A (Aaron, Ashley and so on) she was told that this was because it was a new beginning for her life.

Sources

ORGANISATIONS

New Light Groups   *76 Parkville Road, Withington, Manchester, M20 9TZ, UK* offer to teach basic courses in channelling techniques for those who may feel they can develop this potential.

Concept: Synergy   *PO Box 3285, Palm Beach, FL 33480, USA* is the outlet for the channellings of an entity called Lazaris and offers catalogues and mailing lists of data.

The Voice   *27 The Green, Melbourne, Chelmsford, Essex, CM1 2BQ, UK* is willing to correspond about its source of information.

PERIODICALS

The following magazines cover a range of new age phenomena and include channelling in their brief.

Mind, Body, Soul   *405 Croydon Road, Beckenham, Kent, BR3 3PR, UK.*

Nexus   *PO Box 30, Mapleton, QLD 4560, Australia.*

BOOKS

Of the titles listed below, only the first of Shirley MacLaine's psychic odysseys is included. There have been many others since, all easy to find in bookshops, and several cover her encounters with channelling at least in part. Those by David Icke are from his contentious first book, which sets out his new agenda, and his most recent one which proposes that a conspiracy is afoot. For balance, one by the Reverend Logan is also included. A few of the more interesting Nostradamus titles are listed (the older one is a classic work on which singer-songwriter Al Stewart based his ten-minute song from the 1975 album *Past, Present and Future*, which covers what was then the future, using Erika Cheetham's interpretation of the quatrains – listen to it and see what has since come true). The newer titles assess the as yet unfulfilled prophecies from a 1990s' standpoint and will soon be shown to be either profoundly right or wrong. The medium Ann Walker has written a book about her communications with Einstein and the ecological battle.

Out on a Limb by Shirley MacLaine (Bantam, New York and London, 1983).

Nostradamus: End of the Millennium 1992–2001 by V. J. Hewitt and Peter Lorie (Labyrinth, Durham, NC, and Bloomsbury, 1991).

Nostradamus: The Next 50 Years by Peter Lemesurier (Piatkus, 1993).

The Prophecies of Nostradamus by Erika Cheetham (Corgi, 1973).

The Truth Vibrations by David Icke (Aquarian Press, 1991).

The Robots' Rebellion by David Icke (Gateway Press, 1994).

Paganism and the New Age by the Reverend Kevin Logan (Kingsway, 1989).

Little One by Ann Walker (Century, 1994).

CROP CIRCLES

DEFINITION

The term 'crop circle' is, in a sense, misleading, for these phenomena can form in places other than arable fields and very few of them have ever been truly circular. However, oval and near-circular patterns forming in cereal crops such as oats, wheat and barley were among the first to come to public attention, and it is from these that the term was invented in 1981. What makes the marks appear strange is that they do not resemble the result of weather or some kind of natural effect that might have been caused by animals, for instance. They clearly appear to be artificial, as if a giant cookie-cutter had descended from the sky and bitten into the field.

In the centre the crop is swirled flat in quite a gentle fashion, with a well-defined spiral hub. From above, the effect looks like a Catherine wheel or a view of a distant galaxy of stars. The crop itself is not damaged and can be harvested without ill effect, despite some unsupported scare stories about irradiated grain entering the food chain. At the boundary between the swirl pattern and the unaffected crop the cereal stands erect, almost like a wall, and it too is rarely broken.

Circles have varied in size from a few inches to hundreds of feet across. There have also been gigantic formations, sometimes called *pictograms*, which comprise not only circles and ovals but triangles, straight lines and other geometric shapes. These have covered whole fields and have been up to half a mile in circumference; this one, the largest that has yet appeared, was found in July 1994.

From a high vantage point the effect of a crop circle is dramatic: it stands out sharply against the rest of the field. However, because of their nature they occur only in summer and tend to be short-lived, falling victim to combine harvesters by late August in the northern hemisphere or early February in the southern. Farmers have also been known to harvest early in order to destroy a circle, because they fear that an invasion of sightseers trampling through their fields could damage the crop and make it worthless. In compensation, or simply in a spirit of enterprise, some farmers have charged people small fees to study a spectacular formation at close range. Inevitably a few farmers may have responded to market forces and fabricated crop circles.

Circles were first brought to public attention in southern England, notably Hampshire and Wiltshire. But most cereal-growing countries have now reported them, and what seem to be similar marks have been found in rice, grass, sand, snow, ice, dust and other media. Crop circles are the most common example, because once shaped by whatever force is responsible the crop has a natural resistance against losing this outline. A circle in grass, on the other hand, tends to be blown out by the next moderate wind, leaving less time for it to be seen and photographed.

HISTORICAL REVIEW

There are three distinct histories of the crop circle mystery, which helps to show why the phenomenon is so full of confusion. Two are what we might call 'real' histories and the other concerns our 'social' response to the mystery. This is the most convenient place to start.

A recognisably new phenomenon first appeared in the summer of 1980 when John Scull, a farmer near Westbury in Wiltshire, found a couple of simple circles on his land. He did not take them seriously and harvested the oats before anyone saw the first one. But when the second appeared he made some local enquiries.

Fortunately, an intelligent group of researchers from Bristol called *Probe* visited the site and interviewed the farmer. Nominally UFOlogists, they were headed by the excellent and sensible Ian Mrzyglod. He was used to looking into odd stories of oblique relevance to UFOs and made a good study of this case, taking site photographs and getting samples tested at Bristol University for radiation (although no anomalies were found). He also liaised with Dr Terence Meaden, a local physicist and editor of *The Journal of Meteorology*, to see if he had any ideas.

Meaden suggested a fair-weather stationary whirlwind – the sort that causes piles of rubbish to swirl around in a shopping mall on a hot summer's day, sucking it upwards like a mini-tornado. He proposed that one of these could have formed over the field for a second or two and created the strange mark. To their credit, the UFOlogists preferred this option to the more sensational theory – that a spaceship had landed and left its traces). At the time Ian Mrzyglod was an investigator in my team with BUFORA (the British UFO Research Association) and his reports in 1981 certainly persuaded me and other influential members not to link the circles with aliens.

During the next couple of summers a watch was kept to see if further circles formed, as Meaden felt sure they would if this was a natural phenomenon. Sure enough, a few other patterns appeared in Wessex during July and August of 1981 and 1982. Beyond a little local media interest the matter was not treated to any hype. Everything that occurred seemed to support the whirlwind hypothesis which Mrzyglod, myself and others were now openly endorsing.

However, in July 1983 events took a dramatic turn. Pat Delgado, a local engineer interested in UFOs and associated with the extra-terrestrially orientated magazine *Flying Saucer Review*, had already suggested that there might be something much more exotic within the data. Now he persuaded the media to look at half a dozen circles formed that summer. The national press stories and TV accounts led to international interest, on a small scale at first, but enough to fire the public imagination.

The circles of 1983 were certainly odd. Several of them were in the form of what was called a *quintuplet* – a large central circle with four smaller satellite circles neatly arranged around it. This new design looked far more artificial than the previous simple marks and had Dr Meaden doing some heavy maths to try to work out how the wind could achieve such an effect. He came up with what he thought was a scientific solution, which took account of the ever more elaborate patterns and concluded that stationary whirlwinds were not enough. Something called a *plasma vortex* was now postulated – a new form of atmospheric event similar to a tornado, but with associated electrical effects that allowed complex shapes to be formed. Dr Meaden tried to figure out why these had suddenly started to appear and why the phenomenon was evolving, looking to alterations in the biosphere and farming ecology as possible triggers. Whilst this all seemed plausible, and Dr Meaden retained the support of influential UFOlogists, it is obvious with hindsight that to some extent the theory had lost the simple effectiveness of Meaden's first suggestion, the fair-weather whirlwind.

During the rest of the eighties many variations on the theme developed, including rings and ringed circles. Circle numbers also increased to as many as fifty a year. But simple, single circles still accounted for over 90 per cent of what was being found in fields. This fact allowed Meaden's supporters to cling to his thesis, given that the extreme patterns were rare. Most data fitted easily with his theories. He was also gaining respect from other scientists and a conference was held at Oxford, with meteorologists and physicists attending from the USA and Japan. Paul Fuller and I were the only circle researchers allowed to lecture, as we were then about the only ones not criticising Meaden and not by now seeking some weird force.

Because of the increasing complexity, those who supported that exotic force – possibly alien in origin – began to gain considerable support. Pat Delgado was joined in 1986 by another local engineer, Colin Andrews, and they began a systematic study of the circles in Hampshire and Wiltshire. Media attention was still limited, especially beyond the UK, which probably explains why 98 per cent of all known circles were still being reported in this one small part of southern England where each summer rising numbers of circle researchers would congregate.

Hoaxes

In 1986 Paul Fuller, one of BUFORA's local investigators and a statistician working for Hampshire County Council, and I got together to produce the first publication specifically about crop circles. With BUFORA's backing we published a booklet called *Mystery of the Circles* as soon as the first event appeared that year, and distributed copies to all serious media sources. We also staged a symposium in London, at which (for probably the only time) all factions were represented and allowed to state their case. Terence Meaden put forward his weather-based theory. Colin Andrews and Pat Delgado made their plea for something stranger. Paul and I reiterated the line of our booklet, which backed Dr Meaden but also noted that some of the circles were hoaxes.

In fact Ian Mrzyglod had exposed the first hoax in August 1983, when one national newspaper had tried to fool its competitors by paying a farmer to create a quintuplet on his land. However, media interest was very short-lived that summer and no other news source picked up the story. So the culprits forgot about it and did not publicly admit what they had done until forced to do so much later.

Other examples of hoaxing were beginning to come to light, but, whilst few were taking it seriously (Ian Mrzyglod, disenchanted by the growing media hype, had now abandoned his investigations), even Paul Fuller and I thought it a small part of the problem. However, our campaign succeeded in counteracting some of the hysteria which often spuriously linked circles with UFOs and aliens. We got serious media stories into the *Daily Telegraph* and *Guardian*, and at our London symposium the audience surprisingly backed the weather and hoaxing theories as more probable than any other. The sceptics have since claimed credit for such exposures; although their rational voice was notable by its absence in 1986 and did not surface until 1990, when crop circles suddenly became a hot topic again thanks to a massive media blitz.

As the publicity became more intense and the handful of circle

LEICESTERSHIRE LIBRARIES AND INFORMATION SERVICE & INFORMATION LIBRARY HUMANITIES researchers flocking into Wessex every summer increased to thousands, so the numbers and complexity of the circles also increased. This ought to have been seen as suspicious, but was not. Pat Delgado and Colin Andrews, now sure that something strange was going on, decided to publish a book: publication was planned for July 1989, and its authors aimed to start a revolution.

Aware that it was coming, Terence Meaden decided to self-publish a book attempting to explain his theory. By 1989 he was struggling to accommodate the weird shapes that were turning up ever more frequently, and his book fell halfway between scientific treatise and layperson's guide. Paul Fuller and I much expanded and updated our 1986 booklet and published it, again through BUFORA. It gave a social background to the rise of the phenomenon and justified why we believed that both the weather and hoaxing had to be responsible – although the latter was still under-emphasised. Seven reprints demonstrated the extraordinary public interest in circles at that time.

But all these efforts could in no way compete with the Delgado and Andrews book, *Circular Evidence*, which was a much more expensive, commercial venture and included colour aerial photos of circles. The book barely mentioned meteorology or hoaxing and reached no conclusions other than that a mysterious energy was involved, but was none the less a huge success. Massive media attention rapidly spread around the world. Andrews and Delgado became celebrities and millions were turned on to an interest in these baffling patterns in the crop fields.

In the summer of 1990 a commercial publisher brought out a response from Paul Fuller and myself, which placed more of an emphasis on hoaxing in our joint solution with Meaden's ideas. We also predicted that the phenomenon would change dramatically now that thousands of people were looking for circles and the media had their chequebooks at the ready. We suspected that a hoaxing plot was underway to discredit researchers, and indicated that these people had an urgent need to combat the weather theory with something that was undeniably the product of an intelligence.

The emergence of pictograms

Our prediction was vindicated. That year complex shapes which appeared to resemble picture-language symbols dotted the fields. They soon spread around the world, leaving Dr Meaden's weather theory floundering. Indeed, within a couple of years he had virtually stopped writing or talking about circles. This created the impression, which I think is a false one, that he was completely wrong.

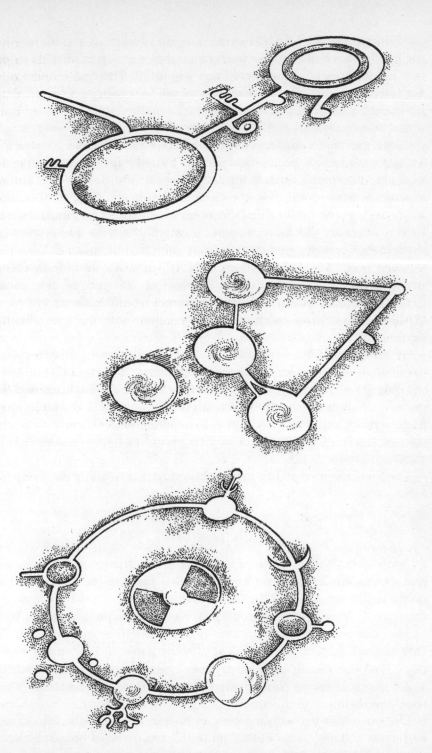

Crop circles – examples of some of the shapes which have been sighted

Although Paul Fuller and I pointed to our prediction as evidence that the pictograms had probably been created by a group of hoaxers toying with circle researchers, we were largely ignored. The real winners were the fast-expanding band of what became called *cerealogists*, who saw these indisputably artificial patterns as a great breakthrough.

For many people, the pictograms proved that some force was trying to convey a message. It had not gone unnoticed that the focal point of this activity was around the mystical sites of Stonehenge and Avebury: the new age movement, already attracted here at the time of the annual summer solstice, soon took the circles to its heart. Conferences were held, circle memorabilia filled shops, mystics made pronouncements or held seances in the patterns, and huge efforts were undertaken to decode the messages – everything from Sumerian to mythical Atlantean was proposed! The Hopi Indians of North America supposedly recognised them as symbols for the ecological collapse of the earth. Channellers even began to dictate messages from the aliens who were creating the patterns – who reported that they looked like an invisible dentist's drill.

By now the circles were seen by many as the most potently visible proof of all that the alien abductees, channellers and psychics had been warning us about for years. The earth was fighting back against the decades of carelessness imposed upon it by humanity. The Medjugorge angelic prophecy of a visible sign to the whole world, warning about the start of the 'end times', was now interpreted as having manifested in southern England.

The media lapped all this up. But everyone was heading for a very big fall.

Confessions

In September 1991 two retired artists from Southampton, Doug Bower and Dave Chorley, secretly approached a national newspaper. They confessed to having faked the circle mystery from the very start, and said they could prove it with photographs. Now they wanted to retire. With hidden cameras filming them, they hoaxed a simple circle in Kent. Pat Delgado was then invited to look at it by the paper, as he had done with countless others in the past. He pronounced it genuine. On the eve of a front page exposé by *Today* newspaper, reporters faced him with the shocking truth.

The two artists had only a couple of days in the limelight, and in fact had never claimed to have faked more than a couple of hundred circles since 1975. They had been responsible for the invention of the

RIGHT
Italian medium 'Anita' uses her left
hand during automatic writing. The
pen is held loosely and the messages
contain information she is not
consciously aware of (see page 40).

BELOW
Painting by trance artist Luiz
Gasparetto, in the style of Modigliani
(see page 48).

The modern crop circles mystery began near the Tully River in Far North Queensland, Australia when this one pictured above appeared in reeds near Euramo in January 1966. British hoaxers Doug and Dave admit this unsolved case was their inspiration (see page 64).

BELOW
A crop circle at Barbury Castle, near Swindon, Wiltshire. As a general rule, the more complex the shape, the more likely it is to be a hoax.

pictograms, citing reasons just as Paul Fuller and I had predicted in our book the year before. They knew that others had copied their tricks, and felt that there could be no real circles. However, Doug and Dave, as they were affectionately known, admitted something very important. They had first got the idea to create the circles after seeing some in the Australian bush during January 1966. They had not faked any of these. Indeed, since the area was populated with deadly snakes, nobody in their right mind would have done so.

Although it was scarcely noted by the media, the two artists were really saying that they had created fewer than 10 per cent of all known circles and that even these had deliberately mimicked a seemingly real phenomenon that had existed before they came on to the scene. Despite the media cries that these men had created the whole mystery, that was not what Doug and Dave's own story implied.

Media interest almost disappeared after the 1991 debacle, but the circles continued to appear as widely as before. Of course, there were many copycat versions of the now retired Doug and Dave's hoaxes. Dozens of candidates, even groups engaged in long-term operations, were exposed, notably by *The Crop Watcher*, a magazine which Paul Fuller launched in 1990. They left massive clues, forging patterns at places such as Fakenham or Littley Green – (the latter being made by 'littley green men'). As ever-sillier shapes appeared, the probability that most were the result of human engineering became all too clear. However, this barely dented the enthusiasm of the cerealogists for a more exotic answer.

The conferences continued and still attracted great crowds. More books and videos appeared. The theory that an intelligence was communicating not only lived on, but new claims surfaced. Doug and Dave were seriously (but in my view wrongly) accused of being pawns of a government disinformation plot. Colin Andrews even addressed a meeting at the United Nations in New York during October 1993. So those who concluded that the loss of media interest signalled the end of the mystery could not have been more wrong. Crop circles simply would not die.

The future of cerealogy

That was the social history of the crop circle phenomenon. Similarly, if you were willing to believe Doug and Dave, the real history was a tale of hoaxing which they initiated very slowly from 1975, which gradually escalated in response to what the circle hunters did and said, and which became ever more elaborate as new tricksters tried to better the creations of the two grand masters. The over-enthusiasm of the press and the wild theories of many cerealogists just added fuel to the flames and by 1991 everyone was investigating a completely fabricated mystery world wide. The marks were produced by methods of greater or lesser sophistication which involved ropes, boards and simple devices flattening out the crop. A fair-sized, good-looking circle could be made in half an hour, as experiments from 1983 had persuasively shown. Everyone knew there were some hoaxes in the data; it was just that no researcher would believe that all of them were fake.

Suffice it to say that no cerealogist accepts this scenario, although many people who have only followed the mystery through the press do. However, there is also a third – most important – history of the crop circle phenomenon. This is only now being pieced together and you can read about it on page 64. Despite the antics of Doug and Dave and media apathy, its growing acceptance may well establish a place for cerealogy as a genuine phenomenon after all.

*E*XPERIENCING CROP CIRCLES

One thing that is not widely appreciated is that there are two types of crop circle witness. Someone has to come upon a pattern before anybody else does. If you are in that position you have important tasks to perform. First, take pictures of this 'virgin' formation, preferably from above – from the air or from a high vantage point – with a telephoto lens. Once people start to tread all over the circle, any signs of hoaxing may rapidly disappear. The first person into a circle can seek out clues, such as a hole at the centre where a pole or stake may have been located. Often tricksters will try to cover this up by filling it in with soil, but if you look carefully you can normally spot it. Just because the crop is not broken does not prove that human beings have not flattened out the circle. They can 'spread the load' using boards or even polystyrene sheets, which act like snowshoes. This allows the crop to be gently swirled and creates the impression that no heavy-booted team of humans was responsible.

The second category of witness is in many respects far more important. These are people who have seen crop circles as they actually form. In some instances, of course, this means bystanders who chanced upon hoaxers at work. Most of their illegal work is done at night in isolated fields in order to minimise the risk of discovery, but 'hoaxbuster' patrols have been mounted by a dedicated few, and other culprits have been caught in the act by sheer fortune.

Nevertheless, there are also around fifty known cases where witnesses have seen circles form without human intervention. A couple walking a dog, for instance, saw an invisible rotation of air create a small circle close by and within a couple of seconds. A case from Warminster in Wiltshire describes how the field suddenly opened up 'like a lady's fan' with no visible source, except the wind rippling through the crop.

There are hardly any accounts of anything truly exotic creating a circle, although one from St Margaret's Bay in Kent refers to a tubular column that was semi-transparent and acted like a beaker placed over the field. It was raining heavily at the time and the water poured down the sides, not penetrating within. A small circle was created under this rotating (vortex?) tube inside a field of grass.

As there are relatively few sightings in comparison with the thousands of crop circles that have been found, this evidence is very significant. If you are fortunate enough to be in the right place at the right time (which will usually mean a cereal field, or adjacent to one, in mid to late summer and possibly during early morning or late evening), take in every detail that you can, record it immediately and report it to a serious research group. There is nothing to fear from seeing a circle under formation. Whilst the occasional buzzing noise or tingling sensation has been reported by witnesses, nobody has been injured by their chance encounter with whatever energy is forming these circles.

RESEARCHING CROP CIRCLES

In my opinion there is not a great deal to be gained by obtaining farmers' permission and visiting as many circles as you can find during the summer. It is diverting entertainment to film and log different patterns, but much of what you come across will be the result of hoaxing and it may be difficult to pick out any that have a chance of being genuine. Countless attempts have been made to set up automatic monitoring stations at likely crop circle sites, but no dramatic evidence has taken us further forward. The occasional instance where something exciting appears to have been filmed is hard to evaluate because of the dark conditions, but in at least one case what was recorded was only the flashlights of the hoaxers.

Similarly, there have been attempts to take samples and test circles for mysterious energies. However, these are hampered by the fact that one can never know what the background readings ought to be, since it is impossible to know how many samples were taken from hoaxed circles as opposed to real ones. Whilst there have been occasional stories about breakthroughs and cell structure changes found inside samples, nothing uncontentious or without a possible alternative explanation has yet emerged. Typical is the huge volume of research that went into analysing mysterious noises tape recorded inside circles. These were eventually found to be emitted by a bird called the grasshopper warbler!

I think that the best possible form of research today is to look at what Paul Fuller has been up to (see *Crop Circles Today*) and try to emulate this brand of historical analysis. Anything uncovered in fields nowadays is tarnished by the spectre of trickery. However, if we look for evidence that pre-dates the invention of the term 'crop circle' and the earliest hoaxes admitted to by Doug and Dave, not to mention the media publicity that changed the ground rules, the chances that we are dealing with real evidence are much higher. Of course, we can never eliminate the possibility of hoaxing, even in the distant past. But it seems unlikely to have been common in the absence of the social pressures that have stimulated it on such a massive scale in recent years.

CROP CIRCLES TODAY

Less than a year after Doug and Dave had made their startling admission, a visitor from the USA was arousing interest again with an extraordinary new approach. Dr Steven Greer, who had developed a process that he called 'close encounters of the fifth kind', began to visit Britain in order to use sophisticated communications equipment to 'signal' into the sky. His aim was to initiate direct contact with the entities that he felt were creating the circles. To this end, in July 1992 a week-long stake-out was mounted by his team at Woodborough Hill, near Alton Barnes in Wiltshire. This was an area where many of the pictograms had already formed, and so hopes were high that the circle-makers might pay a visit.

Dr Greer had already used his techniques to stimulate and film sightings of strange lights in the sky at Gulf Breeze, Florida, a notorious UFO hot spot. Sceptics had declared these to be naval flares or even home-made hot air balloons, but they were certainly flying lights and they did turn up apparently to order.

The CSETI experiment

The cerealogists are a tight-knit community and there was little chance of keeping secret what Dr Greer was up to in Wiltshire. Indeed, that summer Colin Andrews had made a startling prediction on TV that a major event would occur – it probably related to Dr Greer's forthcoming experiment.

Greer's team (known as CSETI) do claim an amazing success. In his detailed report of the events he describes how in the early hours of 27 July they 'had a confirmed, close-range lock-on with a structured space-craft'. Some of the light effects they describe sound to me a little like laser displays reflecting off low cloud, and there was such a show going on at the time some miles away – it might have been responsible for part of the experience. However, other aspects of the story, such as when a huge 'craft' descended towards the group, evidently require more consideration. Unfortunately, rain prevented the cameras from securing any visual evidence of this dramatic event.

Subsequently claims have been made (for instance, in an article published by *Crop Watcher*) that Greer and his team were 'set up' by hoaxers using customised searchlights. In a pre-planned operation, this team were trying to ensnare as many researchers as possible with their technological wizardry. It is worth noting that in the two or three days prior to this incident I received several anonymous phone calls to my ex-directory number. They pressed me to go to Wiltshire, as a 'big UFO event' was going to happen and I would not want to miss it. I thought this simply referred to Colin Andrews' prediction and did not think the expense of travelling such a long distance was justified – even if a space-ship was going to turn up in return. In retrospect, if there was someone trying to trap investigators into an encounter then calls urging my presence make perfect sense.

Certainly the legacy of Dr Greer's extraordinary experiment lives on and he has continued his efforts at two-way communication with the intelligences that he is certain are out there. Perhaps definitive proof will be secured by his team through this novel method, but as yet I have not seen it.

Other efforts, also by an American entrepreneur, have centred on purchasing fields and creating a message in the crops – such as one in English saying 'Talk to us.' His 1992 experiment produced a 'reply' – a nearby field sprouted a series of squiggles which were subsequently decoded by one researcher as an alien language. In 1993 another attempt was made, and this time the symbol for a disabled toilet was later found in a nearby crop. Whilst these are fascinating, if not amusing, efforts to try to make progress, I consider them futile. It is difficult not to imagine a gang of very terrestrial intelligences having a great laugh at the expense of such dedicated enthusiasm.

An ancient phenomenon?

Much more interesting are the attempts to salvage some kind of un-explained phenomenon from out of the crop circle data. Paul Fuller has been at the forefront of most of this, but others, such as Peter Rendall and Andy Collins, have begun to contribute important evidence too. These people are the ones mostly responsible for collating eye witness testimony of crop circles as they form. In addition they have looked for cases from the past – sometimes the distant past – that suggest how crop circles pre-date the hoaxing of Doug and Dave. Given that these two men say their idea came from 'real' circles in Australia, there is reason to suppose that more could exist even before that event.

I have been myself to the Tully area of Queensland, where a farmer named George Pedley found a swirled circle in swampy reeds. Certainly from photographs taken at the time, in January 1966, this does seem to be the same phenomenon as the one under study today (see photo-graph opposite page 59). (The 1966 circle is the one that Doug and Dave admit gave them the idea to try to fake lookalike patterns years later when back in England. Its origin is unexplained and Doug and Dave are adament they did *not* hoax it.) More important, I uncovered local traditions of circles in the area from both before and after 1966, which are well known to sugar-cane and banana plantation owners. Moreover, local researcher Claire Nobel found in an independent study that the aborigines have legends about strange lights in this area which appear to be related to the locations where crop patterns form.

Nor is this by any stretch of the imagination unique. Farmers from all over the world tell tales of finding crop circles from time to time. Paul Fuller and Andy Collins have interviewed several witnesses who, as children as long ago as 1920, were living on farms and can describe these marks. There are even folk tales, legends and woodcuts which indicate that farmers as far back as 1590 were aware of these strange circular impressions flattened into their crop. One of these documents, which is in the British Museum, refers to the cause of the mark as a *mowing devil* – indicating the manner in which these things were interpreted before modern images of aliens and paranormal powers took hold.

A typical case excellently investigated on site by Andy Collins comes from Cockethurst Farm at Eastwood in Essex. In July 1964 the area was a field of ripening wheat, although it is now part of school playing fields. Two witnesses who used regularly to walk their dog in this spot recall discovering early one morning a forty-foot diameter circle with a precise anti-clockwise swirl. As they had passed the spot the night before and nothing odd had been present, it seems to have formed overnight. They later entered the circle and noted how the crop became progressively bleached towards the centre, at which point it seemed to have been dried by considerable heat. This is one of countless cases which gives the lie to the widespread belief that Doug and Dave 'invented' crop circles.

This evidence is now so strong that it is virtually impossible not to accept that some kind of swirled circle phenomenon has been a part of the natural environment for hundreds of years. The hunt for photographic evidence has continued. There are at least a dozen examples from Britain, Canada, the USA and Australia that pre-date Doug and Dave's first hoaxes. Paul Fuller has also begun a systematic study of photographs taking by pioneers who earlier in this century mapped Britain from the air. A number of suspicious features have been found on their photographs, but none has as yet been conclusively proven to be a crop circle. However, there are millions of images to study so this will be a long process.

What is very important is that all the evidence before the arrival of Doug and Dave – the eye witness, legends, woodcuts, childhood memories and photographs – appears to describe simple, single circles. There is nothing even as complex as a quintuplet – and certainly no pictograms. This may mean that the real phenomenon consists only of single circles. Perhaps Dr Meaden's theory of a fair-weather whirlwind was correct after all; much of the eye witness testimony would support that view. The rest of the mystery appears to be a result of massive latter-day hoaxing which has led researchers a long way up the garden path.

The possibility of cheap energy

The Japanese have become particularly interested in circles because they might provide clues to the nature of ball lightning. Scientists such as Dr Yoshi Hiko Ohtsuki at Waseda University have attempted to produce electrified whirlwinds in the laboratory to discover if Dr Meaden's plasma vortex theory might work in a more simplified form. They have simulated what could be ball lightning and, as a side effect, found single circles etched in dust on the metal plates used during the experiments.

More dramatically, larger-scale examples of what could be simple circles have been found by workers in the tunnels of underground railway systems in Tokyo and Osaka. One of these tunnels was closed off to allow scientists to extract evidence: the circles are real enough, several inches in diameter and apparently produced as a result of the rotating air caused by passing trains and the electrical field generated by their propulsion system. The Japanese physicists analysing this data hope that it will enable them to produce artificial ball lightning in a controlled fashion. If so, they might be able to unlock the potential huge energies trapped inside. The economic advantages of such cheap energy are easy to imagine.

None of this will stop a still eager band of people from seeking a mystical truth behind the circles. Indeed, even channeller David Icke has now commented on them, noting that you can always tell a real one from a fake because in a hoax 'the energy is flat', whereas in a genuine circle 'it is like being plugged into the mains by your feet'. He sees the crop circles as a dire warning from the 'earthspirit' that we must reject our consumer society or else face destruction.

SOURCES

ORGANISATIONS AND PERIODICALS

It is amazing how many crop circle societies and magazines have sprung up in a relatively short time. Here are some of those which in my view deserve recognition for their efforts.

Crop Watcher *3 Selbourne Court, Tavistock Close, Romsey, Hampshire, SO51 7TY, UK.* Organised by Paul Fuller, this team coordinates UK research into hoaxing, historical cases and eye witness accounts. Issued quarterly, the magazine supports both the human and meteorological approaches and publishes a lot of hard data (for instance, issue 14 has a database of all then known pre-Doug and Dave circles).

The Circular *13 West Parade, Norwich, Norfolk, NR2 3DN, UK.* Published quarterly by the CCCS (Centre for Crop Circle Studies), this magazine is more broadly based and looks at the more outlandish theories. The CCCS has branches around the world, and for making a photographic record of ongoing circle activity it is unsurpassed.

North American Institute for Crop Circle Research *PO Box 1918, Winnipeg, Manitoba R3C 3R2, Canada.* Covers the whole of North America and, under the tutelage of Chris Rutkowski, has a fine catalogue.

Australian Physical Ground Effect Cases *PO Box 1894, Adelaide, SA 5001, Australia.* Many of the early crop circle cases, some including photographs, come from this part of the world. Keith Basterfield does a good job of sensibly collating activity on to a database.

UFO Sweden *PO Box 11027, S-600, 11 Norrkoping, Sweden.* Clas Svahn has focused on circle activity with this first-rate group and produced some excellent data. There is a long video interview with Doug Bower which is well worth seeing, and his team has also investigated several cases of ice circles – a related phenomenon that also occasionally occurs outside Scandinavia.

BOOKS

The following titles provide a general review of crop circle data. The one edited by Ralph Noyes is broadly based, with chapters from a range of contributors and typical of the CCCS ethos. Also listed is the best work by Dr Terence Meaden, although you may find his early articles in *The Journal of Meteorology* (for address see page 39) more palatable. The Colin Andrews/Pat Delgado book is essential because of its huge impact on public thinking. Jim Schnabel's volume is idiosyncratic and has attracted much controversy, reading like a comic novel based (some feel rather loosely, others say more closely) on the characters behind the circles. Finally, there are the three books by Paul Fuller and myself – ranging from the first-ever booklet published on the subject to the only book so far revised and updated. These cover the sociology, hoaxing and weather theories perhaps more fully than any other publication, and the latest one attempts to make a case for a real phenomenon after Doug and Dave.

The Crop Circle Enigma edited by Ralph Noyes (Gateway Books, 1990).

The Circles Effect and Its Mysteries by Dr Terence Meaden (Artetech, Wiltshire, 1989; by mail order only from Artetech, 54 Frome Road, Bradford-on-Avon, Wiltshire, BA15 1LD, UK).

Circular Evidence by Colin Andrews and Pat Delgado (Bloomsbury, 1989).

Round in Circles by Jim Schnabel (Hamish Hamilton, 1993).

Mystery of the Circles by Paul Fuller and Jenny Randles (BUFORA, 1986; by mail order only from BUFORA, BM BUFORA, London WC1N 3XX).

Controversy of the Circles by Paul Fuller and Jenny Randles (BUFORA, 1989; by mail order only, as above).

Crop Circles: A Mystery Solved by Paul Fuller and Jenny Randles (Robert Hale, 1990; updated softback edition, Robert Hale, 1993).

DREAMS

DEFINITION

Everybody dreams for several hours each night, including those who argue vehemently that they do not. We are simply rather poor at remembering these images because they tend not to enter the long-term memory store of our brain in an easily retrievable form. Experiments have shown that we can train ourselves to recall a much higher percentage of dream imagery than is normal. Some societies consider this a praiseworthy achievement, regarding the dream as a window to the soul. If you can understand the images that your mind conjures up when your conscious brain is idling, you may unlock many secrets about both yourself and the universe.

Dreams are periods of subconscious brain activity that punctuate resting sleep. If you watch a sleeping person you may notice jerking, rapid eye movements. This so-called REM sleep is characteristic of dreaming and is found in some other animals such as dogs, leading to speculation that they too may dream.

The purpose of dreaming remains contentious, but the role-play concept is favoured by many psychologists. They feel that dreams allow the mind to use imagery to act out possible scenes and prepare the dreamer for future events. Others propose a random shuffling of images that are stored in the mind. Psychologists such as Jung considered dreams as highly symbolic, with imagery representing an archetype or belief system. It may even be that a mixture of several options applies.

There are also many kinds of dreaming, some of which step across the boundaries of the paranormal. Flying dreams are surprisingly common and thought to reflect strong psychological urges, although no human beings have ever 'really' flown to give stored images that might allow such visions to be perceived. Mystics claim a strong overlap with out-of-body experiences.

Precognitive dreams (those which foresee the future) have been recorded for thousands of years and, despite scientific attempts to ascribe them to coincidence on the grounds that billions of dreams are dreamt every night and the odds say that some of these should match future incidents, problems do remain. These allegedly precognitive dreams are usually not one-off occurrences and happen to some people quite often. So, if we can put it all down to chance, would not such 'lucky' people win the lottery week after week?

Then there are even stranger states, such as the lucid dream, in which the sleeper recognises that he or she is dreaming and takes conscious control of the imagery that unfolds – the results are near-magical. There are even false awakenings, a related state in which a dreamer experiences waking up, having breakfast and going to work, all in full detail, only to find himself back asleep – the whole thing has in fact been a very vivid dream that matched reality in extraordinary depth.

Indeed, we now seem to be facing the possibility that what we call a dream is but one point on a spectrum of consciousness which includes several other states with very strange properties indeed. The quest to understand the nature of consciousness may well be the most progressive science of the twenty-first century.

HISTORICAL REVIEW

Unusual dream states have been recorded throughout history. Most religious texts, including the Bible, rely heavily on visionary dreams as the starting point of prophecy and mystical experience. Names such as *nirvana* and *reverie* illustrate that most cultures have had a concept of altered states of consciousness. In such a condition communion with other dimensions has been considered very possible. Even lucid dreams were well described in Roman times.

At first there was a strong belief that an actual conduit opened up when the conscious mind was closed off: in the dream state one literally stepped into other worlds and met their inhabitants. The legacy of this centuries-old belief is found in the concept of the 'astral plane', on which consciousness enters a higher sphere and is able to exist temporarily alongside entities who do not need physical embodiment. A similar idea is found in most religions, from the Christian heaven to the afterlife of Spiritualism, and this is the basis of many phenomena such as channelling and mediumship.

The nature of the mind

It was only in the early twentieth century that anyone seriously questioned the nature of the mind and began to apply a more materialistic vision to it. Experimental psychologists stimulated parts of the brain to see what kind of subjective experience emerged, and by this crude methodology our knowledge of the brain and its interaction with the mind developed piecemeal. Two schools of thought developed. The monists saw brain and mind as the same physical organ, whereas the dualists regarded mind as being something immaterial that utilised the physical brain. The battle between these viewpoints remains unresolved, although most psychologists are monists.

Dreams were still seen as something of an irrelevance by scientists, unless they followed the lead of Freud, Jung and Adler and used them to help with psychiatric diagnoses. However, gradually, as we began to understand more about the amazing complexities of the way information is stored by brain cells, attention began to switch towards the different dream states that were reported. REM sleep was identified in 1952, and ever since has been taken as the primary indicator of dreaming. There are, however, still a few who dispute this assumption. At the Oxford psychophysical research laboratories in the mid-1960s, Charles McCreery and Celia Green started a systematic study of assorted dream states and began to look for patterns in hallucinatory, visionary and lucid dream reports. Thirty years later this work continues to push back the frontiers of knowledge.

Dream symbolism

In addition we have learnt a good deal about dream symbolism – way beyond what is contained in those simplistic manuals telling us how to interpret our dreams. Work by dream specialists such as Ann Faraday in the 1970s has illustrated the wonderful creative potential of the sleeping mind, ranging from its ability to pun to the powerful way in which it can express problems with vivid imagery. All of these things can be turned to advantage.

As an example of punning, take the following dream of being caught in a flood, desperately looking for a boat and escaping on the back of an old piano. This typically silly dream takes on new meaning when you study Ann Faraday's research about how a dream symbolises information. We might here suspect that the dreamer's mind, seeking a boat, thought of the shipping line 'P and O' and created the 'piano' in response! In a case such as this the effect is to produce little more than a wry smile, but similar abilities to create powerful images and solve meaningful problems within dreams have led to very positive things. Robert Louis Stevenson is just one of many authors who used this method, piecing together the plot for *Dr Jekyll and Mr Hyde* from a series of dream images. Indeed, he reported that his books often 'wrote themselves' inside dreams.

More explicitly, the chemist Friedrich Kekulé, baffled after weeks of trying to figure out the structure of the benzene molecule, had his problem solved by a dream. His mind had presumably worked out the answer already and wanted to tell him so in a powerful fashion, so it produced a dream of coiled snakes eating one another's tails. On waking, Kekulé quickly recognised this as a beautiful, graphic rendition of the mathematical symmetry that he sought. Other scientific progress has had a similar genesis. Leonardo da Vinci explained that many of his amazing inventions came about this way. The brilliant mathematician Alan Turing created the world's first working computer after seeing its design in a dream. Obviously, there is much to be gained by learning more about how to harness this potential and dream research is perhaps now recognising this possibility for the first time.

Even more dramatic is the possibility that in this state of consciousness time and space may be bypassed. Actress Anne Baxter is the granddaughter of the famous American architect Frank Lloyd Wright. One night she dreamt of a huge bird flying towards her, heading from the light into the darkness. She was terribly saddened and awoke in horror. An hour later, still unable to sleep as a result of the nightmare, she heard the telephone ring. The caller told her that her grandfather had died – seemingly at just the time she must have had her dream. He was then living in the west of the USA, where the sun would be rising, and in the city of Phoenix, named after a large mythical bird. Her dream image seems to have instantly portrayed the knowledge that her mind had somehow detected, in a scene that was powerfully emotive but highly symbolic. Of course, the real question here is how her mind had access to this knowledge from thousands of miles away at the moment the event took place. Did she bypass space, or see ahead through time to the

Examples of common dream symbols

moment when she gained conscious knowledge of the death? Both possibilities exist.

This is a far from uncommon experience, especially when there is some kind of emotional link between two people. It is not unreasonable to call it an everyday occurrence. However, in order to understand it better we need to learn more about the symbolism within more mundane dream states. This ongoing research will provide the clues that may lead to an unexpected paranormal breakthrough.

EXPERIENCING DREAMS

Everyone who has woken from a nightmare knows the shock it can impose on the system. Many people change their plans, even at considerable expense, as a result of dreams which were probably nothing more than that. But so awesome can the sense of reality be that some people do not feel inclined to take chances.

It is difficult to strike a reasonable balance here. Dreams are messages from your subconscious, but it would be wrong to conclude that they are always (indeed, some would say ever) messages from the future. Most of the time they will be random, inconsequential, perhaps cautionary or in response to your fears, but they will not reflect a coming reality.

The best way to deal with your dream life is to become more familiar with it. Nightmares are powerful because they bash their way through your conscious defences in a desperate escape bid. They may be the only dream of which you will become consciously aware for many weeks. If you train yourself to recall a higher proportion of the several hours of dream images that you will experience each night, any one particular dream will become diluted in such a broad context.

It is not difficult to recall more of your dreams. Simply fix on one image as you wake and before you move about or get out of bed. Close your eyes again for a few moments and work around that image. The chances are that more details will flow out. With practice the proportion will increase. If you wake in the night from a dream, try to do the same thing. This should help you to recall more when you eventually awake in the morning.

Just the act of mulling over dream images like this will allow some of them to enter long-term memory store. For greater retention, however, you need to write them into a *dream diary* or, better still, record them on tape – the free flow of speech makes it easier to continue recollection, whereas the act of writing involves too much physical activity that counters dream recall.

Observe the world of your dreams as if you were a naturalist studying strange species. Log them, classify them, seek out patterns and meanings. You will almost certainly discover that some appear paranormal – be they lucid, out-of-body, precognitive dreams or whatever. But it is really the whole structure of your dreamscape that you should be fascinated by, as this will help you to unravel personal codes that might enable you to decipher the symbolism in paranormal dreams. All dreams depend upon your own personal beliefs and modes of thought. This is why they will be highly symbolic and individual. You must decode your own dream history in order to understand how to interpret the obscure imagery that might occur in future dreams.

Finally, bear in mind that dreams appear to occur more frequently if we are having new experiences. This is possibly because the brain has more work to do in recording these events, and so uses the function of sleeping and dreaming in 'data processing'. This means that you can actually stimulate dreaming by trying out new things, visiting different places and watching a lot of TV news reports.

RESEARCHING DREAMS

These days most progressive dream research is the province of psychological or parapsychological laboratories, which have the equipment to make detailed physiological measurements. However, this does not prevent you conducting serious research into your own dreams as just outlined. Moreover, as dreams are the one strange experience that every human being can be guaranteed to have on a regular basis, they are perfect vehicles for your research.

There is also a place for the recording of anecdotal testimony about unconventional dreams reported by others. It is often difficult to do more than log them, but if possible it should be contemplated. Here is a recently reported example. A young woman told me that she had had a weird dream in which she was making banana sandwiches at her Derbyshire home when the phone rang. It was her boyfriend's best friend, calling to say that her boyfriend had suffered an accident on his motorcycle. In response the girl began to laugh, causing the dream to end. This was obviously puzzling to her. Why have such a strange dream? But, more important, why laugh when she knew this was not how she would react were such a thing to happen in real life? When they met at the pub she told her boyfriend and his friend about the dream, and they all smiled about it. But later, after she had gone home and made herself a snack (banana sandwiches, of course) the phone rang. It was her boyfriend's friend. He *did* say what he had said in the dream. And she *did* start to laugh, naturally assuming that he was having a joke. But he was not fooling, and had in fact forgotten about their conversation. The accident (fortunately not serious) had really taken place.

This is just the sort of dream for which you should be on the look-out. It should enter your file of peculiar dreams, as it helps to build up clues for future reference. That dream also poses many questions about how the dreamscape operates. Most specific is the perplexing one of whether the dream forged the reality, or vice versa. For if the girl had never related the dream she would not have assumed that the phone call was a joke and so laughed uncharacteristically in response. But her dream showed an apparent future reaction which depended not only on the dream having occurred beforehand, but on its being remembered and then reported to others. This case crosses what is known as the 'boggle threshold' and throws into utter confusion a very basic principle of physics, that a cause must always precede an effect.

Science presently has no recourse in the face of such a dream other than to call it pure coincidence. However, in this instance you would need written confirmation of their version of events from both her boyfriend and his friend. Yet even if you are lucky it will still remain a story and nothing more. We can never confirm or refute details that are offered from anybody's dream – even your own. All this makes dream research an inexact science, but a fascinating one none the less.

DREAMS TODAY

Research is continuing to unravel the symbolic nature of dreams. One example comes from a Surrey woman who described a vision of a man's face inside a cage, alongside someone whom she recognised as an assistant from the local chemist's shop. This meant nothing until weeks later when she met a man by chance and recognised his face as the one in the dream. In due course he proposed marriage to her, but she had a feeling, not unconnected with these images, that she should not accept. Only then did she discover that he had been under psychiatric care and now had a serious mental illness which required constant medication. The dream image had expressed all this (by showing her symbols of medication and incarceration in a kind of graphic snapshot projected through time.

However, the latest work has also found that emotion provides a strong link to these symbolic dreams. The more emotive the bond and the consequent dream experience, the more powerful it can be.

Stephen from Aberdeen reported how he had had a series of strange dreams in which he was awash with emotions, fighting with his father and holding a knife – something he hated doing in reality. He also felt the shame and sensation of trying to kill someone and being exposed by the press. Such dreams meant nothing at the time, but whilst walking on the beach afterwards he was overcome with similar sensations. He talked about it to a friend. It transpired that a relative of that man had gone missing and a few days later was found dead on the beach near the spot where Stephen had walked. The man had become obsessed with knives and had tried to kill someone, and thus the story was then published; after fighting with his father and holding a knife the man had felt great shame. It appears that Stephen had somehow relived these emotions through his dreams *and* his waking feelings. What are we to make of this experience? Did Stephen read of the murder and incorporate it into a subsequent dream, or did he have a precognition of meeting the relative and hearing the story of the fight at that time? Either way, this shows just how strange and complex dreams can be.

Experiments with prediction

Beyond recording cases such as these and the piecing together of the resultant clues, one can try experiments, especially with people who claim to 'dream true' on a frequent basis. Through a women's magazine I operated a scheme called Project Dreamwatch, which aimed to test regular psychic dreamers by encouraging them to see ahead to any global events during the month in question. Each dream was dated and timed via a post office stamping process, and one or two striking hits emerged.

In October 1994 another experiment was set up by ITV. For the television series *Strange but True?* I had organised a film about Chris Robinson, a man who has had so many strange dreams that seem to predict the future that he has often helped the police with their enquiries. Chris, due to appear on the *This Morning* magazine programme to promote the start of the series, was tested by secretly placing an object in a sealed box and then asking him to describe any dream that might relate to it. He had only twelve hours' notice of this experiment, but, although his dreams normally recur over several nights, he accepted the challenge. He subsequently announced to a live audience of two million that he had seen a telephone box containing a friend who had the nickname 'Dolly', and a post office sack with what looked like lots of presents such as at Christmas. Chris has learnt how to decode his dream images, and immediately suggested that they meant a children's toy had been sealed away.

He was spot on: the object was a child's teddy bear. It had been put there by a programme worker who was born on Christmas Day and whose parents had run a post office. All of this data was neatly encapsulated by the flash images in Chris Robinson's dreams. He only recalled these as often as he did because he made entries in a dream diary each morning, and he had come to understand the symbolism through years of deciphering dream images and matching them against actual events. There is no reason to think he is any different from anybody else. Potentially we all could be Chris Robinsons.

Controlling lucid dreaming

Perhaps the most exciting progress is being made in the quest to control lucid dreaming. It is now known that over 90 per cent of the population have a lucid dream at some point in their lives, but that for all except about one-tenth of them this is an extremely rare phenomenon, probably lasting for only a few seconds. Indeed, at first it was even suspected that the lucid dream might be a waking phenomenon – in other words, that the person who believed he was dreaming and had become aware of that condition was actually still awake and only imagining that he was dreaming.

Nowadays, however, experiments at Stanford University in California and at Oxford in Britain have conclusively established that lucid dreams are real and occur only during REM sleep. Dr Keith Hearne, a British parapsychologist, and Dr Peter Fenwick, a neuropsychologist from St Thomas's Hospital in London, have invented an amazing technique which, when it first succeeded, was described by Dr Hearne as being 'like receiving a message from another galaxy'. What they did was to conduct experiments with people who have more lucid dreams than normal. Using sensitive wiring attached to the eyes, a device can record the actions that a person is making within a lucid dream. The dreamer is set a certain task to perform before going to sleep and, once in lucidity, remembers that he should carry this out. In effect the equipment allows them to send an electronic account of their lucid dream as it is unfolding.

From this work it is now also known that lucid dreaming is a learnable skill. Almost everyone can induce these astonishingly vivid experiences, and so unleash the creative and paranormal potential hidden within. There are many methods available, but some of the simpler ones include reliving old dreams as you start to fall asleep so as to try to retain a degree of consciousness, and (the one that I find best) taking a few moments out before you go to bed each night to imagine that the scene around you is not real but is part of a dream. If you get into the habit of challenging reality like this, it prepares you to question events within the dream state. This can take you over that threshold from uncritical acceptance of a dream as 'reality' into the lucid state where you *know* that it is a dream and can act upon such knowledge.

Dr Hearne's dream machine

Once you are in a lucid state, the way you use the dreamscape at your fingertips is again a matter of practice, but the potential seems to be unlimited. In 1994 Dr Hearne reported that he had developed his experimental work into an incredible practical device called the *dream machine*, which he anticipated putting on to the market in the future.

Hearne's device is a small box that fits by your bed and is attached to your body unobtrusively by a facial sensor. It monitors REM and other factors and can respond when likely states are reached that indicate dreaming is underway. With practice, the scientist believes that the machine will improve dream recall (for instance, by waking you briefly from within the heart of a dream) or will facilitate the ability to have lucid dreams by helping you become aware that you are now dreaming whilst remaining within the dream.

Keith Hearne and his subjects have reported countless strange experiences, from precognitive visions to communications with dead loved ones and wish fulfilment fantasies lived out in a fully lucid state. It is early days yet to know just how successful such a machine will prove when introduced commercially, but dream research is certainly entering a very interesting phase.

SOURCES

ORGANISATIONS AND INDIVIDUALS

Research into lucid dreams occurs on both sides of the Atlantic. For further details contact:

Dr Keith Hearne *London College of Clinical Hypnosis, 229A Sussex Gardens, Lancaster Gate, London W2, UK.*

Celia Green *Institute for Psychophysical Research, 118 Banbury Road, Oxford, OX2 6JU, UK.*

Lucidity Project *PO Box 2364, Stanford, CA 94305, USA.*

ASSISTANCE WITH LUCID DREAMING

Equipment that promises to help you experience lucid dreaming can work, but should be treated with a modicum of caution. A free information pack on their *Nova Dreamer* is offered by:

Life Tools *Freepost SK1852, Macclesfield, Cheshire, SK10 2YE, UK.*

PERIODICALS

ELF Infested Spaces *PO Box 33509, Austin, TX 78764, USA* is a newsletter that looks intelligently at inter-related dream, paranormal, altered states of consciousness and UFOlogical issues.

BOOKS

Of the following titles, John Grant's is the most readable guide to strange dreams of many different types (including mine!) and is written by a non-specialist. Ann Faraday writes well about dream symbolism from a psychologist's perspective. Celia Green presents some of the early work, and Stephen LaBerge from the Stanford Sleep Research Center probably offers the best review of lucid dreaming in a modern context and techniques to assist you in learning how to do it.

Dreamers by John Grant (Ashgrove Press, 1984, and Grafton, 1986).

Dream Power by Ann Faraday (Coward, McCann & Geoghegan, New York, 1972).

The Dream Game by Ann Faraday (Harper & Row, New York, 1976).

Lucid Dreams by Celia Green (Oxford Institute, 1968).

Lucid Dreaming by Dr Stephen LaBerge (Ballantine Books, New York, 1986).

EARTH MYSTERIES

DEFINITION

Anyone who has spent time in the countryside will be aware of the presence of older civilisations. Britain is particularly well-endowed, with many stone circles, burial mounds and other structures dating back thousands of years. The USA contains plenty of examples of special significance to Indian and prehistoric cultures, such as the rock dwellings in Arizona. South America has enigmatic landmarks such as the Nazca lines, criss-crossing miles of desert; Erich von Däniken proposed that an intelligence from beyond earth was responsible for creating anomalies of this kind. There are many other sites of ancient mysteries throughout the world.

The concept of earth mysteries is the mystical sister of archaeology, drawing its power from many strands. According to one of its pioneers, Paul Devereux, it takes a *holistic* approach to these ancient mysteries, not being afraid to combine conventional methods with more controversial ones such as dowsing, altered states of consciousness and the utilisation of data that is overtly paranormal.

Despite the fact that field work on earth mysteries is firmly connected with the past – speculating about sites that may be thousands or just a few hundred years old – researchers often relate their theories to the mainstream of paranormal work and, in some respects, have an uneasy relationship with those who have not adopted such an open-minded stance. Even so, some striking ideas have emerged that are clearly worth integrating.

HISTORICAL REVIEW

We know relatively little about many lost races, and in the absence of written language or lengthy texts we have to rely on studies of their *earthworks*. Archaeology takes a fairly conservative approach, dating these structures by means of scientific methods and digging up bits of pottery and other artefacts whilst attempting to fathom out lifestyles from their distribution. However, this tends to overlook the fact that most of these long-lasting monuments may have been put there for spiritual reasons.

Without understanding this side of things it is never going to be possible to grasp the whole story.

The study of earth mysteries probably owes its genesis to the field work in the 1920s of Alfred Watkins. Whilst roaming the English landscape Watkins came up with the theory of *leys*, often mistakenly called ley-lines, which he perceived as invisible paths that linked ancient marker points such as ancient stones, burial chambers and churches. During the sixties ley research was rediscovered and linked with other esoteric fields, and as a result earth mysteries research was born. It has come a long way since then, and many of the early ideas, including that of energy paths, are now widely discredited. But the research still has a strong power base, particularly in Europe.

EXPERIENCING EARTH MYSTERIES

Farming and other ways of life were governed for thousands of years by the cycles and forces of the natural world. These were largely not understood and so people tended to deify them, treating them with reverence and building fantastic monuments, some of which still survive. Today our very different world struggles to comprehend how significant they must have once been.

Yet it is not difficult to get a sense of all this. Most people live not far from a site of earth mystery importance, and the best possible way to start is to visit it and learn something of its purpose and history. Others enjoy identifying a ley from a map or a book on the subject and then go out and walk it.

It is also possible to adopt a very subjective approach. Those who feel they are psychically aware can attempt to *read* the stones at a megalithic site, for instance. In effect they will be performing *psychometry* – the apparent ability to sense impressions that might be trapped within material objects and visualise their purpose. Whilst this kind of activity is frowned upon by academics, a large section of the earth mystery community is intrigued by these visionary experiences. Their validity can never be proved, but that scarcely matters since they offer a tool that makes earth mysteries distinctive.

There are even studies in hand that combine virtually every kind of research, from the straightforward to the obscure. The *Dragon* project, for example, has been using a variety of methods in an attempt to understand megaliths and stone circles. Sophisticated equipment has been used to measure bursts of power from radiation to ultrasonic emissions that appear to emerge from these stones, particularly at sunrise. Reports of strange sensations, from electric shocks to visionary episodes, are also collected from visitors to such sites.

Other fascinating work is centring upon the dreams recorded by groups of volunteers who sleep inside burial chambers or other permissible areas within earth mystery sites. The experiment is designed to discover whether, in the altered state of consciousness which sleep provides, the mind can tune in to imagery which might relate to the site itself.

Many people attend *moots*, an ancient English term for a meeting, which the earth mystery community (notably the magazine *Ley Hunter*) organise around the country. They combine get-togethers with like-minded people, presentations on the latest aspects of the subject, and the chance to get out and experience the landscape and mystery of the area that has been chosen for that particular gathering.

RESEARCHING EARTH MYSTERIES

You can conduct research into earth mysteries without leaving your own home – poring over maps in search of alignments between ancient marker points, or looking for ground-based figures whose age-old traces might still be visible beneath the blanket of modern civilisation. However, there are probably few people who would resist the temptation to follow this up by going out into the countryside and looking at the reality of what they feel their map-reading may have uncovered.

Researcher Kathryn Preston, for example, spent years comparing older and more recent survey maps of Lancashire, looking for signs of figures from the zodiac. Parts of these might appear as ancient field boundaries, artificial sites, even the layout of very old buildings. It is a difficult and controversial task, because one can never be sure that an identified point is really very old or that the pattern uncovered is not the result of pure chance.

However, there is evidence that ancient people did re-create the shapes of stars in ceremonial designs on the ground, and so the quest to find traces of a missing zodiac still has attraction. As building and technology rapidly encroach on the countryside it is a race against time before such evidence is lost for ever.

Another way to conduct research is from the air. Aerial photography can often show indications of ancient sites, buried beneath fields, which would be completely invisible from the ground itself.

Finally, the reviewing of old texts and mythological literature can be rewarding. This may lead to discoveries about legendary associations with certain locations, and these can help to direct future research or provide the missing clues about some aspect of the landscape which has puzzled earth mystery students for years.

Overall, the scope of work is limited only by the imagination of the researcher, and new ideas are always being sought. The fact that earth mystery work could just as easily concern itself with a strange light seen coming from a megalith last week as with an attempt to fathom why that megalith was put there many millennia ago by a long-dead race of people is one of the subject's greatest attractions.

The entire history of the human race is your province.

*E*ARTH MYSTERIES TODAY

One of the great debates within modern earth mystery research concerns the nature of the straight alignments discovered by Alfred Watkins when scouring the ancient landscapes of Herefordshire and the Welsh borders in the 1920s, and which he named *leys*. When earth mysteries was rediscovered forty years later *ley hunting* became a hot pursuit. For some time the common belief was that these were energy paths within the current of the earth's biosphere – a sort of invisible energy field created by the planet itself. You could only 'sense' them, for instance by means of dowsing rods. Similarities were noted with the *feng shui* or dragon paths of ancient China, which themselves were akin to the *chakras* or routes of energy coursing through the body, which are still used today by acupuncturists. Indeed, the image of acupuncture needles placed into the body at key sites to improve health through tapping its energy field was magnified on to the landscape. Ancient peoples were perceived as placing megaliths at ley energy points to produce similar changes for the good within the entire earth's energy field.

Nodal points – crossovers between leys – were thought to contain enormous energy. This could be used for evil as well as good. Even today there are researchers who believe that accident black spots, which seem to occur for no apparent reason in some unfortunate places, may owe their existence to undetected negative leys passing through the area.

OPPOSITE PAGE *Examples of ley lines: on the left is Old Sarum Ley in Wiltshire/Hampshire, and on the right is Saintbury Ley in Gloucestershire*

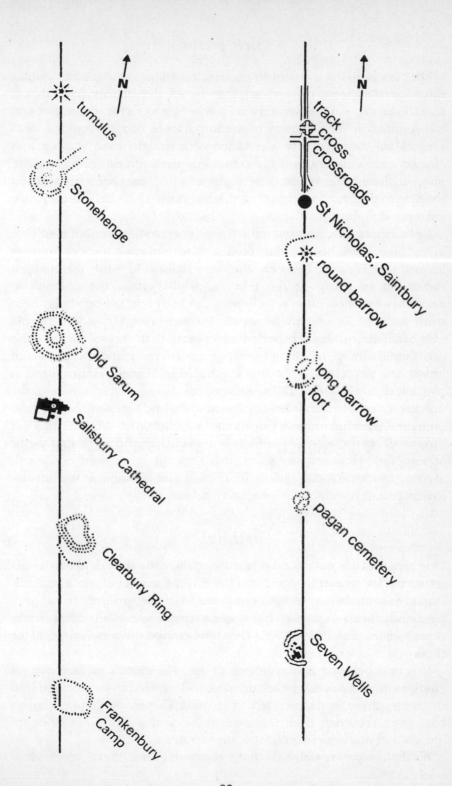

Spirit paths

Whilst this belief is a common conception among the general public, most earth mystery researchers abandoned the energy path theory several years ago. A new way forward has been sought for some time, and has resulted in the discovery of the importance of *spirit paths* or *death roads*. Many cultures have a tradition of a straight road leading to a church and cemetery, and the commonly used phrase 'dead straight' may originate here. Whilst these paths may just have been the shortest route from a village to a churchyard, some researchers believe they have a deeper significance.

Researchers are uncovering the legends of shamans – tribal medicine men, the equivalents of todays mediums, who in most ancient cultures formed the bridge between the material world and the hidden dimension of spirit. At the time of deaths within the community shamans were thought to travel out of the body and swoop along these spirit paths to accompany the dead. Another possibility is that people who had had near death experiences reported to the rest of the tribe the now familiar image of a long tunnel or straight road, and this persistent image was perceived as having mystical significance. Hence straight paths were created to mark its importance.

A great deal of effort is being expended on finding examples of these paths and learning what we can about their traditions. Whether this will directly explain the concept of leys is not yet clear, although that seems a possibility. However, the spirit path concept shows well how earth mystery research today blends traditional archaeological and mythological research with much more spiritual ideas.

Earthlights

One area that has not changed in essence since the rebirth of earth mysteries, but has grown in significance and is the subject of more sophisticated research, is that of light emissions from the ground. These have frequently been reported from stone circle sites and other rocky prominences, and in 1982 Paul Devereux coined the term *earthlight* for them.

It is now believed that at points all over the earth's surface natural energies of perhaps magnetic and electrical nature can be released into the atmosphere and perceived as glowing shapes. Such phenomena have been recorded from mountain peaks and at the times of earthquakes, but not understood, for many centuries.

Earth mystery researchers have suggested that there are various factors which trigger these energies into life. Examples are quarrying and the building of reservoirs which disturb the earth and put it under pressure. TV and electricity pylons also act as channelling points for the energies. Since many of these disturbances are the products of modern society, it stands to reason that earthlights are being seen much more frequently now. These drifting lights are generally perceived as UFOs, which fits with the rapid rise in public awareness of that phenomenon.

Devereux and others such as Fernand Lagarde in France have calculated the number of reports from places above fault lines in rocks below the earth's surface, and statistical calculations by Canadian researcher Dr Michael Persinger implied that there was a correlation. Some, however, still dispute his work, pointing out, not unreasonably, that many of the cases used during this computer analysis probably refer to irrelevant sightings of things such as aircraft lights. Genuine emissions produced by tectonic strain were probably only a small part of his data, heavily contaminated by the countless misidentifications.

However, the earthlight theory is respected in many quarters and the number of active sites the world over where there are legends of such things, where modern sightings concentrate and where the geological and landscape features exist to support the theory, all seem to have established that this research is worth continuing.

An understanding of how earthlights form is still being sought. Experiments by Dr Brian Brady at the Bureau of Mines in Boulder, Colorado seemed to show that electrical signals are squeezed out of rocks when put under stress – for instance, when fault lines move naturally or when reservoirs are at full pressure. These signals ignite atmospheric gases. Filmed experiments in the UK by geologist Dr Paul McCartney duplicated this work: when huge rocks were crushed in the laboratory very transient mini-lights formed. Whether this could be extended to the landscape to produce big lights, persisting for several minutes rather than fractions of seconds, is unclear.

Before earthquakes animals seem to be aware of the coming trauma, and from this it has been argued that gases may be released from inside the earth over a period of many hours before the quake. Research suggests that ions from these gases produce hormonal changes within the animals' brains. Because animals tend to be closer to the ground, where these ions tend to concentrate, they are more likely to detect them than human beings would be. Such ionised gases could glow in the dark to produce earthlights.

Project Pennine, a combined effort between earth mystery and UFO researchers, has delved into the light phenomena reported over many years in the moorland area east of Manchester and west of Sheffield in the north of England. The work of people like Andy Roberts and Dave Clarke has established clear patterns such as phenomena displaying links with local earth tremors, and hot spots having traditional associations with the supernatural reflected in centuries-old names like *Devil's Elbow*.

One of the best-known areas of earthlight activity is around Marfa in Texas. Edson Hendricks, a consultant to NASA, has not only spent years collecting reports from eye witnesses but has seen them for himself and taken some of the best photographs of their form and progression over several minutes. Whilst many earthlights, even these, appear to be mis-perceptions caused by car headlights, refractions and mirages, there is undoubtedly a real mystery. The Marfa lights are beachball-sized and commonly glow red, yellow or white. They drift around the foothills of the Big Bend national park and are seen from surrounding towns and the passing road, where a marker post has been erected to alert motorists. They have been reported since the time of the earliest settlers, and there is reason to suppose that native Americans have known about them longer still. Precisely what this particular earthlight is remains unknown: its persistent but unpredictable nature means that only chance encounters or dedicated stake-outs will result in a sighting.

The same factors apply to all other locations where earthlight activity takes place, but few researchers can be more dedicated than those who hunt the Hessdalen lights in a small valley near Trondheim in a remote part of Norway. In the winter months, when the lights are most often seen, conditions are terrible, with temperatures way below zero. But members of *Project Hessdalen* have mounted several full-scale expeditions to the area and spent several weeks camped out with the sort of equip-ment that most paranormal researchers can only dream about, from spectrographs to radar sets.

The outcome has been spectacular, including many colourful images of the lights at work. It has been discovered that they are a form of ionised plasma, but their cause is, of course, still debatable. Furthermore, the researchers made known some findings which do not sit easily with mainstream science. They claimed that the lights responded to the researchers as if they had some sort of rudimentary intelligence, or perhaps they were interacting with the mind of the observers. This is, of course, not likely to endear earthlights research to science, but it is something not infrequently reported by witnesses at other locations. The dynamic relationship between the energy form and the mind of the witness is now the subject of further intense debate.

At Hessdalen in March 1994 a most remarkable conference took place. By invitation only and held in secrecy, it brought together top scientists from Russia, Japan, the USA and Europe, UFO researchers such as Odd Gunner Roed and Erling Strand of Project Hessdalen, and specialists in earthlights such as Paul Devereux. They created a new alliance to research the mystery with scientific funding and support. One of those attending was Professor Yoshi Hiko Ohtsuki, who during a long quest to understand ball lightning has produced plasma vortex phenomena in the laboratory. He also visited Britain several times to work with physicist Dr Terence Meaden, who had devised the theory that a rotating plasma vortex might have created crop circles (see page 65). The way in which disparate areas of the paranormal – earth mysteries, ball lightning study, UFOlogy and crop circle research – come together here is one of the most promising signs for future progress. It also suggests that there may be something important behind it all, if so many fields of research reached similar conclusions from different starting points.

Images of the earth mother

Dr Meaden has even extended his own work, seeking a natural solution to the crop circles by delving into both archaeology and earth mysteries. He has published theories that stone circle sites such as Stonehenge and Avebury might have been created, not as astronomical observatories as most specialists have believed, but as ways to deify the crop circle phenomenon. What he proposes is that crop circles were occasionally found millennia ago within fields in certain hot spot areas, of which Wiltshire was one. The ancients regarded them as the result of the mother earth being impregnated by a god-like force descending from above (what he would call a whirlwind), and regarded the areas where this occurred as of deep religious significance. So they built the stone circles as a symbolic representation of the effect (the stone impregnating the earth within a circle) to serve as a permanent reminder to their tribe and as a place of sacrifice and worship to the gods.

This ingenious idea has not been well received by the archaeological community, some of whom thought the professor should stick to meteorology! Many crop circle researchers, still clinging to the view that the circles are more mysterious than spiralling energies caused by the atmosphere, were equally outspoken against the theory. Yet circular and spiral designs are deeply imbedded within the symbolism of many ancient cultures. Were they all responding to something perceived in the world about them?

The concept of the earth as a living organism which could be 'raped' by other forces is not confined to ancient history. Indeed under the guise of the so-called *Gaia* principle it has undergone a resurgence. Gaia proposes that all living systems within the earth's biosphere depend upon one another to such an extent that together they may form a larger, autonomous and perhaps even self-aware whole.

Many older cultures that still survive despite the impact of Western civilisation hold such a view. The Hopi Indians of Arizona, for example, reacted emotionally when first shown photographs of crop circles in British fields. Without knowing about the furore surrounding them, they announced that the pictures represented an image of the earth mother responding to attack by human beings!

Aboriginal cultures

In 1991 I spent some time amongst the aborigines in the far north of Australia, and had the rare privilege of entering Arnhem Land. This is a vast area east of Darwin which preserves the ancient culture and way of life and from which visitors, even non-aboriginal Australians, are generally banned.

The aborigines have a beautifully sophisticated image of the rapport between the living land and the people who occupy it. There is a spiritual bond which goes back to the time of *the dreaming*, in which they as tenants can share in the true essence of life. They feel the earth spirit guides what they do and they are a part of it, as opposed to the Western view of humans as taming and bringing to heel a subservient landscape.

The coiled serpent is a key theme of aboriginal lore. They see it as underpinning the earth like a current of energy that binds each piece together. Every tribe has responsibility for one area and learns its importance through songs and pictures which are passed down through the generations. They can link with other tribes by way of the energy paths that bond them. A *corroboree* is a remarkable religious, celebratory, musical story-telling gathering where these sacred trusts are shared. To our eyes this often manifests as supernatural phenomena, and abilities still inherent within tribal initiates are what we would call psychic. They sense danger, have visions and heal the sick. But none of this is strange to aborigines: it is a deeply rooted part of who they are.

However, perhaps the most astonishing culture is that of the Kogi, a tribal society within Central America. When the Portuguese invaded and drove them into a vast, 20,000-foot-high mountain plateau now called the Sierra Nevada de Santa Marta they sealed themselves off from the world. That was in the year 1600.

In 1990 the Kogi suddenly decided to break four centuries of exile and give a message to the world. Alan Ereira, a British film-maker, was allowed to spend time with them and film their story before they sealed themselves off once again. His report is a stunning revelation.

There are eleven thousand Kogi, living in a time warp, with a unique society dominated by the *mamas* – each of whom is part government minister, part priest and part mystic. They have what they call a map stone, like a megalith carved with criss-cross lines. This shows not roads, but paths of thought within the spirit world or *aluna* with which the mamas are in contact. This idea, of course, is exactly what is found in Australian aboriginal traditions, and is yet another example of the 'spirit path' mystique now being investigated by earth mystery researchers.

The reason why the Kogi decided to speak out in 1990 is that they had noticed serious changes to the environment. Because their unique habitat is so large and so far above sea level it contains almost all the ecosystems found on earth, from tropical to polar. They consider themselves to be guardians of the earth spirit, knowing that Western civilisation has deserted these mystical associations. From the way in which the behaviour of plants and birds was changing around them, and from their communion with the earth spirit, they concluded that we had gone too far and were close to despoiling the earth beyond repair. It was not too late for us to put things right, but we had to act soon or the earth would die. This was the message which these simple but profound people wanted Ereira to convey through his film.

He did so, but was disappointed at the lack of positive progress by the greedy West by the time the Kogi unexpectedly invited him back in 1992. They, however, were seemingly content that things were now in motion. Ereira could see real changes had been made. The Kogi had been granted considerable freedoms by the Colombian government. The cocaine plantations that had threatened their hinterland had been razed to the ground by the Americans, and bananas now grew there instead. Ereira even found himself invited to show his film to the Rio de Janeiro world summit on global ecology, where it was received with considerable emotion. There does seem to be a growing awareness of the urgency that faces our need to transform the way we treat the earth. Perhaps at some inner level the Kogi's warning is being heeded after all.

Sources

ORGANISATIONS AND PERIODICALS

There is one place to go first for all research into this field: Paul Devereux and *The Ley Hunter (TLH)*. Its issues, usually three or four a year, are always on the pulse of the latest findings. *TLH* also organises moots around Britain every year.

The Ley Hunter   *PO Box 92, Penzance, Cornwall, TR18 2BX, UK.*

There are many groups, mostly in Britain but also in the USA, who specialise in this kind of research. Most of the following produce magazines, and *GEM*, the one from the Gloucestershire group, lives up to its acronym, providing a superb range of articles that are not restricted to the West Country. The circle organises frequent lectures and trips to visit sites of interest. *RILKO (Research into Lost Knowledge Organisation)* is a charity trust that has provided education on ancient sites, geomancy and earth mysteries for many years.

Gloucestershire Earth Mysteries (GEM)   *PO Box 258, Cheltenham, Gloucestershire, GL53 0HR, UK.*

London Earth Mysteries Circle   *PO Box 1035, London W2 6ZX, UK.*

Northern Earth   *10 Jubilee Street, Mytholmroyd, West Yorkshire, HX7 5NP, UK.*

RILKO   *8 The Drive, New Southgate, London N11 2DY, UK.*

Stonehenge Viewpoint   *800 Palermo Drive, Santa Barbara, CA 93105, USA.*

USA Stonewatch   *334 Brook Street, Noank, CT 06340, USA.*

BOOKS

There are hundreds of books that cover the earth mysteries field, and I can only offer a few of those which are worthwhile. They cover a range of topics featured in this section. Those by Paul Devereux are self-explanatory, as is the report from Project Hessdalen. Ereira writes of his time with the Kogi. Meaden presents his unusual theories about the origin of stone circles. The neatly titled book by Tributsch offers an excellent look at the peculiar energies associated with earthquake activity, and Balfour's is a pictorial guide to the many earth mystery sites found around Europe.

Earthlight's Revelation by Paul Devereux et al. (Blandford Press, 1989).

Symbolic Landscapes: The Dreamtime Earth by Paul Devereux (Gothic Images, 1992).

Project Hessdalen Report by Project Hessdalen (1985; from PO Box 14, Duken, Norway, N-3133).

From the Heart of the World by Alan Ereira (Jonathan Cape, 1990).

Goddess of the Stones by Dr Terence Meaden (Souvenir Press, 1992).

When the Snakes Awake by Dr Helmut Tributsch (MIT Press, Boston, 1982).

Megalithic Mysteries by Michael Balfour (Dragon's World, 1992).

ESP

Definition

There are five known senses: sight, smell, touch, hearing and taste. These are all fairly well explained in the context of biology and our growing understanding of how the brain functions. However, human beings claim a number of baffling experiences which appear quite incapable of resolution within the boundaries of this sensory knowledge.

Amongst those areas, which may be termed *extra-sensory*, are the abilities to detect information in the mind from no known source – that is, picking up images or thoughts apparently coming from others. The term *telepathy* relates to thought transference, whereas *clairvoyance* refers to seeing within the mind images that ought not be accessible – because the person from whom they apparently originate is no longer alive, for instance.

Other aspects of mental phenomena which might be classified as extra-sensory include *psychometry*, the reading from inanimate objects of impressions which normally relate to the past history of that object or its owner. However, the generic phrase 'extra-sensory perception', commonly abbreviated to 'ESP', mainly applies to telepathic exchanges or clairvoyant detection. These are sometimes also described as a mysterious *sixth sense* – although sounds, smells, sensations and tastes are also received paranormally in addition to visual data, so there may actually be several other senses.

Historical review

Throughout recorded history people have claimed to receive information by way of ESP. The hearing of phantom voices that warn the victim of impending doom is a typical example. Someone like Joan of Arc, in the Middle Ages branded either a witch or a saint according to viewpoint, would today more likely be considered an example of a person gifted with ESP.

It was in the late nineteenth century that science began to pay attention to the occasional spontaneous reports of these mysterious powers. In those days, of course, a good deal less was known about the workings of human consciousness than we understand today. The Society for Psychical Research was incorporated in London and over 110 years later still thrives, bringing together researchers from a variety of disciplines who are not afraid to tackle contentious issues head on.

Zener cards

Most of the early work focused on the collation of stories told by witnesses, and it was to be the pioneering efforts of American Dr J.B. Rhine in the 1920s and 1930s that established rigorous protocols for laboratory experiments. The term 'ESP' derived from these tests, which used a set of twenty-five cards each carrying one of five symbols – a cross, square, circle, triangle and wavy lines. These Zener cards, as they were named after their inventor, were then shown to a subject, who was asked to try to project the symbol telepathically to another person across the room.

By chance there is a one in five possibility of guessing the correct card, which means that if you run the experiment over a hundred cards the

The five symbols depicted on Zener cards

person attempting to detect the image might be right on twenty occasions. Anything significantly above this suggested that ESP was at work. In practice tens of thousands of runs were made, but the success rate was rarely spectacular and never enough to persuade science that ESP was real.

A March 1995 experiment illustrates some of the problems that sceptical scientists pointed out. This was conducted from Nottingham during a live Carlton TV programme which had an audience of twelve million. Famed psychic Uri Geller pre-selected one Zener card and sealed it in an envelope. He then stared into the camera and asked the watching audience to pick out the correct symbol which he was sending telepathically to the viewers. Around seventy thousand phoned in and an amazing 48 per cent, rather than the statistically expected 20 per cent, gave the correct answer.

However, in this test the five symbols were laid out in a line before a close-up of Geller's face and eyes. As he knew which symbol he was sending he may subconsciously have let his eyes fix, however briefly, on the right one. Viewers, again subconsciously, may have picked up on this unintended cue in sufficient numbers to be guided to the right symbol.

This in no way suggests that any cheating took place. The better method would have been to have had the psychic in another studio, unseen by the audience whilst he was transmitting the image – but that would have destroyed the impact for TV. On the other hand, a slight change in presentation could have been tried – for instance, showing the symbols before Geller appeared on screen, but not having them in shot during the experiment. That would have prevented any possibility of unconscious cuing. Even if it did not happen on this occasion, the possibility would invalidate the results of the experiment.

Science learnt by trial, error and sceptical criticism to look out for, and try to avoid, such pitfalls, but the perfect ESP experiment was always elusive. To some extent that was simply a failing of the Zener card method. The symbols are boring and no test carried out over tens of thousands of repetitive runs was likely to stimulate ESP.

Unfortunately, as technology improved, this fact was rarely appreciated. Computers that generated random numbers up to six digits were next used to produce the raw material to be transmitted and detected telepathically. The would-be ESP receiver would probably be sent to sleep after a few hours. Again the results failed to impress, although they did outstrip chance predictions a little.

Clues about the nature of ESP were offered by actual experiences. A driver on a motorway would hear a voice cry 'Get out' and would swerve dangerously to avoid an unseen hazard, thus avoiding collision with a truck ahead whose driver had suddenly lost control. A mother would awake in the middle of the night and rush into her child's bedroom to find that she was dangerously ill and would probably have died if left until morning. In all such cases there was some kind of emotional bond, whether it was fear or love. Random numbers and Zener cards could not duplicate these sort of conditions.

Remote viewing and ganzfeld testing

The fad during the 1970s was for *remote viewing*. Person A would visit a location selected at random by computer and absorb the surroundings, endeavouring to project these back to person B in the laboratory who had no idea where person A had gone. Person B then described or drew what he was seeing, and this could be matched against the computer-selected location. This work proved rather more successful than years of effort with cards and random numbers had done.

The update on remote viewing was *ganzfeld testing* named after a German idea. The receiver was relaxed by being isolated from other sensory input, such as sounds or sights. Blindfolds and white noise played over headphones were among the techniques used (white noise is ambient, persistent sound that is played into the ears of the subject both to relax and to block out external stimuli.) In a sense this was artificially creating an *Oz factor* state – that altered state of consciousness found by researchers into UFO and other encounters as the preliminary phase of later visionary experiences. During ganzfeld testing a more emotive stimulus would often be sent, such as a classical painting. Work in this area is still going on in centres such as Stanford Research Institute in California and Cambridge in England, and there are encouraging signs that it may prove worthwhile.

EXPERIENCING *ESP*
—

An ESP experience usually strikes out of the blue and, whilst some people seem more prone than others (we call them *psychic*), it can occur to anyone at any time or in any place. However, there are several levels of experience, some of which it is worth examining here.

Maureen Blyth, wife of the long-distance yachtsman Chay, describes how one evening she was in a restaurant eating a meal when she was overcome with nausea. She just knew that Chay was in trouble, but not how or why, and had to leave the restaurant. At that precise moment, she later learned, Chay's boat had overturned in the freezing Atlantic thousands of miles away and he was trapped underneath for several hours before being rescued.

This is the lowest level of ESP – a sense of foreboding. The term 'PSI-emotion' is applied to it; PSI (pronounced 'sigh') is a word formed from the acronym *paranormal sensory information*, as well as being the Greek letter often associated with psychic phenomena. Here only the mood or raw emotion was seemingly picked up across a vast distance by Maureen Blyth.

A woman in Tacoma, Washington, was observing her husband mowing the lawn whilst she was standing by the sink doing the dishes. Suddenly she had a vision of blood flowing before her. If she had responded in the rationally expected way, she might have assumed that her husband was in danger and banged on the window or cried out to him. In fact, although this image warned her of danger in the most graphic way possible – it was what we term a PSI-vision – she moved away from the window as fast as she could. But why?

This peculiar instinctive reaction seems to have been motivated by the information that her mind subconsciously picked up, because a moment later, in a freak accident, the mower struck a rock and sent it crashing through the window. If she had remained by the sink or tried to warn her husband she would have been seriously injured or even killed. Her ESP controlled her behaviour, and the vision of blood made her actions far more urgent than a mere foreboding would have done. The image ensured that she responded instantly.

Experiences like this suggest that ESP can be used to great benefit and is not something to fear. We should probably all learn to trust our feelings far more than we do.

RESEARCHING *ESP*

Florida psychiatrist Dr Berthold Schwarz described a series of remote viewing experiments which illustrate what to expect if you attempt this kind of research. In one the target was a small mound or hill. However, the receiver drew a woman's breast, seemingly because he was sexually attracted to the sender. He had detected the correct image but his mind had fashioned its own response.

In one test where Dr Schwarz was acting as the receiver he drew a fireman's helmet, but before checking this against the correct picture sent by the other participant he broke for lunch. On impulse, probably with his sketch in the back of his mind, he bought a fire extinguisher while he was in the local shop. After lunch, the doctor learned that the image being sent was indeed that of a fire extinguisher.

Here, probably, the essence of the image was detected by Dr Schwarz but his mind portrayed it in a more graphic form. However, the story has yet another twist, because when he got home that evening his wife was delighted to have the extinguisher. She had suffered a small fire in the kitchen that day, and had wished that she had had one of these devices to hand. It seems that the fire broke out at about the same time as the psychiatrist made his impulse purchase.

The lesson here is to design experiments where the bond between people or some kind of emotional link is an active part of what is being tested. Motivation, too, can be worthwhile. For example, for some years I have run psychic treasure hunts in which people have an incentive to use ESP because in doing so they may win a prize. This makes them rather like participants in a psychic game show, emotionally keyed up, or even paranormal guinea pigs, as in the method inspired by the behavioural psychologist Ivan Pavlov. He offered a reward to dogs that correctly followed his training.

In another test, labelled an ESP-eriment, I worked with the popular women's magazine *She* to gauge remote viewing. Pictures of half a dozen celebrities were printed and at a certain time one of these people agreed to transmit an image to readers, who not only had to tune in to those images but also to decide which of the celebrities was transmitting at the time. The other five celebrities took no part in the test at all.

The results were fascinating. Imagery from the location was not well transferred to readers; emotions and other sensations came through rather better. However, much the best results, way above chance expectation, came with the selection of the correct member of the six possible targets. Nearly three times as many people as chance predicted identified actress Billie Whitelaw as the sender. This high success rate was achieved probably because the readers found it more emotionally bonding to tune in to a famous person than to seek a vague scenic image.

More large-scale tests of ESP are likely to produce even better evidence, but they need to be well designed in order to take advantage of the emotional message that seems to trigger spontaneous occurrences of extra-sensory perception. For example, another test that Carlton TV did with Uri Geller in March 1995 was a version of my treasure hunt concept. He placed the keys from an expensive, brand-new sports car at a landmark in Britain and challenged viewers to use ESP to name it. About forty thousand people tried and, amazingly, so many of them were correct (about four hundred, in fact) that a draw had to be made to pick the winner of the car.

Was this result incredible evidence for ESP? Sadly, I do not think so, because I believe this test was flawed. By selecting a very well-known location – and one that has strong mystical associations – the probability of correct guesses was greatly enhanced. How many landmarks readily spring to your mind? Fewer than you think. I suspect that a guessing game in which forty thousand people were asked to imagine a landmark in Britain as a place where a psychic might well locate an object would produce a significant number of 'Stonehenge' answers. This was just where the keys were placed. I would have put the keys at an obscure but very distinctive location.

Indeed, in an experiment into remote viewing that I ran with magazine readers we later printed a series of photographs taken at a site selected at random by a computer. These scenes, of lock gates on the Manchester Ship Canal and a large vessel steaming through, seemed to stimulate better replies than other experiments where no subsequent photographs were printed. It was as if the mind found it easier to tune in to an image that it would later actually witness than to envisage something that would only ever be described in words.

There is much that can be done to design exciting experiments. But it is important to try to avoid some of the mistakes made by Carlton in their brave but, I fear, sadly misguided attempts.

ESP TODAY

One of the most interesting areas of anecdotal evidence for ESP comes via inter-species communication, where language cannot possibly be used and cues not obviously given in any subconscious form. Evelyn Gregory, for example, has reported on experiments involving dolphins.

Animals

Dolphins are widely considered to have intelligence levels similar to those of human beings. They have a complex language, exhibit social behaviour, can show initiative, develop playful techniques and appear to possess emotions. There are numerous reliable accounts of these creatures placing themselves in danger to help another dolphin that is sick or injured, or even whales and human beings in trouble. It may only be dolphins' lack of technology that prevents most people from recognising them as the first truly 'alien' species that mankind has contacted. Gregory describes the experiences of a woman, blind for twenty years, married to a scientist who studies dolphins. She spends a lot of time swimming with them and has developed a form of mental communication with them. The animals transmit a series of colours to her, presumably by way of ESP, which somehow signifies their relative location in the water. She can use their guidance to 'see' her way around.

There are many other accounts of dogs, for example, changing behaviour or whining at the moment when their owner dies, even thousands of miles away, as if detecting some kind of psychic distress flare. More research into such matters is called for.

Twins

Another area of great interest at present is the possibility of ESP between twins. This is suggested by numerous claims from twins that they seem aware of what each other is thinking. Doreen Hodgson from Wiltshire, for instance, told me that when her twin brother became very ill she shared in his pain, despite being miles apart. At 10.30 one night she suddenly felt free and happy and knew immediately that he had just died. He had done so at precisely this time.

Open-minded sceptic and psychologist Dr Sue Blackmore reported in 1993 on an experiment that she had carried out with Frances Chamberlain at a school in Bristol. They tested twelve twins and twelve non-twin siblings aged between eleven and twenty. In this work the researchers used three experiments, trying to get these young people to transmit and receive a number between one and ten, some freely drawn pictures and then photographs selected out of a set of four.

The experiment was quite complex, but basically divided its runs into two conditions. In one of these the child sending the image had free selection. In the second, the ESP condition, the experimenter picked the target and the child merely transmitted it. At first glance that might not appear to make much difference to the test, but in practice the results suggest otherwise. When freely selecting a number a child's guesses should be correct one in ten times, so a score of 10 per cent would be chance-level. Non-twins scored only 5 per cent, but twins scored 17 per cent – nearly twice such chance expectation. However, when the number was selected for the child the non-twins still only got 5 per cent but the twins, at 12 per cent, were now barely above chance level. With the picture tests nobody scored more than chance when the images were selected for them by the experimenter. Only when the twins could draw a free choice of image or chose their own photograph from the samples did they again score at more than twice chance-level.

Dr Blackmore cautions that these numbers are not statistically large enough to be dogmatic, but they do suggest something interesting. If the higher-than-chance levels which the twins tended to score were due to the influence of ESP, it ought not to matter who picked the number, drawing or photograph. That it did matter infers that something other than ESP was at work here, which Blackmore terms 'thought concordance'. By this she means that twins have very similar genetic make-up and so their thinking processes tend to be very similar. When given a free choice of what number to pick or sketch to draw, they are more likely to think and choose alike than are two children who are genetically less similar.

Scientific encouragement

However, whilst this work may be suggestive of something other than ESP, the mood may still be changing gradually amongst scientists. In 1994 the prestigious US journal *Psychological Bulletin* produced a report favouring ESP, based on many years of research into a sophisticated form of ganzfeld remote viewing experiment. In this work by Daryl Bem at Cornell University and another psychologist, Charles Honerton, working at Princeton in the USA and Edinburgh University in Scotland, computers selected video clips to be used as targets and sophisticated techniques were used to maximise the possibility of ESP. Over two hundred subjects took part in hundreds of trials, and a remarkable success rate of 32 per cent was recorded. Research of this kind may yet legitimise telepathy as a genuine phenomenon.

SOURCES

ORGANISATIONS AND PERIODICALS

Probably the best source of scientific data testing ESP can be found in the regular output of the *SPR (Society for Psychical Research)*, founded in 1883. Its quarterly journal frequently reports on well-constructed experiments with full mathematical results available for analysis by others. The Blackmore work referred to above, for example, appeared in issue 831 in April 1993.

SPR Journal *49 Marloes Road, London W8 6LA, UK.*

BOOKS

Countless titles document theories and research into ESP. Those by Rhine, Schwarz, and Eysenck and Sargeant describe three generations of experimental work by practising scientists. Rattray-Taylor's fine book looks at the science of the brain/mind problem and the role of psychic phenomena at its borders. Heywood's work is an excellent report by a psychic of her own ESP abilities. Bardens considers animals and their potential for ESP, while my own book directly relates what we know about the five senses and the workings of the brain to spontaneous cases of ESP.

The Reach of the Mind by Joseph Rhine (William Morrow, New York 1947).

Psychic Nexus by Dr Berthold Schwarz (Van Nostrand, New York 1980).

Explaining the Unexplained by Hans Eysenck and Carl Sargeant (Weidenfeld & Nicolson, 1982).

The Natural History of the Mind by Gordon Rattray-Taylor (Secker & Warburg, 1979).

The Infinite Hive by Rosalind Heywood (Chatto & Windus, 1964, and Pan, 1966).

Psychic Animals by Dennis Bardens (Robert Hale, 1987, republished by Capall Bann, 1995).

Sixth Sense by Jenny Randles (Robert Hale, 1987).

LEICESTERSHIRE LIBRARIES AND INFORMATION SERVICE
REFERENCE & INFORMATION LIBRARY HUMANITIES ★

GHOSTS

DEFINITION

There is no agreement on whether a ghost is a material form somehow incorporated into our reality, or just a strange type of hallucination. Whichever, it may be regarded as a perception of an apparently living entity that ought not to be visible in the location in which it is seen. Generally, this event occurs because the person encountered is known to be dead. Long-term reports are usually the subject of *hauntings*. These we might describe as being repeated, place-centred appearances by the same ghostly figure – now apparently tied to a house or location with which they were familiar in life. Hauntings of this type can persist for hundreds of years, whereas simple ghost sightings are more commonly one-off experiences that may occur at any point after the person's demise, although most happen quite soon afterwards. However, all apparitions of whatever type are of beings who could not, according to the laws of physics, manifest in the way they do.

There are also a surprisingly large number of living ghosts; the person whose spectre is encountered is definitely still alive but is physically located far from the spot where they are seen to appear. These are sometimes known as *crisis apparitions*, as they often occur when the person concerned is undergoing a life-threatening situation such as being seriously ill. In that state they may somehow be projecting an image of themselves across the miles.

But there are also a number of well-attested instances of a living ghost appearing when there is no evident crisis and, indeed, the 'transmitter' has no knowledge of their miraculous visitation to a distant friend or acquaintance. The German term *doppelgänger*, referring to something being in two places at once, is often used for these strange and fairly rare experiences.

Ghosts of the living are less common than those of the dead, but it is not possible to be more precise than this because of a common fallacy about spectral phenomena. Fiction tends to portray phantoms as semi-transparent forms or wraith-like images and so it is widely assumed that a ghost would be easily recognised by any witness. But testimony shows that most apparitions look completely normal and are also three-dimensional, so at first sight may seem to be ordinary living humans. Only if rapidly identified to be someone who is dead, or if they suddenly do something physically amazing such as walking straight through a wall, is the possibility of their being supernatural even considered.

This begs a question: just how often do people see ghosts which are simply assumed to be another passer-by? Many people could have seen an apparition at some point in their lives and still be none the wiser. All these problems are significant in any attempt to understand the nature of ghosts, which is one reason why one of the most common paranormal phenomena in the world is still the subject of intense debate even amongst committed researchers.

HISTORICAL REVIEW

Encountering apparitions is probably the oldest and most frequent type of paranormal phenomenon on record. Nearly all civilisations which kept written records include stories of visits by spirits of the dead. In tribal societies, the interaction between these ancestor figures and present leaders is often regarded as a source of great wisdom. In more developed cultures, from the Romans and Greeks to those founded on Christianity, the sighting of ghosts was not uncommon but tended to be less revered and more greatly feared.

Dark forces

The medieval Church used this fear to good effect, declaring ghosts to be something evil and regarding those who saw them as witches or being in league with the devil. This was done in order to allow Jesus, who on his resurrection became, in a sense, the most famous ghost of all, to retain a unique status. Indeed, it was this kind of indoctrination which was largely responsible for all study into psychic phenomena going underground and adopting the term *occult*, which literally means 'hidden'. It became a secret knowledge which was dangerous to acquire, not because of its nature but more because of the way it had been associated with evil by less enlightened belief.

The activities of the exorcist stem from these roots. Exorcisms are attempts to drive evil spirits out of people's houses and back into the arms of God – although it is often a poltergeist outbreak that is being exorcised rather than a haunting or ghostly apparition. There are serious doubts that these different phenomena are even connected, and poltergeists may owe their power more to the living than to the dead (see page 162).

Study and investigation

Serious attempts to study ghosts using scientific methods have been undertaken for over a hundred years and began with the founding of the Society for Psychical Research (SPR). A census of apparitions was one of their first major achievements, and even today it remains a vital contribution to our knowledge of the subject. The census was updated in the 1960s by research at Oxford by Celia Green and Charles McCreery, whose detailed analyses of all manner of apparitions are models of how such work should be tackled.

Apart from this kind of social study, the investigation of ghosts has tended to proceed on an ad hoc basis – following up sightings, recording the testimony of witnesses and, with the aid of technology, compiling databases. More direct methods of studying ghosts are relatively recent, but these are one of the biggest growth areas in the field.

Animate or inanimate phenomena?

The typical ghost story is a combination of dramatic legend associated with a building or place, unusual experiences (from cold spots to visions) that are reported by those who have stayed there throughout the years, and popularisation of the story to cement the bond between myth and reality. Most of these things require time to take root, and so the older a building is the more opportunity there will be for spectral legends to attach themselves. It is often said that the British Isles are the most haunted area in the world, but there are ghosts all over the world and Britain's status probably owes much to its large number of old buildings.

There does not seem to be a time limit to legends of this kind. There are stories of what may appear to be ancient Celtic ceremonies witnessed at stone circle sites which could be ghostly hauntings dating back many thousands of years. The famous story of a ghostly Roman legion marching through a York cellar, as witnessed by a workman there 1900 years after such an event took place in reality, again crosses the ages with apparent ease. On the other hand, sightings of very recently deceased people are common, as if they want to make a lingering farewell as they leave this life rather than being wrenched away to the afterlife.

However, an interesting case from Los Angeles in 1993 illustrates another problem. A woman was seen as a ghostly form around an old house, and after much research she was discovered to have been someone who had probably once lived there. In fact, she had moved away half a century before. It was speculated that, although the woman had not died in the building, she might have come to haunt it because of her well-attested love for the place. But a major problem with this theory soon arose. The woman was traced, many miles away, very elderly but still alive! In fact she was seriously ill in a coma, and quite possibly reliving her earlier days in the house that had been most dear to her. After a time her condition improved, and apparitions stopped appearing in the distant house.

This poses the continuing dilemma about the nature of ghosts. Are they animate or inanimate phenomena?

There are relatively few cases in which ghosts appear to interact with living people by carrying out meaningful conversations, for instance. Most often they seem like projected images on a screen, playing the same scene over and over. This has led to the belief that they are similar to a videotape on constant replay – perhaps an emotive moment in time trapped by the surroundings, and run every now and then for an attentive audience. Such a ghost would not in any sense be a living, thinking entity.

But sometimes this view is challenged – for example, when a ghost passes on knowledge that it could only have learnt after death. So an alternative theory sees the apparition as an interaction between the mind of a deceased person and that of a living witness, and that link creates the experience. We still do not know whether this requires a dead person to continue a thinking existence in some other realm, or whether the witness might manufacture the ghost, by way of telepathy, out of information picked up from the environment or from other living people who knew the deceased.

EXPERIENCING GHOSTS
—

Seeing a ghost is probably one of the most frightening things imaginable. But to a large extent this is the result of our cultural expectations and has little to do with the realities of what witnesses say takes place. In fact it can be quite comforting to some people if they find themselves living with a friendly ghost. I interviewed actress Doreen Sloane, who lived with her family in a flat in a large house in Birkenhead in northwest England. During the nineteenth century this building was a family home owned by a wealthy businessman. From the time that Doreen moved into her flat she and other members of her family felt the presence of these long-dead previous occupants. She described incidents of shadowy figures walking through the hall and terrifying their cat, of walk-in wardrobe doors being closed when nobody was nearby, and of phantom cooking smells suddenly appearing and disappearing. These happened so often that the Sloane family were soon persuaded that they shared their home with the original owners.

Doreen explained that, once you accept this premise, the strange presence becomes less frightening. Rather, her family felt pleased that the ghost inhabitants appeared to approve of their occupancy, since none of the spectral actions was malicious. In a sense it was good to feel them around, because it provided a sense of continuity after death – an indication that perhaps there was more to living than three score years and ten. Those who wish to be rid of a ghost are either scared of what might happen, thanks to 'horror' media imagery based on evil phantoms, or have a poltergeist creating mayhem rather than an actual haunting. Doreen Sloane's more encouraging story is by no means unusual among those willing to give their spectral fellow residents a ghost of a chance.

However, paranormal research groups are happy these days to offer advice to people who are sharing with ghosts. There will be no mumbo jumbo, and their association with you will take whatever direction you choose. It may include research into the history of the property to see if there is any evidence of a haunting in the past, or mediums visiting the site and using their gifts to try to tune in to the phantom and understand who or what it is. There are even some psychics who practise what is termed 'psychic rescue'. Their speciality is contacting the ghost and attempting to persuade it to vacate the premises voluntarily and move on up to the afterlife. These mediums tend to believe that ghosts are trapped souls who either do not realise they have died or who cannot bear to leave the earth and their old home behind.

Of course, whether you employ such a person depends upon your interpretation of the ghostly goings on. Many paranormal researchers would not guarantee success, and some residents might feel that, by taking the ghost so seriously, an air of expectancy would be created and strange events might be experienced. However, for some of those living with a ghost anything is worth a try if it means a quiet life after death.

RESEARCHING GHOSTS

These days ghost hunting can be the province of either the hardy or the technologically minded. There is still scope for the staging of ghost watches. Particularly in Britain, organisations such as ASSAP from time to time still stake out old properties where hauntings have been alleged, hoping that one of their researchers might see or hear something. They are equipped with cameras and tape recorders to capture any evidence.

Classic examples were the video footage taken by an ASSAP team at Dover Castle in Kent, which reputedly showed a door being closed by ghostly means, and the sounds of spectral knockings recorded in the Priest's Room at Chingle Hall near Goosnargh in Lancashire, when Radio Lancashire were interviewing ghost hunter Terence Whittaker at this famous site. That night Whittaker had with him a piece of equipment which he called a 'spectre detector'. In effect it measured the temperature in the room and sounded an alarm if it suddenly altered. Many ghostly encounters have been reported to begin with a feeling of intense cold within the room.

This kind of technology has been replaced by clever gadgets, from video camera monitors filming haunted rooms when nobody is present to machines that respond to dramatic changes in the local electromagnetic field and take a photograph automatically whenever this happens. These can be set up in ghost-ridden rooms and left right through the night, after which the results can be studied at leisure.

The ghost in the machine

Another source of ghost hunting today, thanks to modern surveillance equipment, is the ability to access accidental intrusions into our technological environment. For example, at a Christmas get-together in London in December 1993 family photographs were taken as the children were playing. However, when the prints were developed a strange woman's face appeared on the TV screen in the background. Yet, the set was clearly switched off, and the family are adamant that nobody was standing in front of it at the time the pictures were taken. Some people claim that the image looks just like the famed medium Doris Stokes, who had died some years before.

Recent technological ghosts have included a blood-curdling voice recorded on a Manchester answerphone tape (although this may be explained by replay speeds and their effect on the human voice) and a baby alarm in Dublin. The latter was set up to let the parents know if their child began to cry when left alone in the nursery, but it transmitted adult voices from the room when nobody was present.

On rare occasions a security video camera seems to have picked up something more than it was designed to do. In our book *The Afterlife*, Peter Hough and I published an account and photograph of a remarkable case at the Butterflies nightclub in Oldham. Police rushed to the scene when a silent alarm went off in the middle of the night. There was no sign of a break-in, but when they ran the security camera tapes they saw an unknown man walking along a corridor before turning and passing straight through a closed door. The film was recorded at the precise moment that the alarm was triggered, and the building has a tradition of ghost sightings. Clearly, new technology is bringing unusual opportunities for ghost researchers, and we may now have a better chance than ever to get to the bottom of this fascinating mystery.

GHOSTS TODAY

Ghostly episodes can strike anywhere and do not always involve visual sightings. A case reported in April 1995 is a good example.

A family were on a camping holiday on Exmoor in the Somerset and Devon border countries. It was 5.20a.m. and they were miles from any habitation when they were woken by the sound of a child singing, 'plink, plank, plonk'. In the half light nothing was visible outside and they settled back to sleep.

Twenty minutes later the sound returned and the father had had enough. He could not understand how a child sounding so young could be out alone that early. All his own children were accounted for.

Going out into the chilly dawn the puzzled man searched high and low, but could see nothing. He followed the voice, still singing, deep into a wood. Then it suddenly stopped. When he told the rest of the family at breakfast they laughed. However, the experience haunted him so much that he created a piece of music based on the ghostly song to get it out of his system.

But the family's laughter was to become rather uneasy when they met a local historian before heading home. The weird events were mentioned and this man looked shocked. He asked for time to check something out and returned a short while afterwards with an amazing tale.

It seemed that in 1858 a local five-year-old girl had been sold to a childminder by her father. She vanished – being last seen wandering about at 4a.m. The childminder then disappeared himself and it was assumed he had taken the girl with him. However, some time later a passer-by heard a deep sighing noise coming from an underground mine. A search was mounted and the girl's body was found inside. She had been murdered and dumped there. Her father was subsequently convicted of the crime. This had all occurred at the spot where the unseen child's singing had been heard on that eerie morning. That singing had manifested some 136 years later, seemingly on the anniversary of the girl's last few fateful hours of life.

At the other extreme, Erika Davis of Salt Springs in Florida reports a typical visual encounter. Early on the morning of 12 April 1993 her brother arrived and told her to sit down as he had some bad news. Their father had died during the night, at the age of just fifty, and seemingly whilst in good health. His heart simply stopped beating.

Erika's husband then reminded her about her dream. She was puzzled, but it was dancing on the edge of her memory and just out of reach. He reminded her that she had cried out in the early hours as if talking to someone by the window. Her worried spouse had gone to check if there was a burglar but was overcome with icy terror and quickly returned to bed. Erika had stopped talking by then and fallen back to sleep.

This instantly brought back full recall of what had happened. Her father had appeared by her bedside, called her name and said that he had to go. She resisted at first, then said 'all right' and looked at him by the window. He was dressed as normal. Then he stopped talking and vanished. The time appears to have coincided with the hour of death as set by the coroner, making this a classic case of a crisis apparition – with Erika's father appearing to her at the time his life suddenly and unexpectedly ended many miles away.

Cases like this allow us to ponder the truly important questions about ghosts. Clearly Erika Davis can have had this experience in only one of several ways. Sceptics will say it was just coincidence. Her dream was made to fit reality after the facts by the mind's unconscious use of selective memory.

However, assuming that we accept it has a supernatural nature, then there are probably two further options to consider.

In the first possibility, knowledge of her father's death was detected by Erika's mind as it happened and her dream used this incoming data to create an hallucination. It was as if a distress flare crossed time and space and pressed home its message on the woman's sleeping mind. If we acknowledge the reality of telepathic communication, this seems possible, but did her father's mind know that he was dying as the heart attack struck? Could his unconscious mind have sent out such a message? These are questions we cannot answer. But the fact that the event seems to have occurred around the point of death supports this explanation quite well.

In other cases, hallucination was undeniably a factor. A woman at Birkenhead on the Wirral received a phone call from her husband reporting he was far away, in an eerie, sad voice. This coincided with the very moment he was shot dead whilst intervening in a robbery outside his place of work. The big problem is that when the woman regained her composure she realised that her hand was clutching empty air. They did not own a phone and so she had imagined the conversation; although the later arrival of a police officer to break the tragic news demonstrated that it was more than *just* imagination at work.

Another possibility is that, after death, a spirit is able to visit loved ones and say goodbye, presumably utilising a form of thought transference similar to that required for the previous theory to operate. The difference would be that the ghostly images were projected after the extinction of life, whereas in the former theory they would occur at a point immediately prior to death.

In other words whilst the reality of ghosts as disembodied beings is not ruled out by cases such as these, their acceptance introduces an added assumption (that a spirit survives bodily extinction). In that sense the easiest (and so – according to science – the most likely) solution is the telepathic transmission of data at the point of death. If this were correct it would mean that ghost encounters don't require the existence of life after death, merely unusual capabilities bestowed on living minds.

Research into ghostly encounters must also take into account the fact that some cases have conventional explanations.

Malcolm Robinson reported on an excellent study from Falkirk, Scotland in late 1993. A family told how a toy guitar was playing music at the same time each night although nobody was near it when this happened. A vigil was mounted and sure enough the music did float across the room as the guitar sat impassively alongside the wall.

Intrigued by all this, the researchers conducted a full-scale investigation and eventually took the guitar away for tests. But once out of its environment not a peep was heard from the haunted instrument. The terrible truth only dawned when cameras were set up to record the next expected visitation by the spectral musician.

This time the sound was followed by the investigators right to its source and it appeared not to be coming from the guitar at all. Opening up a cupboard another child's toy was found hidden away and the music was emanating from here. This was placed under some household rubbish and was replaying the same song at a pre-set hour each day owing to a slight fault. Everyone – from family members to researchers – had simply assumed that the music was coming from the guitar in plain view, but it was never even involved! It had taken luck and dedicated investigation to find the culprit.

The use of technology has always been a factor in ghost investigations. But cassette recorders and thermometers have been superseded by ever more clever gadgets, from video camera monitors filming haunted rooms when nobody is present, to machines that respond to dramatic changes in the local electromagnetic field and take a photograph automatically whenever this happens.

Such a peculiar device, nicknamed the Spider, is being field tested by renowned ghost hunter Tony Cornell of the SPR. It can be set up in ghost-ridden rooms and left right through the night, with the results studied at leisure the next day.

Unfortunately, tests of the Spider's predecessors have in the past proved disappointing and there seems some evidence that ghosts are camera shy when nobody is around – fuelling the theory that they may need a human witness to manifest, or that they may be largely a product of the mind of the percipient.

SOURCES

ORGANISATIONS AND PERIODICALS

Ghost investigations are carried out by numerous research groups around the world; including some whose addresses are included in other sections of this book (see *Society for Psychical Research, American Society for Psychical Research* and *ASSAP*, in particular).

In addition the following organisation may prove of help to those who suffer from ghostly activity and need advice.

Parapsychology Foundation Counselling Bureau   *228 E. 71st Street, New York, NY 10021, USA.*

Also there are several magazines that report on ghostly activity and often conduct their own investigations. Examples worth checking out are:

Enigmas (Strange Phenomena Investigations)   *41 The Braes, Tullibody, Clackmannanshire, Scotland FK10 2TT, UK.*

Ghost Trackers Newsletter   *Box 205, Oaklawn, IL 60454, USA.*

Ghostwatch Magazine *Box 54, Birkenhead, Merseyside, L43 7FD, UK.*

Spectral *PO Box 18, Aberdare, Wales CF4 8YG, UK.*

BOOKS

Of the many hundreds of books that have been written on the subject of ghosts and hauntings these are just some of those worth examination. They provide a reasonable overview of the topic. The two by Gurney, Myers and Podmore and Tyrrell are classics of the early literature. Price's book concerns one of the most famous haunted house investigations of all time, but is rather dated in its approach and may be flawed as well. The primer by Underwood sets out to be a basic introduction to would-be ghosthunters and the works by MacKenzie offer a perspective on how to investigate cases in some depth, through in-field illustrations. The text by Green and McCreery is an excellent modern statistical analysis of all manner of apparitions and not as dull as it sounds! It is an important starting point for any research project. Evans makes a very good attempt to synthesise a modern theory of understanding about ghostly activity in the light of a century of research. Schatzman's is a remarkable investigation of a modern day apparition case with so many twists it is of great importance to our knowledge. Finally, if you want to put some of these things into practice the books by Coleman and Hough should help. Coleman's *Curious Encounters* includes a listing of haunted sites in the USA and Hough's book has maps to some of Britain's top ghostly spots.

Phantasms of the Living by Edmund Gurney, F. W. Myers and Frank Podmore (SPR, 1886).

Apparitions by G. N. M. Tyrrell (Duckworth, 1943).

The End of Borley Rectory by Harry Price (Harrap, 1947).

Ghosts and How to See Them by Peter Underwood (Anaya, 1993; Trafalgar Square, North Pomfret, VT, 1994).

Hauntings and Apparitions by Andrew MacKenzie (Heinemann, 1982).

The Seen and the Unseen by Andrew MacKenzie (Weidenfeld & Nicolson, 1987).

Apparitions by Celia Green and Charles McCreery (Hamish Hamilton, 1975).

Visions, Apparitions, Alien Entities by Hilary Evans (Aquarian Press, 1984).

The Story of Ruth by Morton Schatzman (Duckworth, 1980).

Curious Encounters by Loren Coleman (Strange Books, Rockville, MD, 1986).

Mysterious America by Loren Coleman (Strange Books, Rockville, MD, 1988).

Supernatural Britain by Peter Hough (Piatkus, 1995).

HEALING

DEFINITION

For centuries doctors have healed the sick with a combination of physical and psychic medicine. Today, however, most of Western civilisation has lost touch with half that equation. As science has become ever more adept at producing ways to combat illness, disease after disease has been eradicated with drugs and technology. The role of the mind in recovery has become overlooked – although to some extent all treatment incorporates a form of spiritual healing.

Whatever medical progress is made, there remains a place for the self-healing process in any cure. Doctors refer to psychosomatic illnesses, where the influence of the will of the patient is paramount. Simply being prepared to fight for health and to believe in one's survival can be a vital factor in the success or speed with which a disease can be overcome. Whilst not all doctors may be willing to admit that mind over matter can strengthen healing, there is some evidence that sufferers of severe or terminal cancer survive longer when they believe in their ability to combat the disease and so fight it off, rather than submit and accept their impending death.

Psychic or spiritual healing is said by its practitioners to utilise such knowledge and help the sick to help themselves. In addition, many workers feel that some form of energy is involved, and they facilitate its transfer.

This also seems to be the focal point of certain other types of healing techniques which are far more controversial in nature. The use of crystals, for example, to channel healing energies is growing in popularity amongst the new age community but has little support from the scientific or medical fraternity, who regard it as a gimmick. However, some theories of earth mystery origin (see page 79) relate to physical phenomena that might result from natural energy forces generated by rocks of crystalline structure. The possibility that such emissions might sometimes prove beneficial to people's wellbeing ought not to be overlooked.

HISTORICAL REVIEW

Professor Stanley Krippner is one of the world's leading experts in shamanism, having travelled the globe to meet healers in their own environment. He has studied them in the remoteness of Siberia and the Zulu townships of Africa. Wherever he has gone, there have been similarities.

Shamans began healing long before doctors existed and before civilisation even created villages, let alone hospitals. They can be traced back almost fifty thousand years, and in some parts of the world are as important as ever to their culture. They believe in two realities, that of physical life and that of the mind, but unlike Western cultures they do not ascribe lesser importance to the latter. Imagination is seen as a gift, not as a sin. Indeed they regard both as real places and think themselves chosen to move – or communicate – between the two. In this sense their similarity with Spiritualist mediums is obvious.

Krippner reports how one modern shaman, Margaret Umlazi, became accepted into the role by her tribe in southern Africa. At school she began to have seizures, possibly epileptic. Rather than having her treated, the tribal elders asked about her dream life. She told of a recurring vision of being dragged to the bottom of the lake by a giant serpent and finding herself able to breathe underwater. This, it was explained by the elders, was powerful symbolism. The serpent was one of her forbears. The deep lake represented that hidden world. This dream showed that she could survive in that world – hence she was to train to become a shaman. However, Margaret had been raised as a Christian and found this idea difficult to accept – until it was explained to her that Jesus was himself a healer and had used his gifts in the same way that she would use her own.

Over the millennia the shaman learned a variety of techniques which are as common today as they ever were. The use of herbs and plants, not only to perfect cures but to induce altered states of consciousness that increased dreaming, ESP and psychic awareness, was frequent. The imagery experienced during visions and out-of-the-body states (see page 152) was interpreted as a conduit between realities and the bearer of important messages about a person's sickness. Above all, shamans invented holistic medicine, based on the concept that body and mind are one, as are earth and heaven and the individual and the planet from which they originate.

It is fascinating to see how much of this has become part of modern society's spiritual healing. Indeed, it seems very likely that much of this knowledge is innate to human consciousness, and the advance of technology has failed to eradicate it completely from our collective awareness. Those who are psychically attuned, and would become shamans if they lived in what we might falsely term 'primitive' cultures, are instead using that capacity for inner knowledge by becoming psychic.

But what do psychics do with knowledge once it is recognised as part of their life? Real problems may be encountered here, because we either disregard such things or treat them like a freak show and reduce them to sensational stories in the tabloids. But the history of psychic healing teaches that they are important and should be incorporated into the very core of our being.

EXPERIENCING HEALING

Healing can be experienced as a patient and as a practitioner.

Many people have a potential for healing. Actor Bill Waddington told me that when he was entertaining troops during the Second World War he seemed to have the capacity to help wounded and battle-shocked soldiers. He recalled a time when visiting a tank regiment that had just been engaged in some vicious fighting. As he performed and the troops' mood lightened, Bill felt energy being sucked from them and into himself. He told me that it seemed as though he was a sponge soaking up the negative emotions and channelling through his own positive power.

Bill Waddington, who breeds horses, does not profess to be a healer. He does, however, possess another ability that seems to be common in those who develop such talents. He can detect emotional distress, knowing, for example, when horses at his stables are unwell even before the staff on duty discover it. Perhaps this capacity to absorb emotion from others is the key to healing ability.

Matthew Manning became a celebrated psychic at the age of fifteen when poltergeist activity, of which he seemed to be the focus, struck his family's two hundred-year-old house in a Cambridgeshire village. This was in 1970, and four years later he was known worldwide for his party tricks, which included Uri Geller-style metal bending and re-creating in unconscious frenzy paintings in the style of famous deceased artists.

However, Manning soon tired of being a performer and felt the urge to use his talents to better ends than bending spoons. So he dropped out of the limelight and spent his time attempting to perfect mind over matter on cancer cells. Once he began to have success he extended his work to helping real people, and is now one of the most undersung and yet sought after psychic healers in the world. He feels that this decision to use his gifts in a practical way was of tremendous importance to his life.

More people nowadays are turning to alternative methods when conventional medicine appears to offer little hope, or when they opt for a treatment free from drugs or surgery and their possible side-effects. Such patients seek out psychics such as Manning, or the countless others who work with foundations around the world.

Most healers do not advise complete suspension of trust in standard medical treatment. They regard what they do as complementary, rather than as a replacement. Nor do they offer false hope. Manning says that he tells his patients there are several possible outcomes, ranging from no success at all through to a complete cure, and he can never predict how a patient will respond.

He does not believe that a person's expectations affect the outcome, and says that some of his best achievements have been with outright sceptics. However, other healers feel that the patient's desire to be cured (aided no doubt by their belief in its probability) does confer a positive advantage. Shamans have also long argued that the mind is a big factor in any cure, seemingly boosted by the number of cases in such cultures where a person can become seriously ill – or even die – apparently because they believe in the pronouncement of the shaman that this will be their fate.

RESEARCHING HEALING

A common method of training as a healer involves relaxing in a meditative environment and picturing feelers of energy coming up from the earth and coursing through your body. This is called visualisation. You should then go immediately to someone in the family with a minor medical ailment, such as a cut finger or sprained ankle, and hold your hands over this position. If you have the potential to become a healer the patient should report a sensation, such as a feeling of warmth.

Of course, during the first few trials it will not be known whether your ability has had any long-term effects. It will need to be measured over time and judged against the results that would be possible from the body's own natural healing processes. These can be quite extraordinary, as doctors rightly point out.

Another way to practise such skills is to try to heal sick animals, although never to the extent that they would suffer because conventional treatment by a vet was suspended. Indeed, Matthew Manning argues that the now established fact that animals can be healed strongly indicates that belief by the patient cannot be the most significant factor.

Presumably animals would not be able to heal themselves through faith in the powers of a human being.

It is also possible to practise absent healing – healer and patient can be thousands of miles apart and not in any sort of direct contact. Physicist Dr Lawrence Le Shan has conducted a number of tests of this procedure after learning to heal by conducting his own laboratory experiments.

In one fascinating example, Dr Le Shan was asked to attempt healing on a man many miles away but whom he would not be able to meet in person on the relevant day. Le Shan agreed and set a time for the test. Later the physicist was contacted by the man's doctor, who explained that his patient had recovered completely and no longer needed the surgery that had once been considered essential. Could the doctor write up this remarkable demonstration of absent healing for the medical literature? A rather embarrassed Lawrence Le Shan had to say no to this request. The problem was that, whilst the patient had evidently put considerable effort into the healing session and felt the apparent benefit, Dr Le Shan's absent healing had had nothing directly to do with it. The scientist had forgotten all about the agreed experiment and had done no healing whatsoever at the prearranged time! As the physicist points out, whatever the truth in other cases where the healer may indeed have a part to play, this case proves that in some instances patients largely heal themselves.

HEALING TODAY

Such has been the progress in the acceptance of healers that these days it is even possible to use Britain's National Health Service to gain assistance from one. Paulina Baume made a breakthrough in early 1994 when she was employed by the Coventry Health Authority as a funded NHS consultant. She is vice-president of the National Federation of Healers and considers this a major step towards recognition for the healers.

Part of her work involves counselling, to help people come to terms with their illness. But she also receives recommendations from doctors, leading her to certain patients who might benefit from pain relief. Paulina considers that the needs of a person to grow holistically – into a single entity with spiritual wholeness – is an important aspect of what she does.

In August 1994 Paulina presented her first progress report, entitled

'Working with Health Care Professionals', to the Federation. Special in-service courses for working doctors were now sometimes including spiritual healing, and allowed them to consider integrating their form of medicine with what Federation workers attempt to do. She feels they approach the same problem, merely from slightly different directions.

Paulina is not alone: several other healers work on an ad hoc basis with GPs. In October 1994 she organised a symposium to bring these people together to discuss working practices and ways of developing matters further. The healing community is optimistic that this trend will continue to grow and, far from being considered as cranks, these workers are respected for their expertise and the real help that they can bring to patients.

Yorkshire-based healer Lorraine Ham (see photograph opposite page 186) took this link even further during 1995. She became an accepted part of a medical team at a surgery in West Yorkshire. Following a TV appearance on the series *Strange but True?* she was swamped with tens of thousands of requests for assistance. Paranormal healing had come of age.

An army on the march

Whilst this form of healing is quietly gaining a foothold, the more dramatic claims continue to provoke controversy within the medical profession. Joe Keeton, a Merseyside specialist who uses hypnotherapy, claims to have helped a young woman to regrow part of her foot which was lost in an accident. Surgeons doubt the possibility but Joe Keeton has a simple answer – the woman's apparent wellbeing. He notes that all he does is use hypnosis to channel visualisation, and from there the body's defence systems take over. He argues that some animals, such as starfish, can regrow severed limbs with apparent ease. There is an energy template which directs the creation of the body from the DNA in cells, and it is possible to coerce the mind into kicking this into action to restore elements of the body that may malfunction.

It may be some time before the medical profession openly embrace this possibility and conduct experiments to test such claims. One renowned psychic, who practises healing as a sideline, upset hospital staff when the father of a young boy, thought to be suffering from a brain tumour, asked him to help his son when it seemed that little else could be done. The psychic got the boy to picture a brave army marching into his brain and killing off the enemy, which was hardly standard treatment.

The philosophy behind this method is simple to see. The psychic picked on a likely topic of interest to the boy and gave him an image to focus on, which may have mobilised his natural resources and allowed them to fight for health. Certainly at the next scan there was no sign of a tumour – although the doctor argued that it might never have been present in the first place, as such diagnoses are tricky. However, it is hard to see how such a healing experiment could be regarded as a bad thing, since at worst it was providing optimism to a young boy in serious distress who was receiving conventional treatment as well.

Monitoring cures

If such amazing cures are possible, modern technology has reached the point where they can now be thoroughly monitored. Such was the case in September 1994 when a remarkable experiment was reported from Japan.

Carol Everett, a healer from Devon, was flown to Tokyo's Denki University to participate in tests with Professor Yoshio Machi. She was hooked up to a series of monitors recording respiration, heart rate, brain wave activity and blood pressure as she engaged in the healing process. This began when a young woman whom she had never met before was introduced and Carol was asked to detect her illness by psychic means. As she spoke and her words were filmed a thermal imaging scope, out of sight of the healer, was probing the patient's body and conveying state-of-the-art – but conventional – medical wisdom to a team led by the Professor. Carol correctly diagnosed a small lump in one of the woman's ovaries, which the imaging scope clearly indicated as being present. The psychic then began the healing process to try to alleviate the 20mm wide tumour.

As the experiment progressed, marked changes were noted in the healer's brain activity: the left hemisphere virtually closed down and most of her energy was now concentrated on the right side and at the back. This is the part of the brain known to control intuitive, creatively visual and psychic experiences, whereas the hemisphere that became inactive is more noted for mathematical, rational and analytical thought processes. The psychic was also displaying alpha wave brain activity, normally recorded only during deep sleep states.

At the same time as these changes in Carol were being recorded, the image of the patient on the scanner was altering radically. The heat intensity of the tumour cooled markedly and the spot reduced in size until, after about seven minutes, it vanished from the scope altogether. Carol felt that healing had taken place, and this multi-million-pound piece of technology appeared to confirm her view. A month later the doctor added that healing seemed to have proved successful.

This test may pave the way for further experiments using similar complex equipment. It is normally too expensive to use in this way and is in any case constantly needed by long lists of patients. However, if Carol Everett's results can be repeated the conducting of further trials with tumours – in operable locations – has to be justified given the potential benefits.

SOURCES

ORGANISATIONS AND INDIVIDUALS

There are many healers now registered with various professional bodies, and it is always wise to consult your own doctor first. The following organisations can be of assistance.

The Matthew Manning Centre   *PO Box 100, Bury St Edmunds, Suffolk, IP26 2DE, UK.*

The National Federation of Spiritual Healers   *Old Manor Farm Studios, Church St, Sunbury-on-Thames, TW16 6RG, UK.*

Dr Stanley Krippner   *Saybrook Institute, San Francisco, California, USA.*

The National Healing Centre   *Roland Thomas House, Royal Shrewsbury Hospital, South Shrewsbury, Shropshire, SY3 8XF, UK.*

The following association claims to offer help and equipment to study the human aura or energy shell, and that this can help in healing and diagnosis.

Auragraph Energy Research Centre   *Box 8378, Wooloongabba, QLD 4102, Australia.*

PUBLICATIONS

Articles on healing techniques can be found regularly in magazines such as *Mind, Body, Soul* and *Nexus* (see page 50). In addition, the following two publications are invaluable. *Psychic News* is a weekly newspaper revealing the latest work of mediums and healers and previewing meetings, sessions and workshops. *Aura Z* is the former Soviet Union's first widely available journal of paranormal developments, reporting on the many fascinating experiments across a wide range of fields including healing.

Psychic News   *Clock Cottage, Stansted Hall, Stansted Mountfichet, Essex, CM24 8UD, UK.*

Aura Z   *PO Box 224, Moscow 117463, Russia.*

BOOKS

Most of the following books are general reviews of healing methods and have self-explanatory titles. That by Chapman and Stemman relates the story of an alleged bridge between a deceased surgeon and a living medium, producing miraculous healing successes. The Levine book consists of a series of interviews about healing with those being helped and their families. Lorraine Ham's work and that of other modern healers is discussed in my book.

Surgeon from Another World by George Chapman and Roy Stemman (Psychic Press, 1977).

Meetings at the Edge by Stephen Levine (Gateway Books, Bath, 1992).

Healing States by Professor Stanley Krippner (Simon & Schuster, 1986).

A Patient's Guide to Spiritual Healing by Eileen Herzberg (Thorsons, 1990).

Spiritual Dimensions of Healing by Professor Stanley Krippner (Irvington, New York, 1992).

Strange but True? by Jenny Randles (Piatkus, 1995).

Hands of Light by Barbara Brennan (Bantam Books, 1987).

Your Healing Power by Jack Angelo (Piatkus, 1994).

ICE BOMBS

DEFINITION

If an ice bomb falls on you, the last thing you would require is a definition. Quite a few repair men might be called for, but the precise cause of the devastation will probably be the furthest thing from your mind.

Ice bombs look like gigantic, often smelly, hailstones that plunge from what may well be a clear blue sky. They can be up to several feet in diameter and are usually at least a foot wide. If you are outside and one falls nearby, it will plop on to the pavement or road surface with a vengeance. If you happen to be indoors, your first realisation might be when the ceiling caves in and a mass of discoloured ice crashes on to your new carpet. The term 'ice bomb' is self-descriptive, because the impact is very similar to that of a bomb. As to whether they really consist of normal ice, this remains to be established. What can be said with assurance is that they are some form of frozen liquid.

Although, thankfully, these events are rare, at least a dozen cases are recorded somewhere in the world in most years – which makes them rather more common than falls of meteorites over inhabited areas. They also do not seem to be a new phenomenon, since sporadic cases have been reported for more than a century. No serious injuries or deaths of humans as a result of ice bombs have been proved, although one possible case is cited below and some minor injuries and very near misses are known.

In many respects this is the archetypal strange phenomenon – utterly unexpected, seemingly baffling, with various peculiar features that defy the more obvious solutions. It is disbelieved by most people – until it happens to them!

HISTORICAL REVIEW

Astronomer Camille Flammarion collected reports of ice falls 150 years ago, at a time when scientists were only reluctantly accepting that meteorites were lumps of rock from space. Previously they had regarded them as being just earthly rocks dug out of the ground by a lightning strike.

In one case cited by the astronomer the ice was said to be fifteen feet long and eleven feet thick, and it was completely impossible for it to have been formed by normal means – for instance like a hailstone, which is created as frozen water droplets plunge through the air. A record example was featured in *The Times*, describing how on the night of 13 August 1849 a huge ice bomb about twenty feet across and weighing almost half a ton had smashed harmlessly into Ord in Scotland.

Charles Fort, the journalist who collected reports of oddities during the first half of the twentieth century, listed numerous ice bombs in his books. The torch has since been passed on to William Corliss, whose 'sourcebooks' today scour the scientific literature for natural peculiarities, among which ice bombs figure strongly.

A sheep was killed by an ice bomb on Exmoor in the west of England in early November 1950, and a possible human fatality occurred when a carpenter working on a rooftop at Kempten near Düsseldorf in Germany fell victim on 10 January 1951. He was found skewered to death by a huge icicle some six feet long that fell from the sky like a spear. Although its origin is strange, the form is not that of typical ice bombs (which are approximately round) and may have been a naturally formed – if remarkably large – icicle.

The role of aircraft

Aircraft have frequently been blamed for the falls, suggesting that ice builds up on the wingtips and tumbles off, particularly in areas close to a major flight path. Whilst this risk was true of early aircraft without de-icing equipment, and occasionally occurs today if this equipment malfunctions, ice build-up on wings is dangerous and significant precautions are taken by the aviation industry. Besides which, the sheer size of some of the ice bombs precludes the idea simply because such a mass of ice would almost certainly have triggered an accident.

Discoloured and noxious-smelling ice is often blamed on the flushing systems of aircraft toilets. If these malfunction and drop their contents earthwards, freezing on the long journey down, such an effect might be possible. A few cases are believed to be due to this. However, all these aircraft theories disregard the fact that ice bombs pre-date the invention of aircraft, so it cannot be the primary explanation.

What was undoubtedly a turning point in ice bomb history came on 2 April 1973, when Dr Richard Griffiths was walking along Burton Road in West Didsbury, Manchester on a cold but sunny day. He heard a single unexpectedly loud burst of thunder, and nine minutes later was startled by the impact of a massive ice bomb crashing on to the road ahead. Recognising both the mystery and the opportunity presented by his laboratory facilities at Manchester University, Griffiths collected the largest chunk from the shattered ice bomb, took it home and stored it in his freezer until he could study it.

Aware of the aircraft theory and the fact that jets inbound to Manchester Airport routinely flew over Didsbury, he checked out the flight logs. But he could trace no aircraft that might have been responsible. Moreover, he ascertained that the ice bomb was composed of water such as might be found in clouds and had been produced layer by layer, rather like a hailstone would form as it dropped thousands of feet through the freezing air. But there were no fewer than fifty-one layers on the ice bomb, and its other characteristics did not fit the 'super hailstone' theory. In the end Dr Griffiths remained mystified about the nature of this huge mass of ice.

EXPERIENCING ICE BOMBS

If an ice bomb falls near you, particularly on to your property, there may well be damage and your immediate thoughts will be on repair. Whether your household insurance covers ice-falls may be debatable, but you should impress on your insurers the fact that it is tantamount to storm damage and therefore ought to be their responsibility.

Since these phenomena are rare and little understood, you should do several things as quickly as possible. First, try to take photographs or video film of the damage and the ice bomb *in situ*, and do so whilst the ice is as intact as possible. This is to preserve evidence of its original appearance, as it will melt quickly in a warm environment. Then take the largest possible sample – the whole ice bomb if possible – and store it in a basin or container inside your freezer. You should seal the sample or remove food from its vicinity just in case it contains any bacteria, although that is not common. Then contact the physics department at your local university, explain what you have obtained and how, and ask them to send someone who might be willing to investigate. If that fails, call your local weather centre or one of the addresses in the sources below.

At the very least, by taking such actions swiftly you will have preserved hard evidence that the media will find interesting. Then, if you do have problems with your insurance claim, you may be able to pay for the repairs by selling your story. This is one of the few areas of the paranormal where nobody would blame you for doing so!

RESEARCHING ICE BOMBS

If you come across an ice bomb report, the physical evidence is obviously your first priority. If you are not on the scene within minutes there will probably be little to see. But even if fluid is all that remains, samples will be important for chemical analysis. It is vital that the analysis is done properly. There will only be one opportunity, so never hand it over to a scientist or laboratory unless they have clearly spelt out what they intend to do – and how quickly.

As an investigator you must check on aircraft movements at the time, as this theory is bound to be suggested as the probable cause. Enquiries at the nearest airport or with the civil aviation authorities have to be made immediately, as records are quickly filed and become difficult and expensive to trace later. Do not limit your enquiries to aircraft coming in or out of any local airport. An ice bomb may well have plunged 30,000 feet from an overflying jet, so check whether there are any air routes above the location that might have resulted in this possibility.

It is also essential to collate the most accurate details available about the weather at the time, not simply at ground level but also data such as the temperature at a range of heights. In addition, peruse newspaper files and police records to check for any unusual occurrences that day – sudden explosions, one-off lightning flashes, odd lights zooming across the sky, in fact anything that might potentially be relevant – all these should find their way into your report.

ICE BOMBS TODAY

There are two main theories today which attempt to explain ice bombs. The aircraft toilet hypothesis still crops up again and again, and in one case in France in 1992 a fall was traced to a faulty flush system on a particular jet. But in the main this theory flounders, especially for un-contaminated ice.

It has long been suspected that these falls occur in some unresolved, but natural, manner. Charles Fort even speculated that there were fields of ice in the sky, just as there are clouds, and that bits can sometimes fall off. Frequent air travel has, of course, dispelled this notion. However, it remains possible that ice bombs form rather as hailstones do, expanding in size just as a snowball grows bigger as it rolls down a hill. The larger the ice bomb, in that respect, the further it may have fallen.

However, meteorologists are not convinced. A fall in Pennsylvania, USA, on 30 July 1957 produced some of the best evidence against the hailstone theory. Two separate milky white ice bombs fell at Bernville, making a whooshing noise as they plummeted. Meteorologists were given the remains to study and found them to consist of numerous little balls pressed together into a single frozen, opaque lump. But they were not formed of water as found in either ground or airborne ice. There were no nitrates and a very unusual level of alkaline salts. The origin of the bombs was baffling, and Paul Sutton, chief of the US weather centre at Harrisburg, was insistent that they could not have been formed by 'any natural process known to meteorology'.

Fish and frogs

So what supernatural processes might be at work? It is interesting to note that ice falls are merely the most common missiles from the air. Many other strange things plunge down. There are countless reliable reports of small fish, frogs, gelatinous goos, bean seeds, even coins raining down from above. The biblical tale of 'manna' from heaven may have originated in these phenomena, which have been recorded since Greek and Roman times.

How do such things occur? One theory is that whirlwinds suck these objects from the ground and then drop them back to earth when the winds lose energy. Could ice form in such circumstances? A rather more astonishing idea is considered necessary by some people, because it is difficult to explain how so little damage is caused to the descending animals – indeed, some are even found alive after they have fallen. Yet the fierce winds in a tornado would surely kill them.

So a new theory contends that these objects are transported through space by some naturally occurring force which we have yet to discover. The frogs may literally hop into this anomaly in one place and hop out again in mid-air many miles away – just as a shoal of herring might swim into this 'black hole' and reappear far away as if teleported from one location to another. Ice may be lifted *en masse* from some point on earth and dropped from above in this way. The idea is undeniably absurd, but the level of absurdity that exists in some of the falling objects may require something as bizarre as this to account for it.

In 1992 an American scientist, Dr Louis Frank, published the latest ice bomb theory. As evidence he produced photographs taken from orbiting satellites, which showed that millions of tiny objects – which were not meteors – were entering the earth's atmosphere from space every day. Dr Frank made calculations which, he says, solve a long-standing scientific riddle: the seemingly constant level of water surrounding the earth. His conclusion is that ice comets only a few feet across are regularly bombarding the outer atmosphere and that some, just as meteors do, run the gauntlet of frictional burn-up and make it to the surface. Those that evaporate account for the input of water vapour to maintain the equilibrium in our atmosphere. This theory remains controversial and is some way from being fully accepted.

Ice bombs continue to fall. One of the most recent occurred on 26 April 1994 in Cheadle, Cheshire. It fell less than a mile from where I was then living, although unfortunately I heard about it too late to obtain any samples.

The Williams family found the foot-wide mass on their lawn moments after their young children had been playing out there. It fell at some point between 8 and 8.40a.m. The object was kept for a short time in the family's freezer to show to aviation experts, as the Williamses believed that the blue-tinged ice-bomb came from an aircraft. Their house lies directly beneath the flight path into a busy airport, and as many as twenty planes passed overhead at about 900 feet during the short period when the ice must have fallen. The airport authorities were unable to say whether the bomb did fall off an aircraft or to pinpoint any culprit – although no aircraft reported any de-icing faults. But they took the matter seriously enough to launch an investigation. After all, as the family pointed out, if the large mass had struck their four-year-old son or crashed through the roof instead of narrowly missing their greenhouse the consequences might have been tragic. For this reason alone study of the ice bomb phenomenon is more urgent than that of many other strange phenomena.

SOURCES

One of the major sources for collating data on ice bombs is *INFO (the International Fortean Organisation)*. This is a membership group which publishes *INFO Journal* and covers a range of anomalies. Much useful data is also regularly recorded by the *Sourcebook Project*, which publishes a series of books based on natural oddities found in the scientific press.

INFO   *Box 367, Arlington, VA 22210–0367, USA.*

Sourcebook Project   *Box 107, Glen Arm, MD 21057, USA.*

In the UK you will find occasional round-ups of ice bomb data in *Fortean Times*. *The Journal of Meteorology* will also be interested in any cases. See pages 158 and 39 for their addresses.

BOOKS

These are not numerous, but the titles by Fort and Corliss are important contributions. The Manak book is a 1994 catalogue of 144 reported ice bombs dating back as far as the year 824. Angel hair is another falling substance, looking like (and sometimes said to be) fine spider's web; he charts sixty-five of these as well. Unfortunately no detailed sources are cited for follow-up work, but the listing and summaries are useful.

The Complete Books of Charles Fort by Charles Fort (Henry Holt, New York, 1941; Dover Publications, 1975).

Tornadoes, Dark Days, Anomalous Precipitations by William Corliss (Sourcebook Project, 1983).

Ice Falls and Angel Hair edited by Allan Manak available from UAPA, PO Box 347032, Cleveland, OH 44134, USA.

LIFE AFTER DEATH

DEFINITION

One of the greatest questions facing mankind is whether any part of us survives the extinction of the physical body. It is an argument that has been debated since we first became a conscious, thinking species millennia ago. Almost every culture on earth has since accepted the answer to be 'yes', and then developed a concept of some form of after-life.

However, the belief in survival of death is an emotive issue. Sceptics argue – not without cause – that we all die and that when we do our brain activity is permanently extinguished. However, they also suggest, this is too awful a prospect for most of us to face – so we invent images of another place where we may continue to 'live'. This serves to reassure our ego.

Of course, one problem is why – if we are simply biological machines – awareness of our own mortality and a consequent need to invent an after-life was ever conferred on us at all. Would it not have been biologically more simple to accept death without recognition of self-extinction?

Again, the counter-argument is that awareness of our own mortality is a response to our selfish genes. These procreate in order to perpetuate – thus bringing a kind of species immortality to us all. We simply misread the signals as individual survival. Of course, on this basis it seems difficult to understand why any self-awareness would be necessary. Would we not all be better off as robots programmed by our DNA to act in the way best suited to evolution?

These are philosophical debates, and it has long been realised that they cannot on their own provide any proof of survival. Obviously, the brain dies, and if our thinking is merely a product of the electro-chemical reactions that go on inside this complex organ (as most scientists contend) there can be no consciousness – and thus no survival – beyond its destruction.

However, many people (including a few scientists) think it likely that the mind is not only the result of signals in the brain but also exists outside our body, almost like a wave of energy. This energy infuses the brain and sparks it into life, causing consciousness to be experienced in the physical world. Our omnipresent belief in survival may result from inherent awareness of this fact.

If we accept this hypothesis, even if the brain dies the energy may still be there – outside the rules of time and space, but without a bodily home and not able to be perceived by the rest of us. If so, there is a real prospect that part of us may live on beyond physical extinction.

However, such theoretical debates can only be resolved with hard evidence to back them up. That is what paranormal research has to offer. We can sift the data and try to see whether hope of survival emerges. Much of this evidence will come through 'mediums', a name that describes their role as a conduit between the physical world and this hypothetical energy field of consciousness. Understanding the messages and assessing the validity of what these people have to say is the basis of most research into life after death.

*H*ISTORICAL REVIEW
—

Sporadic investigations into ghostly and poltergeist phenomena began during the scientific revolution of the eighteenth century. The phenomena were assumed to be spirits of the dead walking the earth, but not much real evidence was available. The investigations consisted of little more than the recording of anecdotal testimony.

Parlour games

In the Victorian era things really changed with the claims of the teenage Fox sisters in Hydesville, New York. In 1848 they professed a link with the spirit world, and messages came to them via knocking sounds and similarly crude methods. Eventually there was such an outcry that they had to leave the place, and by 1851 one scientist claimed to have extracted a confession that their tale was a hoax. They had said they were in contact with the spirit of a murdered tinker who had once lived in their log cabin house. Years later evidence of this murder was uncovered, buried beneath the building.

Whether these two girls were genuine or not, they had incredible impact on the public imagination. A craze for what became known as Spiritualism spread from America to Britain and then across Europe. Many more people claimed similar abilities, either by messages in which the number of raps spelt out words like 'yes' or 'no' or through more sophisticated techniques that used glass tumblers to point to letters and spell out names. These were the forerunner of the Ouija board, still popular today, 'ouija' being a combination of the German and French words for 'yes'.

The first experiments focused either on individuals who believed they could establish such contact (to which the name 'medium' was soon applied) or on a group of people who sat in a circle and tried to pool their individual energies and build a bridge with the spirit world. These early seances were carried out in less than rigorous fashion by hundreds of people, particularly by rich upper-middle-class women for whom it was a parlour game.

Scientific investigation started very soon afterwards. The new materialism of the age, exemplified by Darwin's claim that we were all descended from apes, challenged this perceived nonsense and sought proof that it was all the result of trickery. Much hoaxing was uncovered in this way, and many scientists believed that all mediums worked through conscious (and sometimes unconscious) fabrication.

However, not all scientists were unimpressed. A few remarkable mediums were discovered, such as American socialite Leonore Piper. The messages that she claimed to hear inside her mind, and then spoke out loud, were sometimes found to be astonishingly accurate, offering personal details that it seemed unlikely she could have known. For thirty years she was tested extensively and her reputation held firm, as did that of a few other 'star' performers.

The SPR

In 1882 a group of erudite scientists risked their reputations to launch the SPR (Society for Psychical Research) in London. It was followed three years later by an American equivalent and both still flourish to this day, the oldest paranormal research groups in the world.

The names of those who founded the SPR included some really famous figures of the time, such as physicist Sir William Barrett. Between 1901 and 1903 the president was Sir Oliver Lodge, one of the early pioneers of research into radio and television. Such influential names were the rule rather than the exception among members, which gave the SPR a dry, academic air. As a result many Spiritualists soon left, believing that their honesty was being challenged by intense experimental scrutiny. It was not uncommon, for example, for mediums to be handcuffed and tied to a chair, then asked to perform before SPR members. When Mrs Piper was brought to Britain for several months of testing she exhibited remarkable skills despite such elaborate measures, including being permanently in the presence of an SPR member and never allowed to go anywhere on her own.

The SPR published the positive findings from tests on such mediums and hoped that this would establish proof through science that there was life after death. It did not. The majority of scientists stayed critical, usually refusing even to study the evidence. Their argument, typically, was that the very idea opposed the sweeping materialistic view of the age – so, regardless of what the SPR evidence was proving, it could not be real and there was no point in examining false data. To a large extent this attitude remains.

Although much testimony from sitters with mediums was compiled, it was usually disappointingly banal. The medium would come up with a name, such as Uncle Fred, and the sitter would say they once knew someone of this name. 'Fred' would then tell them he liked the new geraniums in the garden and – as the sitter did have geraniums freshly sprouting – they would go away convinced that Fred had survived death. Unfortunately, a vague and personalised message of this kind has little impact as scientific proof – or indeed proof to anyone beyond the sitter.

Even in truly remarkable cases, where masses of material was produced, the doubts persisted. Lodge's son Raymond, killed during the First World War, returned to tell his elderly father many things that were personally significant. But to anyone else they were almost meaningless, and this remains the key problem of research into survival of death.

What was worse, the SPR scientists soon realised that another possibility might explain what was happening. Since so much of the information passed on to the sitter was known to that person, if the medium had any unexplained abilities at all these might be telepathic. In other words, rather than being told about the geraniums from the late Uncle Fred, the medium could have detected an image of these flowers from the sitter's mind, along with a picture of the name Fred from that person's memory and expectation, and simply assumed that the two were connected and that Fred was their source.

At times much of the evidence given to the sitter by a medium was wrong. This fitted the idea of a medium picking up things from the sitter's subconscious – be they memories, fantasies, dreams or whatever – and churning them all out as a 'message' from the afterlife, regardless of true origin.

The cross-correspondences

During the existence of the SPR only one significant case, the so-called cross-correspondences, has occurred which seems to have challenged this problem. For thirty years from 1901 various mediums on four continents, including Leonore Piper, wrote down messages which came to their minds and seemed isolated, obscure and meaningless. None was aware of what any other medium was up to, and it was many years before the messages were brought together and what seemed to be a pattern started to emerge.

They appeared to interlock, fitting together like pieces of a very complicated jigsaw. No medium could see the broader picture from her own fragments, which seemed to rule out telepathy. The messages seemed to be the clever and elaborate creation of a mind in the afterlife, attempting to prove survival of death. In fact these cross-correspondences often had complex literary themes, and it emerged that their source was purportedly F. W. Myers, a classics scholar from Cambridge who had been with the SPR from the start and had died just before the messages began.

It is disappointing that no case of this level has occurred since, even though mediums are still investigated – albeit with decreasing frequency, as the SPR has tended to focus on other paranormal phenomena such as telepathy and precognition. With the rise in media attention mediums also became stars of stage and screen and acquired a much higher profile not in line with the SPR's academic style. In 1981 a rift developed, with some SPR members believing that the society needed to become more open in its approach and willing to spend time out of the laboratory (the SPR's normal method of investigation was to use random number generators to test subjects *ad infinitum* and not to look at spontaneous cases in the real world).

The result was a breakaway movement called ASSAP (the Association for the Scientific Study of Anomalous Phenomena), whose aim was to undertake the sort of work that the SPR shunned as unscientific. ASSAP still, however, attempted to maintain an air of SPR-like credibility.

Letting in the light

In more recent years, other methods have become available to researchers, notably video cameras with low-light capabilities. Mediums have long preferred to work in the dark, particularly if generating physical energy (known as ectoplasm). This is a sort of bridge between the spirit world and matter, and is reputedly a method that can on rare occasions allow a non-corporeal form briefly to inhabit this matter and appear, wraith-like, in our world.

Such physical mediums are still rare, but are studied by the Noah's Ark Society. A battle is afoot to try to persuade these people to allow low-light cameras to film them at work. Many are reluctant. Sceptics claim this is because such a method would expose their trickery. The mediums usually counter with the argument that the production of ectoplasm is very dangerous and that at least one of their number, Helen Duncan, is believed to have died after being awoken prematurely from a seance. It is hoped that this problem will be overcome and exciting film – perhaps the definitive evidence of the return of a loved one in such a physical form – will soon be captured for posterity.

EXPERIENCING LIFE AFTER DEATH

This is the one paranormal event which comes with a guarantee that we shall all experience it sooner or later. When we reach that point we will discover whether there is some genuine continuance of our existence or whether we merely face oblivion.

Outside the fictional world of the movie *Flatliners*, in which medical students deliberately kill one another and then attempt last-gasp revivals from the rim of physical death, it is not possible to experience such a phenomenon directly and then return (although see page 152 for a major possibility in this regard). At least, most scientists would say this impossibility was a fact. Nevertheless, there are many accounts of dreams (or, more correctly, dream-like experiences) in which deceased friends and loved ones are confronted in pleasant surroundings. To the sceptic these are simply wish fulfilment fantasies based upon memories and mental images. Often the realism perceived by the experiencer leads them to follow the more spiritual view and conclude that these are genuine contacts, because in our deepest sleep our consciousness drifts between the two worlds of life and death.

Unfortunately, this phenomenon is likely to remain elusive and subjective. If you experience such a thing it is best to be reassured by statistics. To sense or even see a close relative after death is by no means a rare event. Almost two-thirds of widows and widowers report such a happening, and generally consider it a happy experience. As many as 80 per cent have sense of some presence in the weeks and months following their loss.

Of course, it may be that years of familiarity with a person's sounds, smells and physical being cause a phantom recognition within the sensory organs – just as people who have a limb amputated commonly say that they can still feel its presence afterwards. But no scientist can be utterly sure of this conclusion, and when it happens to you the feeling of profundity may be more significant than any explanation.

The problem is that nobody can give you a definitive answer, because nobody knows this most secret truth. Scientists will respond in a material fashion, as they are trained to do, giving you a practical solution. If you were to talk to a mystic or Spiritualist they would have an altogether different answer, formed from their own perspective on the universe and neither more nor less valid than any other. Should you consult a religious mentor they will no doubt offer their own blend of comfort, which may even merge aspects of the physical and the spiritual.

All that can be said with any reasonable assurance is that to have such a thing happen in your life is undeniably normal, rather than paranormal, and that the person in the best position to judge how to integrate it into your life is you.

RESEARCHING LIFE AFTER DEATH

The master illusionist Harry Houdini was fascinated by life after death. He spent years researching mediums and psychics, but never proved to his satisfaction that any of them provided genuine proof of human survival. So on his death he told his wife that, if it were possible, he would attempt to return and convey a message to her via a seance. Unfortunately, so far as is known, this never occurred – although there are claims to the contrary. But it is part of a trend that has continued during this century, and a pact of this kind represents one practical way in which everybody can attempt to research this great mystery.

It is easy to assume that all one needs to do is invent a key phrase that will be recognised as the agreed message and seek to pass this on after death to your loved one via a medium whom they then visit. However, if that loved one knows what this message is, the medium could conceivably access it from their mind via telepathy; its receipt during a seance would not therefore constitute proof that it had come from the afterlife.

The problem is to find a way around this difficulty which will not make the message impossible to recognise as a message. Something like the cross-correspondences, where fragments in code needed reference to literary works to be deciphered, would be remarkable, but given the apparent failure rate of most such attempts this may simply be asking too much.

A common type of pact which is easy to operate and offers a high degree of evidence requires each person to take an object and hide it somewhere without telling their partner anything more than this simple fact. Nobody else must know what this object is or where it is located. Then, via the medium, after death they should attempt to convey details of the object and its location so that it can be physically retrieved. If the deceased is the only person to know this information, it is difficult to conceive of any other way in which a medium might obtain it.

One or two anecdotal stories of success in this type of pact have been reported, but what is really necessary is for someone to enter into such an arrangement and then follow it through methodically by video filming a series of interviews with different mediums and shooting all subsequent attempts to locate any alleged hidden object. The failures must be recorded alongside the successes. A series of experiments such as this would be relatively easy to carry out, and any reader of this book could set one up for implementation. Of course, because death is unthinkable we prefer not to bring it to mind for long enough to set up such an eleborate test – which is why very few of these experiments have been carried out to date. And although there are many other ways to research life after death, few beat the potential level of significance offered by this simple operation.

LIFE AFTER DEATH TODAY

Evidence for survival of death comes in many forms and is of varying degrees of persuasiveness. For example, in April 1993 Stockport artist William Turner put on sale the only oil portrait of the late L.S. Lowry. The celebrated 'matchstick man' creator had agreed to sit for Turner not long before his death, and never saw the finished painting. But then a medium told Turner that a man named 'Lower' was trying to get in touch, and it soon became apparent who this persistent character was. According to the information given to Turner by the psychic, Lowry was not painting much in the afterlife but was doing some drawing. He approved of the portrait and advised Turner on its sale for a good cause. It was to fetch a considerable sum for a local hospital epilepsy unit.

This was, of course, personally convincing to the artist, but involving famous people in sittings with mediums is invariably fraught with difficulty. There have been numerous such returns: John Lennon's, to forgive his murderer; Marilyn Monroe's, to explain the real circumstances surrounding her mysterious demise; an experiment to contact the spirit of George Orwell and ask the writer what he thought of the *real* 1984; and even an impassioned plea from outlaw Jesse James attempting to clear his name a century too late. These gimmicky tests are fun and on the increase, but their showbiz aura tends to detract from any serious efforts to prove life after death. The media love them but science not surprisingly shakes its head.

Everyday stories

More useful are the ever-growing numbers of anecdotal stories from ordinary people. However, it is a problem to bridge the gap between what is personally and universally convincing.

For instance, in October 1995 a woman from Lancashire described to me how after her father's death she and her sister went on holiday to the Canary Islands. She awoke at 4a.m. to see a glow in the kitchen and there stood her mother and father, arms outstretched. The women got out of bed – 'not in a physical sense', so presumably out-of-the-body – and floated towards them, conversing in a telepathic fashion. Her mother told her not to touch, but she hugged her father and felt the love. The next instant the woman found herself back in bed, wide awake and overjoyed at this proof of life after death. She has no way of convincing you or me that this was not simply a dream; nevertheless she herself is utterly convinced of its reality, and it has confirmed her belief in an afterlife to the point where she has no fear of death.

Many might consider this next case, concerning a young family, a better example. However, if you think about it, it is just as subjective.

One night a mother found her young daughter talking to an 'invisible man' on the stairs. This innocent act only became mysterious when it was repeated later and the girl insisted there was a real man standing there – she did not recognise him, and nobody else in the family could see him. A few days afterwards it was discovered that the child's great-grandfather, who because of a family estrangement she had not seen since she was a small baby, had died many miles away. His death had occurred at the same time as the first appearance of the man on the stairs, even though nobody in the house knew this fact at the time. The girl added the final piece to the jigsaw later when her mother was looking at the family photograph album. Seeing an image of her great-grandfather, the child's eyes lit up and she said, 'That's the man on the stairs.'

This case, which occurred in 1988, is of the sort that researchers need to seek and document. Again it can never establish proof, being always dependent upon personal testimony and still open to vagaries of co-incidence or other such explanations. But it does seem that, when honesty can be reasonably adjudged, there are few better answers to the events reported than survival of death. Sceptics would, of course, point to self-delusion and imagination.

Experiments to collate evidence via mediums are also developing along more systematic lines. I conducted one for the BBC in which I arranged for a sceptical psychologist to sit with several mediums and record the results. Some months later we reassessed the data, as some of it was supposed to relate to the future. He was completely unimpressed by what occurred, saying that he felt the mediums simply read body language and made guesses. Yet the mediums felt obliged to offer me spontaneous readings which were also recorded, and some of these comments seemed astonishingly accurate. The problem was that, whilst I could identify with some of the images reported – such as that of an elderly woman carrying a banner outside a Sunday school, which matched my long-dead grandmother perfectly – why were they given in the form of a mental snapshot, just as might exist inside my memory? If the medium were picking up an image from my mind, this is the form it would probably take. If she were in actual contact with my dead grandmother, would she really appear only as I recalled her in her last frail years of life?

We might be more inclined to accept survival if a medium said, 'Your grandmother is here', then offered personal details but described her in the way her spirit form might envisage itself to be – surely not as a sick, eighty-year-old woman. Of course, this self-image of a more youthful appearance would not be familiar to me, but I could check it through old photographs – and it would certainly constitute more serious evidence than the somewhat suspicious offering of a description which fits a memory lurking in the mind of the sitter.

There are cases of people missing an arm or leg, perhaps caused by surgery just before death, and then being described in this way by a medium. Does this mean that in the afterlife we carry our deformities and senility with us? Or does it, as some sceptics insist, indicate that the image which the medium sees comes not from a deceased mind but from the very living memory of the sitter?

Psychic artists

Valerie Hope of ASSAP described an experiment in 1995 in which she employed psychic artists. These are people who draw images of the dead spirit which they encounter rather than giving the sitter a verbal description. Coral Polge, for example, is renowned for her sometimes startlingly accurate pictures of relatives presented to an audience during a sitting. Many have professed that she has proven life after death to them in this way, although the same caveat about memory images being unsuspectedly seen could again be applied.

Valerie approached three psychic artists, not including Coral Polge, without ever meeting them. For a fee they offered to send her psychic portraits of spirits who were close to her simply by reading her letter and attuning to it. As Valerie explained in *Anomaly* magazine, the results were disappointing. She received four separate portraits (one artist sent two images for the price of one). None was of a relative and the psychics usually described them as spirit guides – which, of course, unfortunately (or conveniently) got over the need for the sitter actually to recognise any of them. Valerie Hope concluded, 'If I had not already seen examples of very convincing portraits produced in the presence of the sitter, the evidence I received would have led me to believe that psychic art had nothing of value to contribute to survival research.'

My own experience supports that view. I have been sent several un-solicited psychic artworks – all purporting to be my spirit guides looking after me from the afterlife. One was a nun. Another was an American Indian. None of them meant anything to me. Of course, they could all be 'real' – but how can anyone judge them as evidence for life after death?

Electronic contact with the afterlife

So, if these experiments are not proving very much, is there any hope that other ways can be found which might?

Mrs Jones from Surrey tells how, after her father died, she and her husband heard strange noises as they lay in bed, and succeeded in tape recording them. Of course, a faint tape of what sounds like distant voices uttering words that are beyond the threshold of audibility proves nothing to the world at large, even though it may have convinced Mrs Jones that her father (and deceased mother) had returned to offer comfort.

None the less, this form of electronic contact with the afterlife is another modern trend. It began with tape recorders, but has lately extended to specially equipped VCRs to try to produce video signals from the world beyond. Some success has been claimed from Germany and Austria, including the fuzzy image of what is purported to be a scientist working on the project from the land beyond death. But it is fair to say that most people are reserving judgement for the present.

However, this may be the way forward. There are reports of anomalous images turning up unexpectedly on home VCRs when the tape was recording a TV channel that was off the air and only static should have been visible. Time will tell if anything emerges that offers any kind of proof.

SOURCES

ORGANISATIONS AND PERIODICALS

The following list of associations and publications is far from exhaustive – this is a vast area. But it includes most of the major research bodies and some of the better smaller outlets. The *SPR* and *ASSAP* (for addresses, see pages 100 and 28) are major investigative outlets within this area.

American Society for Psychical Research (ASPR) *5 West 73rd Street, New York, NY 10023, USA.*

Australian Spiritualist Association *PO Box 273, Penrith, NSW 2747, Australia.*

Irish UFO/Paranormal Research Association (IUFOPRA) *Box 3070, Whitehall, Dublin 9, Eire.*

Metascience (electronic contact) *PO Box 737, Franklin, NC 28734, USA.*

Noah's Ark Society *Treetops, Hall Road, Cromer, Norfolk, NR27 9JG, UK.*

Northern Anomalies Research Organisation *6 Silsden Avenue, Lowton, Warrington, WA3 1EN, UK.*

Promises and Disappointments *42 Victoria Road, Mount Charles, St Austell, Cornwall, PL25 4QD, UK.*

Psychic News/SNU *Clock Cottage, Stansted Hall, Stansted Mountfitchet, Essex, CM24 8UD, UK.*

Spiritualist Church of Canada *1835 Lawrence Ave East, Scarborough, Ontario, M1R 2Y3, Canada.*

The Skeptic *Box 475, Manchester, M60 2TH, UK.*

Two Worlds *7 Leather Market, Weston Street, London SE1 3ER, UK.*

BOOKS

There are countless books about life after death, and the following are just some of those that I recommend. Lodge offers one of the first classic case histories. Rogo's book provides an excellent introductory summary of the evidence, while Wilson's more in-depth review strikes the right balance of scepticism and open-mindedness. The scholarly work from Lorimer addresses the philosophy of the evidence, and Inglis takes a look at the relationship between science and the Spiritualist quest for truth. Le Shan makes an attempt to blend modern science with parascience into a working theory. An excellent first hand account from an objective medium is given by Heywood. O'Brien is her modern day equivalent. Finally, Raudive and Meek tell the story of early and more recent attempts to prove survival by electronic means.

Raymond by Oliver Lodge (Doran, New York, 1916).

Life after Death by D. Scott Rogo (Thorsons, 1986).

The Afterdeath Experience by Ian Wilson (Corgi, 1989).

Survival? by David Lorimer (Routledge & Kegan Paul, 1984).

Science and Parascience by Brian Inglis (Hodder & Stoughton, 1984).

Clairvoyant Reality by Lawrence Le Shan (Turnstone, 1980).

The Infinite Hive by Rosalind Heywood (Chatto & Windus, 1964).

In Touch with Eternity by Stephen O'Brien (Bantam, 1992).

Breakthrough by Konstantin Raudive (Colin Smythe, 1981).

After We Die, What Then? by George Meek (Metascience, Franklin, NC, 1987).

MIRACLE IMAGES

DEFINITION

Since the invention of photography in the early nineteenth-century some unexpected things have been turning up on film. At first methods and results were crude, and the images that appeared were hard to define. If they looked odd, they were considered paranormal. But as time has progressed, so has the peculiarity of the evidence.

Today many households have camcorders and the production of mysterious images has risen in proportion. Researchers are now used to receiving letters requesting an answer to the mystery posed by the enclosed photograph or tape. Sometimes the image is undeniably present and the photographer has set out to capture it. Of course if someone saw, and then photographed, a UFO or a ghost this would be properly considered under that area of study. But there are occasions when the image is much more difficult to categorise. A strange face may appear on the wall or in the bark of a tree. Clouds may shape themselves into a life-like image. Such things are often known as 'simulacra' or nature photographs, and they are more common than you might imagine.

However, it is more likely that a miracle image will appear from nowhere on the processed film and the photographer will approach a researcher saying, 'I did not see anything when I took the picture, but when the film came back there it was.' These accidental exposures are more tricky to evaluate, but invariably turn out to be caused by some sort of optical illusion. Nevertheless they begin life as a miracle image.

HISTORICAL REVIEW

In 1918 Sir Arthur Conan Doyle set up the Society for the Study of Supernatural Pictures. Tired of writing about his fictional creation Sherlock Holmes, Conan Doyle had become fascinated by strange phenomena of a psychic nature and pursued this interest vigorously in later life. There were already quite a number of alleged 'spirit' photographs taken during seances, but they were almost certainly fakes. The first prosecution, against a Boston photographer who in 1861 faked 'ghostly figures', led to a spate of imitators during the next fifty years.

The Cottingley fairies

But Conan Doyle found himself in the thick of the first truly contentious miracle images in 1920 when, thanks to a colleague, Edward Gardner, he discovered a series of photographs taken by two teenage girls beside a Yorkshire brook. The pictures, taken at Cottingley near Bradford in 1917, were said to depict fairies playing merrily. By the time Gardner and Conan Doyle had finished investigating the case and both had pinned their public reputations to the authenticity of the images, some five photographs – including one with a gnome posing boldly upon it – had been taken. But after that time the girls were unable to produce any more, and they separated when one of them moved to South Africa. The Cottingley fairies entranced the world for many years, even though few people took the images as seriously as Conan Doyle and Gardner did. Attempts to prove them a hoax largely failed until, with the availability of modern computer technology in the 1970s, enhancement work suggested – as most people had long suspected – that the pictures were two-dimensional.

The two girls, by now elderly ladies, issued ambiguous statements about their photographs. They said, for example, that they were pictures of 'figments of the imagination' – yet still real. Only shortly before their deaths did they admit that the photographs had been faked as an act of revenge on the parents, who had not believed them when they said they had seen fairies by the river back in 1917. After that their tall tale got more and more out of hand, and once Gardner and Conan Doyle had become involved it proved impossible to challenge the views of these famous men. The fairies and gnome were in fact cut-out sketches based on a popular children's book of the day. More extraordinary still was the fact that, although the photographs were a hoax, one of the women insisted on her deathbed that they really had seen fairies by the stream.

This was not a very auspicious start for the study of miracle images, but more curious things followed. For example, many people photographed a peculiar image that appeared in damp patches on the walls of Christ Church, Oxford, in 1923. It bore an uncanny resemblance to Dean Liddell, who had died in 1898. Coincidence seems improbable. So could such a thing be hoaxed? Many people wonder what other explanation there could be for such a freak effect.

Conan Doyle also assessed the first photograph of Christ, which has been seen in tabloid newspapers ever since. Taken over the Himalayas in 1920, the image, constructed by the eye out of patches of white snow and dark rock, is an impressive, classic simulacrum. Thirty years later a similarly impressive image was captured by an American bomber crew over Korea – nothing was seen at the time as they filmed fellow aircraft during their mission. Only after processing did the 'holy' image appear from the shapes within the clouds (see photograph opposite page 187).

EXPERIENCING MIRACLE IMAGES

I have lost count of the number of times someone has sent to me a picture of a 'demon' or 'elf' lurking in the trees. If you look very hard you can see what they mean, but the image is an illusion caused by the effects of light and shade, and its success depends upon both your ability to see sharply and the extent of your imagination. To be blunt, if you do not see anything strange whilst you are taking a photograph and it simply turns up on the print after development, the odds are extremely high that it is just an illusion.

Light and shade effects are the most common, but they are by no means the only ones. A cloudy mass floating in the sky may be a drying mark or the result of light entering the camera at some point between the shutter being pressed and the film being processed. Something called a lens flare – where a bright light source bounces inside the lens system and creates a stray but weird-looking image – is equally common. And even very innocent objects, such as birds flying across during the fraction of a second that the shutter is open, can be misleading. You would probably not notice them at the time, but the camera can sometimes freeze their motion into very supernatural-looking poses.

It is always worth looking for unusual images in your photographs, and researchers are likely to be interested in them even if they do have a conventional explanation. However, it is wise not to put too much faith in their being more than just a curiosity of the filming process.

Of course, if you see something that looks peculiar any photograph of it is bound to be more impressive than your story on its own. It seems obvious advice to go and get a camera, but you would be surprised how often witnesses in a position to do so fail to heed this simple rule. They stand there watching in amazement and only think about getting their camera when the moment has gone for ever. A picture, as they say, is worth a thousand words – and since the tabloids love to exploit the supernatural you might also find it is worth a thousand pounds.

Yet, if you do see something and film it, be prepared for logical explanation. In 1988 I received a series of colour images taken by a woman near Rhyl in Wales. She saw clouds light up in a spinning blaze of glory that reminded many people of the alleged miracle of Fatima in

October 1917, when thousands reputedly saw the sun plunge from the skies above this Portuguese village after a promise made by the Virgin Mary to local children. Sadly, the miracle of Rhyl was the result of an unusual combination of sunshine, ice particles in clouds and natural laws of physics and meteorology. It looked intriguing, but it was not paranormal.

RESEARCHING MIRACLE IMAGES

Thankfully, the days when photographs were automatically considered proof of something paranormal have long gone. Not only have many hoaxers faked pictures for fame and fortune, but the desire to see how many people can be duped is a great temptation.

In 1963 a ten-year-old boy from Sheffield in Yorkshire filmed some blobs of paint on a sheet of a glass, through which he then filmed the sky. This simple act produced a vaguely puzzling picture which had UFO researchers talking for years. It was featured in the press and even led to an invitation to talk to the Ministry of Defence about his 'evidence'. When ten years later he owned up to having fooled everyone, researchers – certainly in Britain – changed their tactics. Now a photograph was considered suspect and had to be proven to be unusual by a series of tests and experiments, rather than being automatically regarded as genuine until anything came to light to suggest otherwise.

This may seem unfair, and it runs the risk of offending genuine people who may feel that you are challenging their honesty. But it is a necessary precaution. No photograph can stand alone, without the support of extensive analysis of the witness's story. It is not always easy to set up such analysis work, and it can be expensive. However, contacts should be courted because no photograph is worth much until it is investigated.

Professional photographers and laboratories may well be just as intrigued as you are by a truly baffling image. For example, in May 1964 a Carlisle fireman took a lovely colour shot of his young daughter holding a bunch of flowers on the marshes by the Solway Firth. Only when he got his developed film back from the chemist's did he notice a strange white-suited figure sticking up at a peculiar angle behind the girl's head. Over three decades later this photograph remains one of the most bemusing miracle images ever taken. Theories about drying marks that happen to form the shape of a space-suited figure, or double exposures involving a fellow fireman in a protective suit, have been assessed and rejected by countless experts. Hypotheses as to its nature have ranged from aliens via time travellers to extraordinary projected images of someone at a nearby nuclear power station. The British Ministry of Defence was concerned enough to send two men to interview the photographer.

The truth is that nobody knows what produced this bizarre image, but Kodak offered free film for life to anyone who could solve it to the company's satisfaction. So far as is known, nobody could rise to the challenge.

MIRACLE IMAGES TODAY

Hardly a week goes by without the paranormal research community receiving a new miracle image from some source. Even camcorder sequences are now becoming common. Of course, most videotapes show misperceptions of lights in the sky or reflections. In November 1995, for example, national newspapers featured an image of a key-shaped light filmed over eastern England that month. There was undoubtedly a light present to be photographed, and it may have been unexplained, but the shape depicted was caused by the fact that the internal iris system of most video cameras distorts an out-of-focus point light source. Researchers had learnt of this feature the hard way, after mistaking similar patterns for assorted strange phenomena such as ball lightning and UFOs.

Sometimes the images can be quite odd, such as the one on a photograph taken in the summer of 1994 on the beach at Rhyl by a holiday-maker from Lancashire. The eerie white figure bending over was analysed in great depth by the research group NARO, with the help of workers at the University of Manchester Institute of Science and Technology. They concluded it was a flare-out effect caused by sunlight on certain clothing and the limitations of some camcorder lens systems – but it certainly resembled a ghost.

There has also been a trend for automatic security cameras to record sequences when nobody is present. In one case, a floating white mass moved along a corridor in an Oldham nightclub and went through a closed door in very spooky fashion, even though the locked building was deserted at the time. If a still camera had been at work, this ghost-like photograph would have provoked speculation about tricks of the light or processing faults appearing supernatural. The human mind certainly has the ability to seek out and read patterns in random images, and

LEICESTERSHIRE LIBRARIES AND INFORMATION SERVICE
REFERENCE AND INFORMATION
LIBRARY
HUMANITIES

some ghost photographs probably result in this way. But such a theory does not work with moving images, nor when it is known that at the precise time of the filming the silent alarm went off at the local police station. Lens flare simply does not trigger electronic systems.

The face on Mars

The miracle image of the moment is the so-called face on Mars (see photograph opposite page 187). Is this simulacrum a natural illusion, or proof that we are not alone in the universe? The face turned up on two photographs taken in July 1976 by the Viking probes that filmed the surface of the planet in detail for the first time. Amidst numerous rocky outcrops in the Cydonia region was this mile-wide monolith that resembled a human face with eyes, nose and mouth staring up into space. It was just at the level of resolution at which telescopes on earth could never have seen it. You would have to be orbiting mars to spot it.

NASA staff were dismissive, shrugging their shoulders at the remarks made by the few who noticed the image among the sixty thousand photographs taken by the spacecraft. It was just an effect of the angle of the sun shining on the rocks, they said – a simple illusion. There were thousands of mountains and crevices, and from the interplay of light and shadow one was bound to resemble something by chance.

Several years later, between 1979 and 1981, two computer specialists, Vince DiPietro and Gregory Molenaar, followed up their personal interest and established the truth. They found other shots of the face, taken from different angles and with the sun in new positions, which suggested that the image was not a trick of light but a real three-dimensional object on the surface of the planet. It may have been a natural illusion, but it was really there on Mars.

The next step was to use computer enhancing techniques to clean up the image, and this proved even more intriguing. Sharpening up the picture did not destroy the illusion, as one would expect from a natural effect; instead, the face came into clearer focus. From this discovery they were certain that it was a real object, and speculation mounted that it could be an artificially constructed monument like the Sphinx on earth.

If so, who made it and why? The human-like appearance, curious tie-in with Egyptian culture and mathematical patterns found within the structure were akin to those in the Pyramids, which led to suggestions that some ancient race had built both it and perhaps even these ancient earthly wonders. Maybe the fact that it was of just the right size and stared upwards into space indicated that it was a calling card left on Mars millennia ago by some space-travelling race, meant to show that they had been here, had seen us at the time when our great civilisation was in the Middle East, and had wanted us to know of their presence should our technology ever take us to Mars.

In 1983 the fascinated computer experts involved Dr Richard Hoagland, a NASA scientist who saw the significance of their work. A team was set up to study the evidence and to pressure NASA into going back and taking better photographs of the Cydonia region, something that they seemed curiously reluctant to do.

Hoagland won converts. In 1991 I met Dr Brian O'Leary, who told me his story. As a physicist and a NASA astronaut, he was being trained for a manned flight to Mars. Then budget cuts suddenly scuppered the plan. Given his particular expertise, he was the best person to assess the face on Mars. He had been dismissive of the early stories about it, but he admitted this was not based on any first-hand study. Hoagland, DiPietro and Molenaar convinced him by their careful analysis and evidence. Dr O'Leary showed me the enormous blown-up images that he had obtained of the face and the rocky area around it. I saw his point. My suspicion that this simulacrum was just a trick of the eyes was certainly given a knock by the impressive appearance of the structure.

Since 1991 much else has occurred. Computer analysts claim to have found further detail – such as an eyeball in the eye socket and teeth in the mouth. I have my doubts about some of this evidence. The 'teeth' seem to me to coincide with the resolution dots on the photographs, for example. However, Hoagland is also certain he has found other objects, such as a giant pyramid, nearby in Cydonia. He has now turned his attention to the moon, where similar straight-sided and non-natural objects have allegedly been found during intense scrutiny of close-up photography.

In 1992 Hoagland and his team petitioned the United Nations to try to get NASA to make a commitment to send their Mars Orbiter craft, due to head for Mars that autumn, to take new photographs of Cydonia. With the advantage of two decades of new technology the cameras on board would produce such vivid images that the true nature of the face would be exposed. If an illusion, its crudity would show up. If a genuine monument, as Hoagland and others were now certain (even producing three-dimensional computer maps to 'prove' their point), that too would be revealed. Either way, here was the chance to end the debate.

Again NASA were strangely reluctant to commit themselves. Lowell Martin reported on a seminar that he attended, given by NASA leader Dr Daniel Goldin and noted cosmologist Dr Carl Sagan at Caltech in Pasadena as this controversy raged. Martin eventually extracted an agreement from Goldin that they should look into the possibility of taking more pictures. Also of concern were claims that NASA would prevent live transmission of the images from the spacecraft and only release them months later after careful study. This had never happened before in the history of space exploration, and led those who believed in the Mars monument concept to claim that the US government wanted to vet the data before releasing it to the world. Did the authorities suspect that proof of life on Mars would be found? Goldin denied that there would be any scrambling of the transmissions, but would not confirm that pictures would be broadcast live.

The NASA mission left without any guarantees, but on arrival in orbit around Mars in August 1993 something happened as it was about to switch on its complex equipment and begin the in-depth survey work. All contact with the spacecraft suddenly disappeared. NASA said later that they struggled for months to regain control, but all to no avail. The mission was over.

What happened is still unclear. Many things could have gone wrong, such as a meteorite strike or a major computer malfunction. It certainly was remarkably timely that the failure coincided with the beginning of the photography. The spacecraft had successfully operated for a year as it crossed between earth and Mars. On the other hand, as the complex equipment was unfrozen and fired up in readiness this was strategically the moment when most things could go wrong. Naturally there are those who believe that the project was deliberately shut off to prevent having to face the Cydonia riddle. Others even argue that the failure is a sham, invented to prevent NASA from having to share its results with the world until it could properly evaluate them. NASA, of course, reject both arguments, saying that accidents do happen and unfortunately this one proved very costly.

Any plot to prevent this craft from filming above Cydonia would be ultimately futile, as future missions will return to Mars and sooner or later film the face in sufficient detail to end argument one way or the other. For now the face remains a miracle image of epic proportions whose origin is unresolved.

SOURCES

ORGANISATIONS

Photographic assessment work on miracle images is readily carried out by Dr Vernon Harrison for *ASSAP* and Dr Bruce Maccabbee for *FUFOR.*

ASSAP   *31 Goodhew Road, Croydon, Surrey, CR0 6QZ, UK.*

FUFOR   *PO Box 277, Mount Rainier, MD 20712, USA.*

The team researching the face on Mars is:

Mars Mission   *31–10 Skytop Gardens, Parlin, NJ 08859, USA.*

For sceptical analysis of the face on Mars and other mysteries a good source is:

Skeptical Inquirer   *Box 229, Buffalo, NY 14215–0229, USA.*

PUBLICATIONS

There are regular examples of miracle images in editions of *Fortean Times*, published monthly.

Fortean Times   *Box 2409, London NW5 4NP, UK.*

BOOKS

Few good books on miracle images are available, but here are three.

Simulacra by John Michell (Thames & Hudson, 1979).

Photographs of the Unknown by Bob Rickard and Richard Kelly (NEL, 1980).

The Monuments of Mars by Richard Hoagland (North Atlantic Books, Berkeley, CA, 1987).

OUT-OF-BODY EXPERIENCE

DEFINITION

At present we do not know whether brain and mind are separate. Some biologists claim that the mind is an illusion fostered by the workings of the bio-mechanical computer that is our brain. In the minority is a rival view that mind, being some sort of ethereal phenomenon, exists in its own right and uses the brain just like steam drives a turbine to produce power.

If mind is only the by-product of the brain, all our consciousness will cease when that brain no longer functions. Death will then prove terminal. On the other hand, if mind is a distinctive field of energy that flows through the most complex organ in the human body and creates our conscious experience along the way, it can still exist even if that organ is destroyed. It may simply lose the ability to root itself in our physical world.

Central to the debate over which theory is correct is the question of OOBEs, or out-of-body experiences. These are allegations by human beings that they have travelled outside the physical limits of their body. The implication is that mind really is able to exist free of the brain.

The OOBE manifests as the centre of consciousness – the 'I' which represents each human being – moving away sharply from its normal abode 'within' the body and finding itself temporarily elsewhere. I can best summarise this with my own report of an OOBE, the most powerful and seemingly paranormal phenomenon that I have ever faced.

It was January 1971. I was nineteen. My grandmother, whose many psychic experiences had first alerted me to the paranormal, had just died in our living room. The night before the funeral I was staying with a friend in a strange bedroom in an unfamiliar house in Manchester. In the middle of the night I woke up. The room was dark, yet I could see it in accurate detail. I was floating perhaps ten feet in mid-air, but I was also looking down at 'me' in the bed below. The recognition of this dilemma – my mind being in one place and my body in another – aroused great fear in me. In an instant I snapped back into my body as if I were at the end of a huge elastic band. I sat bolt upright staring into the gloom. Sleep was an impossibility, for my mind was racing with what had just taken place.

This is a typical ordinary low-key OOBE. Sceptics will say it was just a dream. Indeed, I have subsequently had dream-like OOBEs, including some that were lucid and very realistic. Yet the difference between those later experiences and the reality level of that January is huge. The others felt real, but I knew they were dreams. This felt real, and I knew it was real.

Of course, it may still have been an illusion brought on by stress. All I can say is that anyone in my situation would have been sure that they really did float up above their bodies, but would not be in a position to prove that conviction to someone else. This is the essence of an OOBE.

HISTORICAL REVIEW

The OOBE is the essence of mystical experience in a wide range of religious beliefs, and records of it date back thousands of years. Usually the event was perceived as the person having come close to God, and many saints and religious leaders have described OOBE-like events as a turning point in their lives.

In the early days of psychic research, during the late nineteenth century, OOBEs were recorded, but the rather remote and cerebral nature of the phenomenon made it difficult to investigate. So these cases were not given much consideration.

In 1965 Professor Charles Tart of the University of California reported on the first significant OOBE experiments with a woman patient who claimed to enter the state regularly. He suggested that she write a series of numbers on pieces of paper, fish one 'blind' out of a hat each night and hide it about the house. Then, if she had an OOBE, she should attempt to read the number. This primitive test has been adapted many times, with increasing sophistication. Tart's success rate with this woman (in about one in four alleged OOBEs she apparently got the number correct) is typical and indicates that, whilst there is evidence of something going on, it is by no means reproducible to the extent demanded by science.

Grant-funded research during the next ten years, mostly via the American Society for Psychical Research, but with some tests at Stanford in California and Oxford and Cambridge in the UK, developed this work. Sophisticated symbols and patterns were placed too high to be seen from ground level. Good subjects (those to whom OOBEs reportedly occurred quite often) slept in the laboratory and attempted to 'see' these patterns. The experiment scored numerous failures, but enough spectacular successes to suggest that something was occasionally happening.

Parapsychologist D. Scott Rogo next participated in some interesting experiments at Duke Medical Hospital in North Carolina. Here, the person attempting the OOBE was particularly fond of animals, as many psychics are, and it was decided to see whether in the out-of-body state that person could influence the behaviour of a kitten in a distant room. Considerable success resulted and Rogo followed up with tests using – of all things – a vicious snake. These were less successful, possibly because even in a disembodied state one is unlikely to want to announce one's presence to a viper!

Bright lights and tunnels

Meanwhile, in 1975 an American psychologist, Raymond Moody, published a little book that would raise the debate to a new level. He had come across reports of OOBEs from patients who had suffered a life-threatening situation such as a car accident or major surgery. They would describe themselves surveying the scene from above, and some would add further details. There were accounts of a feeling of peace and euphoria, stories of bright lights and tunnels that sucked them along, and even some cases where witnesses believed they entered heaven and met deceased relatives or God before being given the choice to return. To everyone's surprise Moody's book was a smash hit world-wide even though it was very anecdotal. It evidently struck a chord within society. Paranormal researchers realised that their records already held some examples of these deeper-level OOBEs, which became known as NDEs or near death experiences. But Moody's book implied that they were rapidly increasing.

Systematic studies, many set up by sceptics, were launched during the next few years. One by one they actually verified Moody's findings and greatly expanded upon them. It appeared that, as medical science pushed back the frontiers of death, more and more people were being revived from what were once irreversible conditions and describing what occurred in those last moments before life ebbed away for ever.

From basic OOBE to full NDE

By 1980 psychologist Dr Kenneth Ring had established that there were several levels of NDE, beginning with a sense of joy, moving on to the basic OOBE, passing through visions of the light and tunnel, then images reviewing moments in one's life like a rapid memory slideshow and ending with the transient visit to another world. The deeper into this chain of events a person went, the less common the reports became.

A photograph taken by the Revd R W Hardy of White Rock, BC, Canada at Queen's House, Greenwich, London. It appears to show a ghostly figure on the Tulip Staircase.

Dover Castle – one of the most haunted castles in Great Britain (see page 107).

About one in five people had a basic OOBE at some point in their lives, but only one in twenty of those reported the deeper levels of the NDE. In the final phase the patient frequently reported a conscious choice to return to earth rather than to stay in the new pleasant surroundings, as almost all of them said they would rather do.

Later Ring and a team of researchers in Europe and the USA discovered that NDE patients were recovering from their adventure with a brand-new philosophy. It seemed not to matter whether they were religious – virtually all became convinced of survival after death, and returned with a renewed love of life and ethical standards. In a small way they all became saints.

Countering the sceptics

Dr Michael Sabom, a cardiologist from Georgia, spent the early 1980s attempting to verify the prime sceptical theory that the OOBE or NDE was a hallucination caused by lack of oxygen to the brain when it was close to death. However, he found cases where the amount of oxygen reaching the brain had been recorded and yet an OOBE was still reported. He had another surprise when he tabulated the detailed accounts of witnesses who had described medical procedures taking place during their out-of-body state. He expected these to match ideas gleaned from TV medical dramas, complete with errors; instead he found that witnesses were often astoundingly accurate, recalling precise feature of rooms, unusual methods of treatment, unexpected items of clothing worn by theatre staff and specialised equipment. It seemed difficult not to conclude that these people really had witnessed the events described, from an out-of-body position.

Yet still the sceptics fought back, arguing that not enough was understood about anaesthesia or coma, and that in these conditions some patients could be aware of what was going on around them whilst seemingly unconscious. They might imagine they had observed a scene, details of which they had simply overheard whilst the medical team worked on them. This led to a hunt for cases in which witnesses had seen precise details that could not have been viewed other than in a disembodied state. Some OOBEs provided evidence of just that.

A five-year-old described a plastic valve which had been inserted into his heart but which he had never seen. A woman quoted a conversation between two relatives in a room some distance from where she lay unconscious, fighting for her life. Another patient told of a discarded shoe lying on a ledge outside the hospital, invisible from the bed in which he lay.

Within thirty years of the first serious OOBE research and twenty years after the publication of Moody's trailblazing collection of NDE stories, these related phenomena had become established as the most exciting and rapidly advancing area of paranormal research.

EXPERIENCING *OOBE*s

If all of its forms are taken into consideration, the OOBE is one of the most common paranormal experiences in the world. About two-thirds of the population, according to surveys, feel that they may have had one at some point in their lives. But it is not often a regular occurrence.

The NDE is the rarest form. Of people who suffer life-threatening traumas, no more than 10 per cent describe any OOBE symptoms. OOBEs in other circumstances – occurring spontaneously whilst a person is relaxing or meditating, say – are more common; also certain drug-induced states, for instance after taking LSD, are reported to have similar effects.

The most widespread form of OOBE occurs during sleep. It can range from the basic flying dream, in which the person experiences aerial mobility in an obviously dream-like state, to more lucid dreams in which they seem to drift out of their body and float about their real surroundings but remain deeply asleep. Then there are the sudden OOBEs that occur from within sleep and end with the person fully awake as they appear to re-enter their body. This is probably the type of experience that I had in 1971.

It may be that all these dreams represent different degrees of OOBE, and that our description of them as dream or reality depends upon our state of consciousness at the time. This is not to say that all OOBEs are necessarily merely dreams – it might equally mean that flying dreams are to some extent real OOBE.

There are many alleged methods of inducing OOBEs. They usually involve relaxation techniques and, it is claimed, you can 'astral travel' (as such dream-like OOBEs are sometimes called) almost at will when you become practised. Trips next door or even to other planets have been claimed in this way. Some regular astral flyers have even assisted intelligence services such as the CIA in America, reputedly 'spying' out-of-body on distant foreign installations. Ingo Swann and Keith Harary, among others, have inferred that an OOBE can produce better results than a multi-million-dollar spy satellite.

Overcoming the fear that comes with an OOBE seems to be the major obstacle to experiencing them repeatedly, but – according to those professing to teach such methods – it is possible to do so with practice. Recording your adventures while in the OOBE state is important, as are experiments to verify details. For example, if you have any control over the situation endeavour to travel to a location where it is possible to verify as soon as possible afterwards details of what you have seen. If this is somewhere practicable, such as a nearby street where you can note the cars parked there and their registration numbers, evidence can be readily collected. Obviously, if you choose to visit the moon, establishing whether your OOBE was imagination or reality will be more difficult!

RESEARCHING *OOBE*S

The OOBE is one of the few areas of the paranormal where you can conduct research by trying to induce the experience in yourself. If rigorous methods of checking any evidence are maintained, preferably with independent assistance, there is nothing wrong with this approach. Indeed, simply establishing the blurred relationship between OOBE-like dream states and spontaneously occurring, full-blown experiences will be a worthwhile project.

Collecting reports from other people who believe that they have had an OOBE is more of a problem. Usually these will be unverifiable and you will have little more than ancedotes to work with.

NDEs are more productive, particularly if they have occurred recently, because you can talk to medical staff to check the accuracy of a person's statements against the actual circumstances. Recording an NDE just as a person's story has limited value. If you can back this with testimony from doctors and nurses which seems to confirm what the patient saw in an out-of-body state – but which ought not to have been visible given their condition – you have much stronger evidence. This is particularly so if information is offered that could not have been reconstructed by guess-work simply through overhearing a conversation whilst apparently unconscious.

If, for example, a person says doctor A turned to nurse B and discussed inserting a catheter, this could have been recalled by the person even if unconscious. Deep-coma patients are believed to detect sounds and stimuli. However, if the precise type of catheter used and the way in which it was inserted are also described, this is more difficult to explain and constitutes stronger evidence that the person was really out of the body and watching the procedure.

Those whose work brings them into first contact with someone liable to experience an NDE – ambulance crews, police officers or hospital emergency staff – have the best opportunity to collect data. Of course, it will not be high on their list of priorities at the time of the crisis. But if the chance arises immediately after the trauma, take it. Seize on any strange remarks or descriptions of experiences made by the patient, and attempt to document them.

*OOBE*s TODAY

Many researchers feel that OOBEs may provide the key to the ultimate questions: do we possess an independent mind or spirit, and if so does it survive bodily death?

The dying brain hypothesis

One person who believes that both these questions have negative answers is psychologist Dr Sue Blackmore, who became interested in OOBEs after having a personal experience whilst at university.

She has conducted tests over many years in a search for verifiable evidence, but has concluded that there are basic medical and psychological reasons why OOBEs and NDEs occur. Dr Blackmore has identified a series of individual solutions to the various reported phenomena and gathered them together under the heading of the dying brain hypothesis.

In essence, she says that the sense of wellbeing described by witnesses results from natural endorphins released into the brain by our bodies during a crisis; that the tunnel and light images are the product of randomly firing neurons as brain cells disintegrate; and that the out-of-body sensation results from the person's loss of ego as the mind breaks down and desperately attempts to create some kind of structure for input still flowing in. Opinions on this theory are divided. Many sceptical scientists consider it a great achievement, but NDE researchers are unpersuaded. Their strongest arguments against it are, first, those cases where verifiable evidence is apparently seen whilst out of the body and, second, the lucid, decision-making frames of reference described during the latter stages of an NDE, which seem inconsistent with a mind on the edge of destruction.

Sue Blackmore acknowledges the importance of verifiable evidence 'seen' whilst out of the body, but is unconvinced by the case histories that she has studied so far. However, she agrees that modification to her theory would be necessary if enough data of this kind was both available and reliable. Her objectivity has won her many friends, and various attempts to provide the evidence that she rightly requires are underway.

Work with children

In Seattle, Dr Melvin Morse has worked with seriously and terminally ill children for many years and has specialised in obtaining their evidence of OOBEs and NDEs. Even at a very young age they describe experiences difficult to distinguish from those of adults. Whilst this does not negate the medical theories suggested by sceptics, it does lessen the impact of cultural conditioning. These children are typically too young to be expected to describe hallucinations that fit the expected stereotype of heaven. Dr Morse's work may establish that the main aspects of the OOBE and NDE appear to be real events, needing a natural (or supernatural) answer, and are not imagined experiences. He has also uncovered a number of verifiable stories, for instance that of a child who in the NDE state saw a person who was dead but who the child did not know had died.

The search for objective evidence

Cardiologist Dr Michael Sabom has collected evidence across the southern states of the USA and conducted an interesting new study. He interviewed people who had not had NDEs but had almost died from heart attacks, asking them to describe the techniques they thought had been used to revive them. Some of these patients had long medical histories and had inevitably picked up some information on the methods used. Yet their accounts were shallow and often inaccurate compared, he reports, with data offered by NDE patients, who invariably give graphic and correct detail about how the medical team brought them back from their close encounter with death.

Kimberley Morley-Smith, a senior nurse at a Northampton hospital, reported in 1994 on results of studies in the coronary care unit. A team questioned patients after recovery from a medical crisis. Then, to test whether they were simply hallucinating their OOBE visions, a bold but simple plan was set in motion. Numbers were attached to the overhead light on the beds. This was not visible from the bed, and its presence would not even be suspected from ground level. Yet nearly every patient who claimed to have an OOBE during resuscitation had seen the number and, when asked, gave it correctly to the nursing staff.

An extension of this project has been implemented by a team of NDE researchers led by a London neuropsychologist, Dr Peter Fenwick. Various symbols have been secretly located in hospitals around the UK, in places where they could only be seen by someone floating up by the ceiling. A long-term project to collate reports from patients is underway and, if the Northampton claim proves a guide, may provide powerful evidence that something truly is going out of the body.

Further evidence comes from Oxford University, where in 1994 Dr Charles McCreery reported on OOBE experiments at the Institute of Psychophysical Research. Here the researchers induced OOBEs, with an 80 per cent success rate, by getting subjects to relax whilst all sensory stimuli were being blocked out – for instance, their eyes were covered and soothing noises were played incessantly. The OOBE witnesses were also connected to brain wave recording devices to discover what changes occurred in brain activity whilst they reported that an OOBE was taking place.

A considerable increase in activity was noted within the right hemisphere of the brain, the area known to control the emotive, imaginative, creative and psychic areas of mental life. Unfortunately, it was not possible to judge whether the experiences described were hallucinatory or genuinely out-of-body. Dr McCreery's request to refine the experiment to seek verifiable data that might prove a true out-of-body state was turned down. Perhaps, in these cost conscious times, it is only academically acceptable to study OOBEs under grant funding in the context of abnormal psychology.

SOURCES

ORGANISATIONS AND PERIODICALS

Research into OOBEs and NDEs is being conducted by Sue Blackmore and Kenneth Ring, respectively, at the following locations.

University of the West of England   (*Department of Psychology*), *Bristol, BS16 2JP, Avon, UK.*

Department of Psychology   *University of Connecticut, Storrs, CT 06218, USA.*

The International Association for Near Death Studies also publishes a journal:

IANDS   *PO Box 193, London SW1K 9JZ, UK.*

BOOKS

Tart and Moody's pioneering work and the psychological, cardiological, paediatric and sceptical approaches of Ring, Sabom, Morse and Blackmore respectively have been described above. Ring's later book draws a startling parallel between NDE witnesses and those claiming alien abductions. It may prove nothing more than that both occur during altered states of consciousness, although he perceives a deeper link at a spiritual level. Kubler-Ross has probably had more experience with terminally ill patients than anyone and, whilst not specifically about OOBE or NDE states, her book is full of insights into the state of consciousness close to death. Monroe claims to be able to go out of the body almost to order, and tells you how to do it.

Out of the Body Experiences by Charles Tart (Putnam, 1974).

Life after Life by Raymond Moody (Bantam, 1975).

Life at Death by Kenneth Ring (Coward, McCann & Geoghegan, 1980).

Recollections of Death by Michael Sabom (Corgi, 1982).

Close to the Light by Melvin Morse (Souvenir Press, 1991).

Beyond the Body by Sue Blackmore (Granada, 1983).

Dying to Live by Sue Blackmore (Grafton, 1993).

The Omega Project by Kenneth Ring (William Morrow, New York 1991).

On Death and Dying by Elisabeth Kubler-Ross (Macmillan, New York, 1969).

Far Journeys by Robert Monroe (Souvenir Press, 1986).

POLTERGEISTS

DEFINITION

The word 'poltergeist' is German and means 'noise spirit', which immediately suggests the more colourful and popular interpretation of its nature. A ghost is behind the boistereous poltergeist activity, perhaps playful, mischievous or simply over-zealous in its attempts at communication.

Poltergeist attacks can appear in many forms. They can be rather obscure, such as strange sounds and pools of water suddenly appearing on a landing in a house, or coins vanishing from one spot and turning up hidden under a bed. Sometimes they are violent, such as furniture being moved or small items tossed about a room, frequently when nobody is looking. However, they may also be more benign, for instance household objects can be lovingly rearranged in a neat and tidy fashion.

It is sometimes difficult for those unfamiliar with the supernatural to distinguish between a haunting and a poltergeist outbreak, but the two are quite distinct. In a haunting a phantom figure is seen or heard on a regular basis and is assumed to be tied in with the location, usually an old house. Rather than being a one-off apparition, it becomes a repetitive ghostly encounter, possibly spread over hundreds of years and seen by many people who inhabit the building at different times.

Poltergeists, on the other hand, only rarely step across that boundary and involve apparitions, or display any obvious connection with a known or assumed ghost. Moreover, they are people-centred events, rather than place-centred as in the case of a haunting. If the occupants of a haunted house leave, the ghost normally stays put. In a poltergeist case it tends to make little difference if the owners move, and it is not unknown for the trouble to migrate with a family wherever they go.

Another major difference is in the duration. Poltergeist outbreaks rarely last for more than a few weeks and certainly do not persist over months, years or longer before transferring to a new generation or any other family that might move into the haunted location.

Although poltergeists may seem destructive and dangerous, it is rare for anyone to be injured – even slightly – by one. In essence they are like attention-seeking children, not really spiteful or intent on causing harm, but simply bent on someone taking notice. Once their perceived cause of discontent is recognised, they quickly weaken in effect and fizzle out. Many paranormal researchers regard this characterisation as strong evidence of the cause of this phenomenon. It is now rare for them to attribute a poltergeist event to some outside, spectral source. They tend instead to look for the answers closer to home – perhaps still paranormally, but certainly on the earth plane.

That said, some parapsychologists doubt the wisdom of this modern trend and feel it is wrong to exclude the possibility that a poltergeist may depend on some post-mortal intrusion. As a result, exorcists – priests trained in 'driving out evil spirits' – still on occasion visit the scene of poltergeist attacks in addition to their more usual role of winkling out demonic forces in haunted buildings.

HISTORICAL REVIEW

Reports of poltergeist activity can be found from at least six hundred years ago, and researcher Jerome Clark records a brief passage from the annals of King Theodoric which date back to the year 530. For a short time his palace was attacked by stones that seemed to be hurled by an invisible assailant – classic poltergeist behaviour. In 1599 one of the first true poltergeist investigations was conducted by Martin Del Rio. Given the cultural climate of those days it is not surprising that he referred to the force as a type of demon which was 'wont to occasion various commotions and annoyances . . . [such as] clattering of pots and hurling of stones'.

It was in January 1905 that the current view of the poltergeist really began to take shape, when a farm at Binbrook in Lincolnshire suffered a series of fires that sprang up out of nowhere but were quickly put under control. The presence of an emotionally strained young woman at the focus of the activity was noted, although she did not seem to be deliberately starting the fires. The same factor was present in the infamous Fox sisters' 'rapping sounds' that had given rise to the Spiritualist movement in New York sixty years before. When other poltergeist cases were looked at, a pattern seemed to be emerging. Were young girls somehow unconsciously responsible for the attacks?

This proved to be a simplistic, but not altogether inaccurate, way of viewing things. Certainly teenage girls were present in many cases, but by no means all. Some involved young boys, not girls. And a few had no element of children – although menopausal women were considered another likely group.

Psychokinesis

During the 1960s experiments began in earnest to test for what was called PK – psychokinesis. This is the apparent ability to move physical objects by the mind alone. The concept was highly controversial because it seemed to fly in the face of the laws of physics, which insisted that any motion must have a physical force behind it. Yet in laboratories witnesses were apparently doing precisely what Sir Isaac Newton had long decreed to be impossible.

The relevance of this research to the poltergeist outbreak was clear. If stones or a table shoot across a room and nothing seems to be responsible for moving them, some hidden force must be doing it. That force could, conceivably, be PK – and the origin of that PK might be a person present in the room at the time, even if they were unaware that they were doing anything.

The Rosenheim affair

An instructive poltergeist case occurred at Rosenheim in Germany in 1967. It affected the office of a solicitor, where all manner of strange things happened for a period of several weeks. Light bulbs swung violently in their sockets. Photocopiers spewed out paper. The telephone behaved most oddly, running up fantastic bills thanks to countless calls to one number that nobody was actually dialling. That number was the speaking clock.

Professor Hans Bender, a leading paranormal researcher at Freiburg University, investigated the case and discovered that one person had been present during all these events – a nineteen-year old woman called Anne-Marie Schaberl. Bored and frustrated, she had taken to constant clock-watching. Bender suggested that this had somehow 'leaked out' and translated into swinging light bulbs and calling up the speaking clock every few minutes – acts which all occurred without any physical activity on her part but as a result of the subconscious release of intense PK. Naturally, this theory was controversial. But it was interesting that when Anne-Marie got married and settled into a happier lifestyle the poltergeist attacks stopped immediately.

The notorious Enfield outbreak

Of all the poltergeist cases that have been documented during modern research, in dozens of countries, one of the most dramatic was at a small house in Enfield, north London. Between August 1977 and September

1978 a family was driven close to despair by the longest-lasting and most consistently aggressive outbreak on record. Objects as huge as sofas were tossed around the room. The two teenage girls in the family claimed to be levitated into the air, sometimes in front of witnesses. Countless small objects were thrown at researchers and journalists who were all endeavouring, with some success, to put the barrage of evidence on film.

During the case SPR researcher Maurice Grosse, and to a lesser extent his colleague Guy Playfair, lived with the afflicted family and steered them through the worst of the trauma, which ended as quickly as it had begun. The Enfield case remains the most studied investigation on record and, whilst some sceptics claim that the children were inventing the phenomena (and it is likely that something of this sort went on at times), the research team are adamant that they witnessed numerous genuine and seemingly unfakeable happenings. The full case is indeed very impressive.

Once again, the Enfield poltergeist suggested that the presence of children, especially young girls going through the physical changes of puberty, was a central factor. The poltergeist began to be recognised almost like a psychic temper tantrum, or the unconscious expression of sexual tensions and frustrations. It was a safety valve that let off steam, allowing the bottled up psychic energies within a person to find some way out into the world.

However, in the Enfield case there were also some indications of a real 'ghost' at work – a gruff voice speaking through the vocal cords of one of the girls professed to be an old man who had died in the house (and who really had existed, as research established). Was this evidence that some force was simply using the emotionally fragile victim to express its own aggression? Perhaps it will prove so, but experiments being carried out in Canada offered another possibility.

A ghost named Philip

In 1972 a group of Toronto researchers (see photograph opposite page 27) decided to invent a ghost. They created an entire life history for a phantom cavalier whom they called Philip, and met frequently to discuss his non-existent life. They wanted to see if they could make him real enough to manifest, thus proving that ghosts might emerge from within the collective mind. Despite considerable effort they never succeeded in making Philip visible, but poltergeist events began to plague their sessions and when they asked (via one rap for yes, two raps for no) who was responsible, the fictitious cavalier claimed due credit.

In the Toronto case the fabricated ghost had adopted a degree of independence that no one individually could terminate. Once let loose, the ghost came 'alive'. The team argued that this experiment demonstrated the reality of ESP and PK but put a whole new perspective on hauntings and poltergeist cases. It is certainly easy to see how, in a case such as Enfield, PK at a prodigious and persistent level over many months might be blamed on a 'ghost' who could adopt sufficient life to join in the ongoing activity as a self-fulfilling part of the phenomenon.

In how many other cases where a ghost is allegedly responsible for physical acts are those acts really down to human beings at the location? Is the ghost a surrogate creation of their belief system, fuelled by their latent PK? Does it serve as a way to transfer the blame for these strange events onto any external agency (the poltergeist) rather than to accept that the forces which power them may originate within one's own sub-conscious mind.

If true, this concept has a far broader implication. We tend to assume that any supernatural manifestation is either real or unreal. If witnesses believe that they have been abducted by aliens, either this is true or they are imagining it. But what if an alien can be conjured up into a form of proto-existence simply by way of a strong enough belief spreading throughout the community? Can it be magicked into temporary and semi-physical reality as a result of the PK abilities of witnesses? Would this not be an excellent way to explain how any seemingly absurd phenomenon, which is in line with cultural beliefs and has too many human-like foibles to be 'real', can display at least some apparent attributes of independent existence?

As with aliens, so with ghosts and who knows how many other supernatural entities who are blamed for paranormal events. Might not this blame lie at the door of the potentially extraordinary PK abilities of the human mind? These are the questions raised by the poltergeist debate.

EXPERIENCING POLTERGEISTS

Suddenly to face the apparent wrath of a vengeful spirit must be an extremely harrowing paranormal event. From all accounts the witnesses feel personally victimised by the relentless assault of physical acts, from the trivial to the terrifying, which hit them day in and day out.

Telling them that they are not really being visited by a spiteful ghost, but that the events are caused by some sort of energy seeping out from one of their own family members, will probably get short shrift. Even if it is considered a credible argument it will not stop the phenomena from occurring or lessen their impact. This, almost always, is what the witness actually wants. In such circumstances, of course, understanding the poltergeist is the key to ending its activities. To know that it is likely to be a transient experience, lasting weeks or perhaps only days, is also a comfort.

From what we know about poltergeist attacks there are two ways to handle them. You can try to get rid of them or try to harness their power. Your choice may depend upon how brave you are willing to be.

Studies have shown that exorcism probably works because the victims believe in its efficacy. So if you are a religious family which accepts that a priest can call on the love of God to drive out evil forces, seek that sort of assistance. Your church will be able call on trained exorcists who travel the country performing this age-old ritual even in the 1990s. If it works for you, don't mock it.

However, there are good grounds to suppose that an exorcist is not always necessary. Researchers have found that simple rituals that can be performed by oneself are just as effective, provided they are believed in.

One witness, fed up and frightened, grew angry and let out a tirade of four-letter abuse at the offending 'spirit'. It never troubled him again. TV actress Doreen Sloane told me how she became annoyed at the attacks, which sent her pet cat scurrying under the table. So she cried into thin air that the ghost was frightening her animal and it should go. It promptly did. In another case I helped a child who was suffering frequent problems in her bedroom by suggesting she should keep a camera handy. I told her the apparition would not want to be photographed and so it would stay away. It did.

In such cases an element of trickery is involved. But it is only necessary for the person who may be responsible for the phenomena to accept subconsciously that this form of magic spell will end the manifestation. When children are involved, or suspected of being involved, that is easier than it may seem.

Moreover, there is good evidence that, if PK energy is leaking out to reflect the inner tensions of the victim, this energy can be channelled into something more positive. Subjects of poltergeist attacks have cured themselves by practising automatic writing and seeming to channel strange messages on to a piece of paper, or drawing pictures, or writing stories of surprising creativity, all appearing to come from some unknown source. Others have developed healing skills, finding that by touching or massaging sick animals and people they can somehow transfer energy from within themselves.

RESEARCHING POLTERGEISTS

Poltergeist cases can be very demanding on a researcher. Maurice Grosse indicates that he would probably never have involved himself with the Enfield case if he had realised that he would need to devote so much of himself to the family for month after month. Thankfully, most poltergeist outbreaks are less taxing – indeed, so short-lived that by the time a researcher hears of them they are virtually at an end. Although this means that speed is essential if any meaningful data is to be gathered, it does mean that long periods away from home and work will not be called for.

Fortunately, a lot can be done with modern equipment. A house prone to poltergeist attack can be fitted with a video camera which will continuously record what happens, and various monitors can be set up to log temperature changes, electrical and magnetic fields and other indicators which research suggests may be critical during PK outbursts. It is even possible to be prepared and monitor homes where there are children approaching puberty and who have previously displayed psychic abilities.

Since technical equipment of this kind has been more readily available no truly classic poltergeist case such as Enfield has yet happened. But if the opportunity arises we should learn a great deal about the phenomenon. In the meantime there is a good deal still to be done in seeking patterns and trigger factors in older cases. This will involve in-depth interviews with families to check on details of their lifestyle or other small clues which might prove significant. It can be difficult, because you may easily appear to be prying or you may get out of your depth asking questions which are really the province of a psychologist or psychiatrist. Equally, the family might regard probing questions as tantamount to disbelief or evidence that you are challenging their sanity. It can be hard to persuade people that suggesting that it may be they themselves, rather than a ghost, behind a poltergeist attack is not the same as making accusations of fraud and deception.

Some insight has been gleaned from this work. Activity has been seen to focus around times when emotional and hormonal changes are occurring in the physical body. People who are creatively visual – for instance good at painting or storytelling, which probably means a well-developed right hemisphere in their brain, also seem unusually prone. More surprising has been the discovery that witnesses often have migraine and, to a lesser degree, epilepsy, in their medical history. As these conditions both seem to be based on rapidly changing hormonal and electrical activity within the brain, this may prove a significant factor.

Another very useful thing that researchers can do, even after a poltergeist attack is over, is to conduct tests with the witness who is suspected of being involved and see if they are capable of automatic writing or healing. If the theory is correct, they should be several times more likely to perform well at such things than are people who are not prone to PK experience.

What is also intriguing is that researchers into witnesses of alien abduction, apparently a very different phenomenon, have found many similar clues. This may imply that a person is capable of experiencing both these events, according to circumstance. Indeed, one of the most common elements in reports by alien abductees is that they have a life-long track record of other paranormal phenomena, with PK and poltergeist activity high on the list.

POLTERGEISTS TODAY

Research into poltergeist activity has undergone something of a revolution in the twentieth century. It has also probably made more progress than most other areas of the supernatural – in other words, we think we understand the whys and wherefores rather better than we do with many other strange phenomena.

A typical modern case occurred at the Same Yet Inn in Prestwich near Bury, Lancashire in the north-west of England. In March 1994 a fire broke out in the middle of the night, causing extensive damage but leaving things cold to the touch in the morning. The fire brigade called it 'very strange'. One wall was completely unaffected – a wall in which earlier a shadowy image of a man had mysteriously imprinted itself.

The tenants for ten years described many odd things that had occurred in the room, from bottles propelling themselves off shelves to tills opening up on their own – classic small-scale poltergeist activity. Local legend, however, associated the events with the reputed haunting of the place by a farmer who had died in a robbery in that area some 150 years before.

Strange faces

The curious story of a man's 'shadow' imprinted on the wall brings to mind miracle images and simulacra (see pages 143–51). It is also another pattern found, though rarely, in poltergeist cases. For example, on 23 August 1971 at the little Spanish village of Belmez de la Moraleda a man's face turned up, seemingly having formed overnight in the concrete on the kitchen floor of an old stone building. Six days later, the superstitious family dug up the slab and destroyed it, which hardly suggests that trickery was at work.

However, over the next few months further faces started to form on the whitewashed floor. These were not random effects, nor hard-to-see illusions. The faces are clear and precise, although they all faded with time, and cannot have been due to chance. Either they were fabricated, or some supernatural force was at work.

Local people saw them often, and their interest drove the family to try to cover them up or destroy them as their lives were being disrupted, but the mayor decreed that they had to be preserved. In November one face was cut out and mounted behind glass. It is still there. Then the kitchen floor was dug up to seek a possible cause. Some human bones were found, and the restless spirit of their owner was blamed for the appearance of the faces. This at least got the media off the backs of the family, but in fact almost every house in the village had bones underneath as the place had been built on an old graveyard.

Even after a new kitchen floor was put in faces continued to form, and experts from all over Europe flocked to the house to assess the mystery. One researcher kept a photographic record of a face that formed, crystalised, then faded away again all in the space of one day.

In May 1972 poltergeist researcher Hans Bender travelled from Germany and noted that it was not possible to remove the faces from the concrete even with bleach or heavy scrubbing. Despite further experiments, no cause for the faces was ever found. After about twenty of them had turned up the outbreak stopped for ten years before beginning again as suddenly as before. They have continued to appear from time to time, including a full-size human image in 1989.

Surprisingly little physical research has been carried out. Cesar Tort and Luis Ruiz-Noguez reported to the SPR in 1993 on their field trip to the village, and published the only chemical tests carried out on one of the faces. No obvious paint or colouring agent was traced, but they could not eliminate this possibility and sceptics will always suggest fraud as the most likely cause.

The other possibility that Tort and Ruiz-Noguez discuss is thought-ography – the use of PK to impose images on unprocessed film, presumably by manipulating the chemical agents to create patterns that are determined at an unconscious level by a psychic. A similar process could print images on to concrete, and these would eventually fade as water seeped in. However, as the investigators point out, proving this is much harder than establishing fraud, and the case is likely to remain unresolved. It is in obvious need of deeper study.

Thoughtography

Research into thoughtography has gone on for more than thirty years since Ted Serios in the USA regularly projected images on to an undeveloped film simply by pointing the camera at his head. After a period of producing well-defined images, he was only able to come up with what he called 'blackies' and 'whities' – amorphous blobs with no obvious photographic cause.

Serios was never caught cheating and several other cases followed. They included Stella Lansing in Michigan, who experienced a whole series of PK, poltergeist and other psychic adventures as well as finding numerous odd images turning up on both still and movie film. Psychiatrist Dr Berthold Schwarz spent years studying her case but never found a rational explanation.

Claims of thoughtography continue. Peter Hough investigated a case for ASSAP in July 1990 when a Lancashire woman provided various photographs which contained dark blurs, semi-transparent tubes and curious green globes. These are unlike the common effects such as when a set of beads accidentally dangles in front of the camera lens and is reproduced out of focus in a rather ghostly way, or when a processing mark or stray light spoils an otherwise good shot. ASSAP's photographic consultant, Dr Vernon Harrison, assessed the evidence and was puzzled. But Hough's experiments – he gave the woman unprocessed film to use – all failed to provide any new evidence, although occasional images still turned up on her own shots.

Experiments in Russia

Meanwhile Russian psychiatrist Dr Gennady Krokhalev was working with patients at a hospital in Perm. He fitted still and movie camera lenses to their eyes and encased their heads so that no light could intrude. All the patients were suffering visual hallucinations, either through medical conditions or as a result of alcoholism. As the film was taken, their reported hallucinations were transcribed.

Krokhalev claims extraordinary results. He says that in 87 of 203 patients tested anomalous images were recorded, which often matched the accounts they gave of their hallucinations. Reproduced images do show what look like blurred shots of the moon or animal horns and – if

171

we take the researcher's word – this is remarkable evidence that the mind can affect photographic film. Perhaps the unusual state of consciousness during which the hallucinations were occurring facilitated this ability. Krokhalev claimed that alcoholics were the best thoughtographers, suggesting some rather interesting (if ethically dubious) experiments for which volunteers might not be hard to find!

Russian optical scientists have been working on perfecting the technique and determining exactly how it works. Their speculation centres on manipulation of quantum mechanical effects whereby all actions – including thought processes – cause sub-atomic particles to change state and issue packets of energy (quanta) which are theoretically capable of interacting with the particles inside an adjacent film. In fact, at the sub-atomic level of physics action without obvious physical cause is not only likely, it is virtually the rule. The cause occurs within particles sub-microscopically and is only detectable to us at the level of measuring statistics across millions of events. It is not visible on a one-off basis.

The importance of emotion

The uninhibited state of alcoholics may offer a clue as to why such people seem good at PK. It is known that emotion is one of the strongest triggers to any kind of psychic phenomenon. The bond of love brings people close together and makes them more likely to share ESP. Anger and frustration may be channelled as a destructive poltergeist attack.

Paul Lounds reported on an experiment conducted at the University of Nottingham in 1993, in which forty-two students from the department of psychology were given twenty images of varying emotional content – some pleasant, others very nasty. These were shown to them in a computer-generated random order, but the set-up allowed for PK to control the frequency with which the good and bad images were screened if the unconscious was able to unleash this ability.

Two tests were conducted with each subject. In one they had theoretical control over four of the randomly selected images. In the other they were asked to pick four slides according to their emotive impact, including the one they liked the most and the one they hated the most. This should have offered an incentive to try unconsciously to select the most liked and deselect the most hated. By chance 210 examples of each slide should have appeared. When no emotive choice was on offer nothing significant happened – 212 of the most liked were selected. When there was a choice this figure rose to 238, with only 199 of the most hated slide. These results were not spectacular, but were enough above chance level to suggest that more research of this kind might one day scientifically demonstrate an emotional basis to PK.

That energy transfer is occurring during PK is strongly suggested by measurements made during experiments in which gifted people seem able to move small rotating targets inside vacuum-sealed jars. In some cases temperature drops of up to 5°C and weight loss of several kilograms have been recorded, before and after, suggesting that this is the physical basis for the energy required.

Physics argues that energy is never destroyed, simply changed from one form to another. Perhaps it is the latent energy within a human body that provokes PK and poltergeist activity. Certainly many poltergeist victims are physically and emotionally drained after their experience; and it may not necessarily be because of the stress of the terrifying episode.

SOURCES

ORGANISATIONS AND INDIVIDUALS

Research into PK and poltergeists is conducted by *ASSAP*, the *SPR* and the *American SPR* (see pages 28, 100 and 141 for addresses). You may also find it helpful to contact *Dr Alan Gauld at the University of Nottingham* (who works with Tony Cornell and Maurice Grosse as the SPR poltergeist expert team) and *Professor Arthur Ellison* at the SPR, who can organise physical testing of PK.

BOOKS

The first three texts are acknowledged classics of general literature in the field. Matthew Manning describes what is probably the most remarkable benign PK outbreak. Harrison's work is a book-length case investigation. Owen and Sparrow write about the experiments to create an artificial ghost. Guy Lyon Playfair's book discusses the Enfield poltergeist case. Thoughtography is dealt with in a book-length section of Schwarz's mammoth work. Evans reveals a fascinating sideline to PK: its involuntary effects on street lamps.

Can We Explain the Poltergeist? by A.R. Owen (Taplinger, New York, 1964).

The Poltergeist by William Roll (Doubleday, New York, 1972).

Poltergeists by Alan Gauld and Tony Cornell (Routledge & Kegan Paul, 1979).

The Link by Matthew Manning (Colin Smythe, 1974).

The Signatures by Dr Vernon Harrison (SPR, 1994).

Conjuring Up Philip by Iris Owen and Margaret Sparrow (Harper & Row, New York, 1976).

This House Is Haunted by Guy Lyon Playfair (Souvenir Press, 1980).

UFO Dynamics by Berthold Schwarz (Rainbow Books, 1988).

The SLI Effect by Hilary Evans (ASSAP, 1990).

PRECOGNITION

DEFINITION

Literally translated, precognition means 'knowing in advance'. If someone becomes aware of a future happening which later turns into a reality they will have had a precognition – but only provided there is no obvious method by which that foresight could have taken place. For example, if you put a car on a slope, release the handbrake and watch it roll towards the edge of a cliff you might well have a vision of it plunging into the sea. But that would not be a precognition, because the event is almost certain to occur. It is utterly predictable by ordinary methods of perception. If, however, in the seconds before the car topples over the edge you have a sudden image in your mind that all four wheels will fall off and the hulk of the vehicle will then grind to a halt in the long grass without falling over the cliff, that would be regarded as a precognition if this highly improbable circumstance were then to take place.

It is usually assumed that precognition means 'seeing' the future, by way of a vision. But that is only one method. Foreknowledge more often comes in the form of a simple gut reaction or foreboding (officially termed a *presentiment*), and the hearing of sounds or even smelling of odours ahead of their real occurrence is by no means unknown. The term 'precognition' covers a wide range of sensory perceptions depicting something that you should not be able to foresee.

True foresight or inspired guess?

But there are problems inherent within this definition. For instance, what do we mean by an event happening after the foreknowledge? If you have a vision of an earthquake and one happens tomorrow, that might seem strange. But if your vision is followed by twenty uneventful years before an earthquake occurs, can it still be argued that you saw the future? After all, most of us probably dream about an earthquake at some point in our lives, and many such events do occur. For a meaningful precognition something precise must be foreseen, and the timespan between this foreknowledge and the event must be realistic, not open-ended.

Ironically, some might feel almost magically, within hours of my writing the above paragraph (in November 1995) psychic Dave Mandell (see page 184) announced that he was selling his London home because

175

he has dreamed that it will be damaged in an earthquake during 1996. That is a specific precognition, made stronger by the huge improbability of such an event striking a geologically stable area like London. It has also been recorded in advance in an indisputable way, as all precognitions worth their salt must be. If this prophecy is fulfilled, Mandell's visionary gifts will have to be taken seriously.

But was the fact that I wrote these words the day before this announcement a precognition of the press report? It is tempting to accept this conclusion, but I was not really specific enough. Had I mentioned an earthquake in London, things might have been different. You see how difficult it is to determine whether a precognition should be counted as true foresight or a lucky guess. Let me offer as an example one precognition that I am very sure about. It occurred on 8 March 1968 when I was sixteen, and was recorded in writing in advance (as I awoke that morning). In my dream I saw a paper mill beside a bridge apparently on fire, a very curious and precise scene. Twenty-four hours later, whilst I was passing through Preston at 4a.m. on a sponsored walk for charity, the image was duplicated in reality. The odds of such a coincidence are so fantastic that precognition is a better explanation.

Because billions of dreams are dreamed every night, sceptics rightly argue that some of them must come true. Statistics prove it. Occasionally, four card players are dealt hands that consist of the four complete suits. The odds against this are fantastic, but because so many games of cards are played around the world each day such a freak event is bound to happen from time to time. Seeing the future is a bit like getting dealt a full suit of cards, except that we all dream many dreams every night and so the odds of a match with future events are really rather better than they seem.

If precognition were a flimsy, infrequent occurrence the sceptics would have a strong case. But it is probably the most common paranormal event of all, experienced by most of us a few times during our lives – indeed, some research cogently argues, probably by *all* of us hundreds or even thousands of times. You will very likely dispute that fact, because you will not recall most of your minor precognitions. But you can do something to prove it (or disprove it) to your own satisfaction; more of that later.

HISTORICAL REVIEW
—

It is not hard to find stories of precognition from the distant past. We read about them at school, and they fit into the same two basic groups found today. On the one hand we have the legends of mystics, seers and soothsayers, such as the Delphic Oracle of Greek mythology. These were wise people or entities supposedly endowed with such great gifts of precognition that they were consulted regularly by kings and generals as well as by ordinary people who needed to decide what action to take at important points in their lives. Claims of spectacular successes for such oracles are legion – but they were often wrong as well. The other type of precognition found millennia ago was the spontaneous vision or aware- ness of the future which occurred to someone out of the blue. It most often happened during a dream, and was so powerful and lucid that the dreamer tended to accept it as foreknowledge and tried to act upon it or warn others of its consequences. Many ancient texts are full of stories of this kind – the Old Testament of the Bible, for example, is packed with them.

Modern world, ancient beliefs

Until about a hundred years ago precognition was seen as part and parcel of everyday life and, outside the rational, techno-science ethos of Western civilisation, this is still the way it is. So-called 'primitive tribes' around the world regard visions of the future as fundamental to their day-to-day existence. But precognition still holds extraordinary fascination for us all, as evidenced by the fact that the visions of Nostradamus (see page 41) have, despite their opacity, been in print ever since the sixteenth century. And even though computer analysts, statisticians and business forecasters now weave their magic spells through mathematical and scientific means, it is amazing how many of us still consult our horoscopes in daily newspapers.

Hidden failures

Experiments have shown that, when put to the test, those who profess seer-like abilities are very hit and miss in their performance. We hear much about the successes and very little of the failures. Jeanne Dixon, perhaps the most famous living seer, clearly foresaw the death of President John F. Kennedy even before he was elected, and this was well documented in advance. But she also saw Russia getting a man to the moon before the USA and a female US president who never was. The tendency to recall the hits and forget the misses creates an impression that the success-to-failure ratio is better than it is. These seers, like most of us, seem to have a dramatic precognition now and then, but flounder when forced to perform on a regular basis.

Pure precognition

Precognition works best in its pure form – happening unexpectedly to those who do not seek it rather than being forced to occur so as to fulfil our hunger for predictions. As a consequence, most study of the subject has concentrated on strong one-off cases rather than on the dubious prowess of those who may have taken their abilities too much for granted.

There are many such case histories. The sinking of the *Titanic* inspired quite a number from passengers who died, as well as from those who cancelled their trips and survived. A novel published fourteen years earlier by Morgan Robertson (the author described being in an altered state of consciousness as he wrote it) was called *The Wreck of the Titan* and is a close approximation of the coming event.

President Abraham Lincoln had a dream of his own assassination; although in it he saw his ghost wandering the White House trying to find out why everyone was in mourning. Indeed, there is plenty of evidence from such stories that what a precognition foresees is not an actual event but a person's future state of consciousness when they experience that event. This may seem a moot point, but it is a profound discovery for several reasons.

For example, in my dream of the paper mill there was a fire. When the event took place there was no fire – merely the glow of furnaces reflecting off low cloud. But several people in the group I was with saw the dancing orange light, wrongly assumed it was a fire and hurried off to check more closely before realising the error. Clearly here my dream perceived that error, not the true event. There are many other examples on record: a wrong address for a dead person, explained because the obituary column that the dreamer first read contained a typographical error; a volcanic eruption that was seen as having killed four thousand people, when the truth was nearer forty thousand – the dreamer wrongly heard the news as four thousand when he came into contact with the story. This helps enormously in our efforts to comprehend how precognition might work, and also poses significant questions about certain cases.

The Aberfan precognitions

In October 1966 a slag heap at Aberfan, in a mining area of Wales, collapsed and flattened a school. Many children were killed, probably without knowing what hit them. Psychiatrist Dr John Barker collected sixty cases of people who seemed to have had a precognition of some sort, and was able to verify that many of them were recorded in some way in advance. Time and again they displayed evidence that the foresight was of the person's first contact with the news, through television reports or newspaper stories that day.

Perhaps the most remarkable were two precognitions by Eryl Mai Jones, a nine-year-old girl who became one of the 144 victims of the tragedy. Two weeks beforehand she told her family she was not afraid to die because she would go to heaven alongside two of her playmates, whom she named. On the morning of the disaster she dreamed of a black mass falling on the school and causing it to disappear. Aside from the terrible reality that these images foresaw, the real question is: what future state of consciousness did the girl perceive? From inside the school, how could she have an image of the sudden event that killed her? Moreover, how could she know that she would be buried in the mass grave between the two children she named? This incident occurred days after Eryl Mai Jones had ceased to exist as a conscious entity – unless some part of her did still exist somehow, somewhere. What this implies is that precognition of events after one's death may turn out to be unexpectedly strong evidence for survival – perhaps better than many messages from mediums relaying the thoughts of dear departed Uncle Fred.

Since 1966 various attempts have been made to set up a premonitions bureau to record precognitions from the public. With modern computers, the dedicated assistance of the media, preferably television, and the willingness to give the experiment enough time, quite remarkable results might be achieved.

EXPERIENCING PRECOGNITION

If you had a precognition, would you recognise it as one? The answer seems to be that very often you would not. Contrary to expectation, most foresight seems to be about the mundane trivia of life and so is rather quickly forgotten. If it should occur during a dream, you are unlikely to recall it as soon as you get out of bed. This is why most people seem unaware of the extent to which they probably experience precognition during their lives. It is relegated to the deep subconscious.

The most powerful events are those charged with emotion. It is as if we are on the edge of a pond with someone dropping stones in the water on the far side. Most of these produce tiny ripples and we barely notice them unless we pay special attention. Occasionally a really big rock is dropped in, and the waves that reach us are sufficiently strong that we cannot miss their effect.

In the same way a vivid precognition tends to be recognised because of the emotional impact. It shakes us awake, its raw energy lingers even as we struggle towards consciousness. Of course, vivid nightmares can be like this as well and they are nothing more than imagination. Mistakes will be made as a result, but it is worth taking seriously any lucid and vivid experience of this nature because some may turn out to be pre-cognitive.

Should we adopt a fatalistic view? Is our future mapped out and unavoidable? Nobody knows the answer, but some evidence suggests that we can act on what we foresee. In one classic case, a woman had a dream of her baby playing by a river during a picnic, of going away for a few moments to fetch something, and of returning to find her child face up in the water, drowned. Soon afterwards – having forgotten the dream – they did picnic by a river, she did forget something and, just as she turned away to get it, the memory of the dream came back. Her child was wearing exactly the same clothes. The scene was being replayed. She stopped herself from leaving, saw him wandering towards the river and no tragedy resulted. Here, you might say, the precognition saved a life. But sceptics say that, as the event was unfulfilled, it was not a pre-cognition in the first place!

However, far more often there will be no full memory of a dream. Had I not written down my paper mill vision it would have never mani-fested as a precognition, because during the fulfilment of the experi-ence I only had a sense, rather like the common feeling of déjà vu, that I had seen this moment somewhere before. Without my notes from twenty-four hours earlier to jog my memory and prove the dream, this would have been just another example of precognition that went unrecognised.

Heeding your instincts

For this reason it is important to pay heed to feelings, gut reactions and instincts. Often these can be an awareness at the subconscious level of a precognition that we are not able to appreciate consciously. If we ignore the feeling – assuming it is strong enough – it may prove costly.

In May 1979 actress Lindsay Wagner and her mother were checking in to board an American Airlines DC-10 at Chicago's O'Hare airport. Such a feeling struck and they switched flights. Moments after take-off the plane they should have boarded lost an engine and crashed. Everyone on board was killed.

Hundreds of miles away a man called David Booth, with no connection to the flight, had spent a week living with the intensely powerful dream of a plane crash. So strong were the images that he finally called the aviation authorities, pleading with them to stop similar-looking aircraft from taking off. He saw many details that were accurate, seemingly based on TV images of the disaster, including a still photograph of the crashing plane taken from the airport. But he could not name the airport nor give the date (then just two days hence) and the aviation authorities could not ground every plane, no matter how sure he was about his unexpected precognition.

After the fact the fulfilment was obvious and David Booth, for whom this was a one-off event, felt the burden of failure very heavily. But what could anyone have done? He had tried his best. Perhaps, had there been a computer-based premonitions bureau collecting dreams like this and scoring them for quality, others might have foreseen the tragedy and a warning could have been issued rather like a weather forecast. Then, if you had a presentiment of disaster as you waited at an airport and knew that the premonitions bureau had forecast the imminent probability of a crash, you could make an informed judgement on whether to trust your instinct. This may be the best – if not the only – way to try to harness the uncertain yet undoubted power of these various forms of precognition.

RESEARCHING PRECOGNITION

Paranormal researchers tend to approach precognition in a curious way. Rather than appreciate how it operates, they feel a need to apply scientific methods to prove the case. So they stick a guinea pig in front of a random number generator and ask that person to predict a six-digit figure that the computer will churn out. Then they do this again . . . and again . . . and again.

Unsurprisingly, little probative evidence has been gathered in this way. This kind of test bores the participant and takes no account of either the emotive component of many precognitions or the way in which the person will sense their own future state of awareness. If they never see the number generated by the machine there is no future awareness to sense and the experiment is doomed to failure. It would be far better to develop the computer-based premonitions bureau discussed above, because this would focus on people seeing future news stories on TV with a strong emotional element. The computer could be programmed to sift these and ascribe weightings, and, given enough input, it could issue probability forecasts as mentioned above.

Be your own guinea pig

The true advantage of researching precognition lies in the fact that we do not have to hunt for super psychics to aid our work. We ourselves are perfect subjects for an experiment. Each one of us dreams several dreams a night, and it is simple to train yourself to recall them better. Normally, 95 per cent of them are forgotten within moments of waking. When talking about dreams (see page 72) I explained the benefits of keeping a dream diary – perhaps the best way of showing that we all have precognitive experiences on a regular basis. Experiments have shown that at least one dream a week per person probably refers to a future event. The frequency may be much higher than that, but even if you spend a lot of time recording notes of your dreams you will still miss out a good deal.

Also keep notes in your diary of any times when you experience déjà vu. This term, from the French meaning 'already seen', describes a common sensation of having been somewhere, or lived through a brief moment of time, before. It is experienced by most of us once or twice a year. Scientists are not sure what causes it, although they have theories about neurons firing in the brain in patterns similar to earlier firing sequences, thus creating a feeling of familiarity. The possibility that a déjà vu experience reflects subconscious awareness of a consciously forgotten precognition is as viable as any theory that biologists have come up with.

The best way to kick-start premonitions into your dream life is to use two alarms. Set the first to wake you an hour before you need to get out of bed, and when it rings switch it off immediately. Then fall straight back to sleep whilst awaiting the second alarm. The state of consciousness which you enter in this way seems to draw forth a higher percentage of precognitive images. Since the length of dreaming increases progressively throughout the night, much of this pre-waking hour of sleep will involve dreams. These will be readily recalled for your dream diary when the second alarm goes off.

The chances of precognition also increase if you take a new route to work, visit a new club or simply have new experiences of some sort. Probably because the brain is forced to process novel experiences more thoroughly and because things are felt more emotionally when new, the scanning ahead needed for precognition may happen more often.

Finally, if you want to increase the number of dreams which do not relate to personal trivia but are more associated with world events, get into the habit of watching the TV news broadcasts for half an hour or so each morning soon after you wake up. If precognition works by sensing your own future state of consciousness, you need to experience images of major events, if only on TV, to have any real likelihood of foreseeing them in a dream.

Of course, precognition does not only take place during dreams – it can flash superimposed on your normal perception without any warning. But you cannot control this. The reason why dreaming is excellent for this kind of research is that we all do it every single night. It is a perpetual experiment that we do not have go out of our way to perform, and there is never any problem finding a suitable subject.

PRECOGNITION TODAY

Cases that verify the suggestions from this ongoing research are not hard to find. American John Riley described how on 11 September 1981 he had his precognition. He was taking a very early flight from Rochester, New York to Chicago, then on to Albuquerque and finally to San Francisco. He had to get up before dawn, and so fell asleep almost as soon as he settled into his seat. He was awoken at 5.40a.m. by the stewardess serving breakfast. During those few minutes' sleep, as he told the stewardess and many other passengers, he had a dream so vivid it was like being there.

In this dream Riley saw a helicopter plunge from the sky like a stone and crash on to a coastal freeway, although it did not burst into flames. So charged with the emotion of the disaster was he that he could not stop talking about it and bought the latest edition of the local news-papers at every airport *en route* – without finding news of any such crash. Only when he reached San Francisco and was driving from the airport did a news flash interrupt the music on the radio to describe the tragedy. It had occurred nearby, at Fremont. The newscaster used almost exactly the words and images with which John Riley had besieged his fellow passengers all day long. But the crash had happened six hours *after* his dream.

Interestingly, when Riley later saw details of the crash they differed from his dream in minor ways – the weather in reality was more misty, for example. What seems to have occurred is that in his dream he visualised the crash from his first contact with the news hours into the future – the moment that had the maximum emotional impact upon him. As that

LEICESTERSHIRE LIBRARIES AND INFORMATION SERVICE
REFERENCE & INFORMATION LIBRARY HUMANITIES

was via a radio report, the words used on air fitted into the dream, but he had to draw in the scenery from his own imagination. He therefore got the broad details correct, because these were described by the newscaster, but was inevitably wrong in small details that his future self would not know and had to invent.

In another case, Arctic exploration scientist Dr Peter Wadhams described to the SPR a dream he had on 27 May 1994. He was in his childhood home, holding a double-barrelled shotgun and performing several tasks. The vivid dream impressed him on waking, but he had no contact with guns of any kind and so this element seemed odd. The dream occurred just before he awoke, at 7.20a.m. An hour later on the breakfast TV news he saw an item about police recovering guns from a raid; it contained a scene with a police officer holding a double-barrelled shotgun and doing exactly what he had done in his dream. It seems that his mind detected his future view of the TV news item and jumbled this up to form a dream scene in the way our minds often do.

A problem with cases such as these is that they tend not to have much more than the word of the witness to back them up. David Mandell, a London man who dreams vividly and (he says) very often of the future, has developed a simple way around this problem. As well as making notes of any dream that he feels to be precognitive, he draws a sketch of what he sees and then photographs himself holding this up in front of a bank or building society digital clock which displays the exact date and time. He can then log these pictures with witnesses, to prove just when he had his precognition.

Mandell has often demonstrated remarkable abilities. A classic example is of a series of dreams in which he saw 'four square lights' rising up from parked cars and fall to earth on a 'river or runway'. His sketch, with the bank clock to date it well before the coming event, were even discussed in a TV interview twenty-four hours before the fulfilment. That event, on 9 March 1994, was the IRA launching mortars bombs from parked cars outside the airport perimeter that then fell on to the runway at Heathrow. This unexpected and unique attack fits extraordinarily well with David's illustration and description, somehow seen ahead of time.

Dreams of the lottery

A question often asked of such people is this: if they can see the future so clearly, how do they not win the lottery by visualising the right numbers? In the summer of 1995 Dave Mandell was invited to join an HTV programme which set out to test this idea. He explained some of his most stunning dreams, including one in which he changed a train ticket at the last minute to avoid travelling on a London to Swansea express which subsequently crashed. He showed the audience the ticket, altered by the booking clerk at his insistence. The 'pick the lottery numbers' experiment involved all manner of prophecy methods, from a numerologist to a tarot reader, and the six numbers chosen were entered into the draw. Sadly, nobody got rich as a result. Only two of the six numbers came up in the seven out of forty-nine possibilities, which was slightly better than chance but not even good enough to win the smallest prize.

Things worked a little better for Margaret Bramley of Darlington. When her husband went to bed late one night he heard her talking in her sleep, muttering a series of numbers. He woke her up, and Margaret recalled her dream of putting an additional line on her ticket that week with numbers they did not normally use. The Bramleys decided to trust their luck and five out of six came up, with the sixth being the bonus number. As a result they won quite a large amount of money.

This teaches us several things. First, attempts to force precognition to operate rarely succeed. It works best when it happens spontaneously. Second, it is almost certain that Margaret would not have remembered the dream in the morning but for the act of being woken from it by her husband. Third, Margaret Bramley saw an imminent event in her life – writing a new line on her ticket, as opposed to what might have been considered the more emotionally stunning moment of seeing the numbers come up to confirm their win. However, that was several days further into the future than the act of writing the ticket.

Does this suggest that the probability of seeing into the future increases the closer one comes to an event? Research seems to have verified that conclusion. Several experiments indicate that over ninety per cent of all precognitions fulfil themselves within forty-eight hours and less than three per cent seem to relate to events that are more than two weeks into the future. Indeed, well over half of precognitions occur within a day of the event being foreseen. Both American researcher Alan Vaughan and British physicist Danah Zohar have effectively proved this with detailed statistical experimentation.

Precognition and memory

Vaughan and Jack Houck, reporting in 1993 to the SPR on another experiment, described how precognition seems to act like a mirror of memory. Recent events are remembered well, but quality falls off rapidly the further back in time one goes.

Memory research by psychologists also suggests something else which has been tested against precognition and found to be duplicated. Emotionally strong events that create outstanding memories are far better recalled even many years later than are unemotive ones. It is well known, for example, that many people who were over the age of ten in November 1963 can recall, like a snapshot in their mind, the moment they heard about the assassination of President Kennedy. But ask them what they were doing on the same day in November 1973 or even 1993, and very few will have any clear recall. The emotion of the moment tagged the memory and made it stick.

Precisely this effect is operating with precognition, causing emotive events to produce more visions and also to cast their shadows further in advance than more trivial matters. This strongly implies that both memory and precognition operate in a similar way – through the obvious common denominator of human consciousness.

Dissociation

A survey in 1993 by the *Journal of Nervous Mental Disorders* also gives pause for thought. Two Canadian psychologists, Colin Ross and Shaun Joshi, set out to discover whether phenomena like precognition relate to a well-attested mental state known as dissociation. They found good evidence that it did – and also that 17.8 per cent of the population felt they had once had some kind of precognition.

Dissociation is, in effect, our ability to focus away from the outside world and look more inwardly, paying so much attention to our consciousness that we can get lost in its imagery and even perceive this as reality. Of course, this does not prove that those who are expert at dissociation are hallucinating. They may simply be more able to pick up on internal information which gets blocked out by more outward-looking people. That information could be valid and significant, not just illusion.

Indeed, the idea that it can be more than useless fantasy is suggested by data collected by American parapsychologist William Cox. He analysed the number of people travelling on trains that were subsequently involved in crashes and found that there were markedly fewer on these than on similar trains at the same times, or on the same trains on other days when they did not suffer an accident. A good way to account for this is that subconsciously some of those who could dissociate sensed the impending disaster and were motivated to take another train or means of travel.

Ross and Joshi also remarked on recent findings by psychologists

Lorraine Ham demonstrating her healing technique on the Revd Alan Kitchen, whom she successfully treated for neck problems (see page 119).

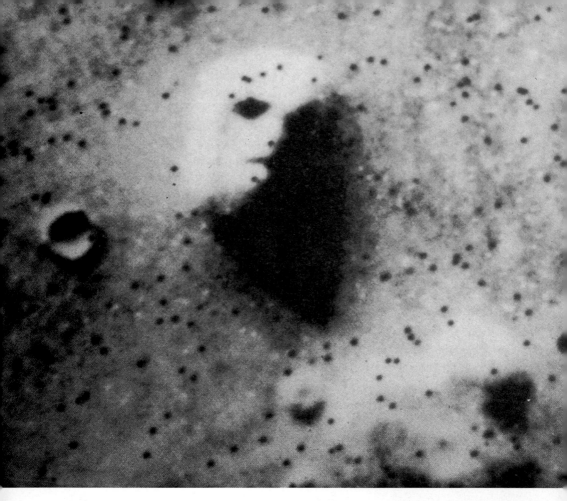

ABOVE
The so-called face on Mars,
photographed by an orbiting
spacecraft in 1976 (see pages
148–50).

RIGHT
A photograph taken in the
skies over Korea in the 1950s
by the crew of an American
bomber. Only after processing
did they notice the image of
Christ appearing from within
the shapes of the clouds (see
pages 144–5).

alleging that witnesses to ESP and other strange phenomena, notably alien abductions, suffered a higher than expected level of child abuse in their early lives. Sceptics have sought a way to make these impressive results 'explain away' the paranormal. The Canadian study does not propose a direct link between child abuse and later experience of weird phenomena. Rather, it can be argued, those who have suffered abuse are known to develop a strong ability to live within themselves as an escape route from the traumas of their day-to-day lives.

Do these people learn to dissociate and pay more attention to what occurs in their inner consciousness? Part of the price may be increased proneness to fantasy, but they may also become more sensitive to things like precognition. The rest of us are taught to ignore inner experience as 'just imagination'. Trusting our feelings is considered far less important in modern society than making rational judgements. That repression creates imbalance and may well cost some of us dear.

SOURCES

ORGANISATIONS AND PERIODICALS

New precognitions feature regularly in *Fate* magazine, which is published monthly. *PSI Researcher* carries more detailed accounts on a less frequent basis, while *Theta* is concerned with research into mental phenomena. The *SPR, JSPR* and *ASSAP* (for addresses see pages 100 and 28) also publish research papers from time to time.

Fate   *PO Box 1940, 170 Future Way, Marion, OH 43305–1940, USA.*

PSI Researcher   *49 Marloes Road, London W8 6LA, UK.*

Theta   *Duke State University, Durham, NC 27706, USA.*

BOOKS

Timeslips are a peculiar phenomenon which may well illustrate how precognition and ghosts are closer to the same phenomenon than we imagine. In the former we appear to see the future and in the latter a scene from the past, but if time is either symmetrical or even (as some people contend) non-existent at the level of consciousness, these two phenomena may be different sides of the same coin. In a timeslip the witness becomes so absorbed in the experience of past or future, and the imagery is so powerful, that they actually feel as if they slip in time and travel there before returning to the present. Such cases are rare, but some have been well documented by Joan Forman.

The Mask of Time by Joan Forman (MacDonald and Janes, 1978).

In the following list about precognition, Dunne explains his own unique mathematical theory while Priestley offers a different version. Zohar gives a more current interpretation in the light of quantum mechanics, well expressed by a physicist who takes precognition seriously. Oxford scientist Shallis has some interesting observations on déjà vu and Penfield reports on the findings from years of experimental brain research. Rattray-Taylor, on the other hand, provides a fine review of what we are struggling to learn about human consciousness and problems outstanding. For spontaneous cases both Greenhouse and Bardens establish the wealth of data. My own book is a general review of claims to travel in time, with ideas about experiments you can try for yourself.

An Experiment with Time by J.W. Dunne (Faber & Faber, 1927).

Man and Time by J.B. Priestley (Aldus Books, 1964).

Through the Time Barrier by Danah Zohar (Heinemann, 1982).

On Time by Michael Shallis (Burnett Books, 1982).

The Mystery of the Mind by Wilber Penfield (Princeton University Press, NJ, 1978).

The Natural History of the Mind by G. Rattray-Taylor (Secker & Warburg, 1979).

Premonitions by Herbert Greenhouse (Turnstone, 1973).

Ahead of Time by Dennis Bardens (Robert Hale, 1991).

Time Travel by Jenny Randles (Cassell, 1994).

REINCARNATION

DEFINITION

'Do you believe there is such a thing as reincarnation?' I once asked a researcher. 'I hope not,' he replied. 'Who wants to come back as a tin of milk?' Behind this joke lies a debate about one of the strongest and most universally accepted belief systems in the world: that after we die some inner self (call it mind, consciousness or soul) has the capacity to return to earth and infuse a new material body to make us live again.

Although this belief is shared by more than half the world's population – Christianity being one of the few major religions not to embrace it – ideas about the exact nature of the way reincarnation operates differ considerably. Whilst returning as a can of evaporated milk is probably beyond the scope of any belief system, it is not a long way beyond. Some people envisage rebirth in the animal and plant kingdom, or even a steady progression from one form of life to another. This becomes an evolutionary spiral of the mind to rival Darwin's theory of the survival of the fittest.

Most people who accept reincarnation presume that we return as another human being, often with the purpose of improving on last time around or even atoning for our wrongdoings by suffering appropriate consequences. This is the essence of the law of karma – what we do wrong is visited upon us with a relevant misfortune in some future life.

However, there are major differences in opinion as to whether we always return as one sex, and whether we reincarnate immediately after death or after a lengthy sojurn in the afterlife. One of the few constants seems to be that when we are reborn we do not recall our past lives – except deep inside our soul. The idea is that we must make better progress because we believe it is right to do so, not because we are bullied into action as a price for previously remembered indiscretions. Some also argue that we can map out our next life and choose to go for maximum growth or to put right many wrongs. Others say our path is planned for us by God and we must make the best of it.

Until recently, much of Western culture considered reincarnation a primitive belief, but the media-inspired interest in hypnotic regression to so-called 'memories of past lives' has now become a popular aspect of modern society. Today belief, even amongst Christians, is spreading fast.

189

This has forced sceptics (and, to a much lesser degree, science) to look at the question and see if it has any actual support beyond an unprovable philosophy of life.

Yet perhaps reincarnation's greatest point in its favour is the universal nature of its appeal. Even Christianity once included it as part of its teachings. Does its ease of acceptance stem from mere wishful thinking? Indeed, is the idea of returning to the many hardships of life something to wish for when heaven is supposed to be such a wonderful place? Or does it reflect an inner knowledge that we all share at some level of our deeper mind because we have all lived many times before?

HISTORICAL REVIEW

Belief in transmigration of the soul, as reincarnation was originally termed, dates back at least five thousand years. Its history is probably a good deal older, but no documentation exists. We know that the druids believed in it, as did the Ancient Greeks and most cultures in the Far East.

Sceptics suggest that the belief sprang from observation of nature. Most early cultures relied for their survival on farming and astronomical calendars, which epitomise the system of cycles. The sun rises and sets and then rises again, as if reborn. New plants grow, mature, wither and die, only to produce green shoots from their decaying remains just a few months later. It may well have seemed that human existence would surely follow this same natural order. Just because we had died did not mean that we would not rise again in some way and at some time.

Great philosophical debates created the major doctrines of reincarnation which in some countries are still very much a way of life. Many poor peasants in India derive some comfort from knowing that next time they may be reborn into a better lifestyle. Twentieth-century Tibetans still choose their spiritual leader, the Dalai Lama, on the basis of the ancient belief that on his death his soul will have instantly passed on to a new child, for which specially trained priests scour the country in a remarkably discreet search.

A recent revival

The attractive and seemingly apt nature of reincarnation was lost to Western society when it was outlawed by the Christian Church fourteen hundred years ago, but it has only taken four decades of media interest to generate a massive revival of the subject. As recently as 1955 no attention had been focused on it at all, beyond a couple of virtually unknown psychic experiments in France and Britain earlier in the century. But since the fifties hundreds of thousands of people have explored one of the countless methods which supposedly discover your past lives. So deep is this fascination that it shows no sign of being a passing fad. A slumbering giant of a belief system has awoken from more than a thousand years of repression.

The case that truly popularised the subject was the experiment carried out by hypnotist Morey Bernstein on a Colorado housewife, Virginia Tighe. During his routine therapy on the woman she spontaneously regressed to a life as an Irish woman more than a hundred years earlier, and gave the name of Bridey Murphy. Countless sessions followed to drag out more detail, and a remarkably consistent story of a fairly humdrum life was extracted. Bernstein published a book in 1956, and a movie followed. There was huge media interest, and the search for more past lives by the same method has never abated.

But as with alien abductions the use of hypnosis to retrieve repressed memories is fraught with difficulty. Although research shows that it can sometimes facilitate recall, hypnosis is just as likely to stimulate a person's ability to fantasise and invent vivid experiences. Since most past life memories prove uncheckable because they describe ordinary people living lives that may have left no mark, it is impossible to judge whether a past life memory is a true memory, or a fantasy, or even a little of both.

Rival newspapers battled for the truth about Bridey Murphy. One sent a reporter to Ireland and found some details that supported the story. Another dug into Virginia Tighe's childhood and discovered that, even though she denied any conscious memory of such a thing, she had some contact with a woman of Irish ancestry and in this way could have heard about earlier life there.

Cryptomnesia

The theory of cryptomnesia became the sceptics' main weapon. They knew that the brain seemed to have an amazing capacity to store information – indeed, that perhaps every memory of things seen and conversations overheard, perhaps years before, may be stored somewhere in the deep subconscious, normally out of reach of our recall. If hypnosis allowed access to this hidden store, fantastically realistic stories might be conjured up. These could offer verifiable 'past life' data with which a person would quite legitimately claim to have no conscious contact.

Welshman Arnold Bloxham tape recorded many sessions with people who were hypnotised to past lives during the 1950s and 1960s, and this proved a turning point. A star subject, Jane Evans, recalled several past lives, often quite romantic ones and all as women. Two in particular commanded attention. In the first she remembered a life as a Jewess during a well-known terrible massacre in York in 1190. She came out with so much information that a historian specialising in the era was impressed, arguing that few people would know the kind of detail she offered. Jane even described a crypt in a church which at the time of the hypnosis did not have one. Later an old crypt was found at the location. This impressive case was matched by another life in which she was the wife of a Roman nobleman based in Britain. Alongside much accurate information Jane told of things unknown to scholars, yet reasonably credible and consistent with the facts that were on record.

Both these cases stood as great evidence of reincarnation, until determined sceptic Melvyn Harris had the fortune to find a novel about the Roman occupation of Britain by Louis Wohl, written fifty years earlier. It told a story identical to Jane Evans's 'real life memory', and even included the names of people whom she had recalled as friends and companions but whom historians had been unable to trace in contemporary records. This is hardly surprising, since Louis Wohl had invented these people as fictional characters in a book set against a background of real historical events. Jane Evans cannot have known them because they never existed.

There seems almost no doubt that Jane Evans's Roman life was a product of cryptomnesia based on this novel, even though she seems not to recall having read it. Nobody is charging her with fraud, and it is of course fascinating, – and almost supernatural in itself – that the human mind could remember such exact detail from a book probably read and forgotten several decades earlier, and then out of this subconscious memory create such a realistic life history.

More to the point, what are we to make of Jane Evans's life in York eight hundred years ago? Is this also a product of as yet untraced cryptomnesia? Indeed, are all past lives – even the very best hypnotically produced ones – simply play-acting based on long-forgotten fragments? A systematic attempt to find out was launched in 1960 by University of Virginia psychiatrist Dr Ian Stevenson. He is still seeking the truth about reincarnation.

Stories from Asian cultures

Stevenson's work, published not in books but as scientific research papers, rejects the doubtful methods of hypnosis and concentrates on spontaneous memories of a past life. He has collected hundreds of these, although the vast majority are from countries such as India, Burma, Thailand and Sri Lanka where children are indoctrinated into acceptance of past lives almost from birth.

Whilst the psychiatrist has published research into many seemingly impressive cases, he has not claimed that they prove reincarnation. A typical example would be of a child who, when perhaps four or five years old, describes a prior life. Often this involves remembering details of a family who are still living locally and to whom the child can give sufficient detail about a lost loved one to make it seem that he or she is a reincarnation of that recently deceased husband or wife.

However, there are significant problems. These cases suggest almost instant rebirth and virtually always in the same sex as before. Moreover, the migration is never from country to country and frequently involves a distance of just a few miles. These conditions do not seem to be duplicated by reports of rebirth in other cultures, in which sex change, varying-length gaps between lives and long-range migrations are all fairly common. But they do match the belief system regarding reincarnation found in India.

This has led to a sceptical reappraisal of Stevenson's data by Ian Wilson, one of the most thorough and objective researchers into the subject. He has noted that all too often the child comes from a poor family and that the past life remembered is of a person who was from a higher social caste. Random accounts of reincarnation would make this pattern seem highly unlikely and to Wilson it is clear evidence of only one thing – a motive.

Given the social acceptance of reincarnation in these cultures, were a family to concede that the child presented to them is really their dead relative they would feel an obligation to help the new parental guardians of this soul. Fraud for financial reasons must always seem an option in many cases that Stevenson has investigated, even though he himself disputes this conclusion.

Déjà vu

Another way to address the problem is to assess the growing number of cases where déjà vu and past lives seem to interact. To illustrate the point, American researcher D. Scott Rogo describes a personal investigation into an experience which occurred in 1971 to a woman who had just moved from Virginia to New Jersey, a state she had never visited before. As she was driving north on the New Jersey turnpike with a friend, a powerful sense of awareness hit her very hard. The feeling of familiarity was so intense that she told her friend about the scenery they were about to drive through and about a house a mile or so down the road in which she felt she had once lived.

As she was doing all this, a vision in her mind enveloped her present-day thinking processes and placed her as a girl of about six just before her death around the turn of the century. She saw and felt the experience in precise detail – from her grandmother fastening her shoes to herself playing on a swing in the garden. She also described walking down the street to a drugstore. It was all very real. The two bemused women drove into a little town and found the house in question, although it had no swing. There, too, just as directed, was the drugstore – now all boarded up and empty, but with its structure pretty much as she had just seen it during her vision.

What are we to make of events like this? In the discussion of pre-cognition (see page 175) it was explained that déjà vu could relate to a memory of a dream that may have previewed the future and is buried in the subconscious mind. The fact of having seen the house in a previous dream may have been bursting to get out when the events started to unfold in real life, thus creating a sense of familiarity. Could a cryptomnesia memory of, let us say, old photographs of this town at the turn of the century also have lodged in the mind and provoked a vivid experience such as described? Or was a memory of some real past life lurking in the deepest mind of this modern woman, only to be reactivated when she drove past familiar scenery for the first time in seventy years?

Whichever explanation we consider, the mechanism by which such a remarkable process takes place still leaves unanswered questions. At the very least it tells us that the human mind has extraordinary untapped potential. Perhaps cases such as this – which are far from uncommon – offer the best way to explore the possibility of reincarnation.

EXPERIENCING REINCARNATION

If there is such a thing as a past life memory, it seems probable that we all have many of them buried in our subconscious mind. The trick is to access this information, which probably means that you will only see images of a past life whilst in some altered state of consciousness. How would you recognise such evidence amidst the dreams, memories and fantasies of your present life? The most likely source is by way of vivid dreams or images that flash into your awareness very unexpectedly, perhaps when you are daydreaming or just idling away a boring journey.

Since childhood I have had a recurrent vision of a cottage in a wood. It is not a house that I recognise, but it has a range of distilled emotions attached to its appearance. More than once it has entered my mind when I have been fully awake – like a picture thrust in front of my eyes for just one instant. It freezes out every other image or feeling, and is incredibly vivid despite being so transient.

Researchers into past lives argue that this could be a fond memory from a prior existence – perhaps a house I once lived in. I have come across many people whose exploration of a past life begins like this, from a single image. It is often something anomalous and clearly dating from before their birth in their present life. This discrepancy forces them to confront the reality of a possible earlier existence. But my cottage is sufficiently timeless that it could exist today as easily as being a memory from years ago.

However, on a long train journey that I do very often I was once staring out at the rolling landscape passing before my eyes and possibly entering a light hypnotic state without intention. Suddenly I saw a different image that was very clear. I was standing in a square in Manchester, a city I knew well, watching trams go past. I saw the scene as if through my own eyes looking at the trams. The image, fantasy or memory lasted only a moment, but it shocked me. I had been born several years after the last trams had run in Manchester and could not have really witnessed such a scene. Where did this image come from?

The chances are fairly high that you too will have an unusual dream or flash image that has cropped up at least once in your life. Whether you will be motivated to explore a possible past life as a result of what you see is much more improbable. Certainly there is no way I could decide whether the source of the cottage scene is just a fantasy of somewhere I would like to live, a distant memory of a real cottage seen way back in my childhood, or a true image from another lifetime.

The tram scene is different. Could it be a fantasy I created around a desire to have once seen a tram in Manchester – perhaps based on a film or TV drama? Curiously, some years after my vision Manchester brought back trams and they ran right past the spot where I was standing in my vision. I have stood at that point in reality in recent years and watched the trams go by, trying to relive that one-off occurrence, but have failed dismally to recapture the vividness of the image and emotion. I am fairly sure, too, that this was not a precognition, since the trams in my vision were very old vehicles. From investigations in library records I would probably date the scene as the mid-1930s.

As you can see, many complex possibilities arise from one simple, momentary image. The mind is such a fascinating area of exploration that nobody really knows how some experiences begin. Hunting for a past life to decode a fleeting image is one option that could be followed, but there are also many other possibilities to take into account.

Emotional triggers

One man from Norfolk told me of his starting point – an image of a German soldier in an unusual uniform that kept cropping up throughout childhood and adolescence. He had not studied the Second World War, which had ended well before he was born. Moreover, the uniform was not like those shown in war films and so seemed inaccurate. But he kept experiencing the same image and eventually chose to dig deeper.

This act of exploration seemed to open up the locked images within his mind, and as the years went by he had more vivid and complete dreams. The more he checked these images against history, the more they were verified. He 'knew' he was killed fighting a certain battle on a given date in 1944. Much of the detail proved correct. Then he stopped seeking the real existence of the clearly remembered soldier whose name was embedded in his mind. He had gone as far as he wished to go.

Only you can decide whether a dream or vision – or even a memory induced by other methods, such as relaxation therapy or hypnotic regression – feels powerful enough to be potentially a past life. This is a very subjective judgement, but there seems little to lose by starting to explore the possibility of a genuine memory. If nothing else it might free the trauma it reflects, which could be important if the image is an unpleasant one such as a sudden, violent death – and that is not infrequently the case.

Indeed, the predominance of violent or emotional memories as the trigger for these possible past life images is itself most intriguing. Emotion is frequently the apparent trigger that sets a paranormal event in motion. If a past life is a real memory, emotions and traumas from those days would be just the scenes we might expect to break out from the subconscious mind – just as they seem to do when generating precognition or ESP.

RESEARCHING REINCARNATION

Whilst the exploration of your own past lives is the most tempting to carry out, from the viewpoint of meaningful research it will always be tainted. Thanks to a nurse practising relaxation therapy I probed my cottage and 'relived' a life from two hundred years ago in the Forest of Dean – a place I have never visited. The village I named does exist, but had I seen it somewhere on a map or in a book?

It is much better to try to investigate the memories of other people and seek verification. Hypnosis should be avoided; unless you are medically qualified it is not a good idea to incite such a volatile state of consciousness. Evidence also suggests that much of what emerges from hypnotic regression is fantasy and cryptomnesia (and potentially all of it may be). However, there are a few cases on record where a humdrum life seems unlikely to be fantasised, or details emerge that were unknown to anyone at the time and yet were later verified. So it is not fair to be too dismissive.

Nevertheless other states of consciousness offer access to alleged past life memories just as readily. The so-called Christos method works rather like the conditions used for remote viewing experiments: a deep state of relaxation is imposed and the person describes into a tape recorder the images that come into their mind. The problem is that some guidance is necessary to direct the experiment, but once you start suggesting that a person relives past lives he or she may unconsciously fabricate something simply to fulfil that request; I sensed this during my own foray into my 'past'. Therefore any past life memory deliberately provoked into existence risks a high level of distortion and fantasy. You may have to be prepared to track information on dozens of cases before any event comes to light that is potentially real.

Another problem concerns the time, effort and extreme difficulty involved in trying to verify evidence. Two cases which I explored for the BBC make the point. In the first a woman described brief scenes from her life in London earlier in the century, working at a publisher's office and living in a certain street. Much information was given, which could all be checked out through obscure reference books and calls to the office of the publisher, which still existed although under another name. Sadly no matching facts ever came to light and in some instances the past life recall was simply wrong. Things were not like they were said to be at the time and place in question, so the memories must have been fantasies.

Another woman came out with a memory of life as a pig farmer's daughter centuries ago. She spoke in a rich accent, later verified and located geographically. She described her pigs, gave their names, and talked about the local woods and how they made cider at the nearby inn. But names, dates, places and verifiable information were all elusive, despite weeks of effort. There was simply no way to prove or disprove this young girl had ever existed. All too often that is the case.

Despite the sceptics' view that past life memories tell of famous or romantic characters, that is not generally true: the majority are remarkably mundane. Unfortunately, since their reality can never be established the few colourful ones gain most attention because they are easier to confirm or deny.

REINCARNATION TODAY

Recent exploration of past life stories has developed in curious directions. A number of theories are emerging that do not blame the experience on a genuine reincarnation but seek a different paranormal source. Even some of the best-known witnesses refuse to go on record as saying that they believe they really were the person whose experience they describe during a 'past life memory'.

Some researchers believe that the reliving of a past life serves as a therapeutic tool, and it is a technique that is being used increasingly to help patients suffering from phobias. Not all the therapists who champion its value believe that their patients do recall a past life; some feel they are tapping aspects of our own psychology out of which a drama is built. Yet the act of living through that drama can help to check a problem that is associated with a person's fragmented subconscious mind.

Small details

Hypnotherapist Joe Keeton, who has no set view on whether there is genuine reincarnation, worked with a woman (now his wife) to try to help her with her deep and irrational fear of the sea. Since she lived close to water, on the Wirral peninsula in the north-west England this was a potential problem.

Monica O'Hara described a detailed past life in which she had been born in 1895, over fifty years before her real date of birth. This was in in a Cornish village of which she had never heard. Much specific information was given, including her name, that of the house where she lived, details of her relationship with a farm labourer and her family's disapproval of this liaison. When she was seventeen they ran away together – unfortunately booking passage on the maiden voyage of the *Titanic*! Monica described her traumatic death aboard the stricken liner, an event which had left a lingering fear of the sea eighty years later.

This witness was sufficiently intrigued to travel over 300 miles to Cornwall and investigate her own memory. She found the house, now a hotel of the same name, and described a pond in the garden which was no longer present. The current owners agreed that it had once existed but had been filled in. Whether this verification proves cryptomnesia or that Monica O'Hara recalled a genuine past life is less important than the way in which its unravelling greatly reduced her fear of water.

Researcher Jim Alexander published his findings in an even more detailed case. A woman born in 1952 suffered powerful nightmares. His therapy for these led to a series of dramatic memories of the short life of Janice Kershaw, born in 1920 in Leeds and dying there with intense head pains at the age of thirty-one. A huge wealth of information was provided about the slums of a city that the present woman does not know at all. She gave exact details of streets, houses, pubs, cinemas and so on in an area largely redeveloped in 1954.

As Jim points out, we can never be sure of the origin of such information but it certainly indicates the extraordinary nature of past life memories. This was no wonderful life. It is the sheer number of verifiable trivialities about Janice Kershaw's day to day existence that are so impressive.

Challenging cryptomnesia

Verification of an alleged past life came to Ken Llewelyn in 1994 by very different means. Dreams and hypnosis were but minor aspects of his story; much of the impetus that drove him on came through messages reputedly conveyed to him from the spirit world.

Ken was a senior public relations officer with the Royal Australian Air Force in Canberra. He had a desk job because his desire to fly was thwarted by a phobia that struck whenever he was at high altitudes. Desperate to find out why, he undertook a long quest that suggested he had been shot down over England as a German bomber pilot during the Second World War.

After considerable effort he located the time and place where he believed that his Dornier had crashed and he had been decapitated trying to escape. Bit by bit his evidence began to match facts painstakingly uncovered from obscure sources. Finally he traced and met a member of his crew whom he had ordered to parachute out of the doomed aircraft. As the only man to get out of the crash alive, only he knew exactly what had occurred inside the plane. The account which Ken Llewelyn offered – supposedly from his past life memory – seems to fit in every significant detail with the co-pilot's recall of the actual event.

Jenny Cockell's story

Cases such as this seem to challenge cryptomnesia. In perhaps the most astonishing reincarnation story yet told, the chances of cryptomnesia seem almost zero. Once again hypnosis was not much of a factor; it was used in a limited way and only after much of the detail had emerged.

Jenny Cockell, a mother and chiropodist born in Northamptonshire in 1953, grew up with a series of visions and dreams of fleeting images. These seemed to be of a time and place she could not identify but which she felt was very real. She worried them around so much that she never lost recall, as she believes many children do with similar memories of past lives as they grow older. Eventually Jenny set out to find a house, a jetty and a seaside location in these images.

After much exploration she linked the experience to Malahide, a town near Dublin in Ireland, a country which she had never visited. Masses of new information flowed out and she became convinced she was a woman called Mary who had died young from illness, leaving a large family. The name O'Neill emerged out of hypnosis.

Jenny decided to seek her children from this past life. It turned out that a woman called Mary Sutton was the source of her visions. Her children had been adopted and scattered across Britain and Australia after their mother's death. Jenny felt that it was this 'guilt' at splitting her family that made the memory of her past life so persistent.

In the end, the TV series *Strange but True?* took her to Ireland, where she was reunited with some of her children, now grown up. The way in which she could swap anecdotes at the ruined site of the cottage where the family had lived during the 1920s and 1930s was truly astonishing: tiny details of daily life that would never have been written down anywhere were remembered.

For cryptomnesia to work here we must suppose that Jenny, as a small child, somehow and somewhere overheard talk about the life of this obscure, scattered family and then for some inexplicable reason let this become the source of a powerful lifelong fantasy. Even if one can accept this idea, the wealth of verifiable information seems difficult to explain away.

Since Jenny told her story in 1993, more information has emerged. Under hypnosis she had come up with the name O'Neill, rather than Sutton, and this had baffled her. But on a trip to Malahide she was contacted by a garage owner who told her that Mary Sutton had earned some money by working for a family in a local house. These well-to-do folk were the O'Neills.

Whilst the Jenny Cockell case is extraordinary, a lesser-known aspect of it seems even more bizarre. For Jenny has other images in her mind which she believes relate to further lifetimes, and she has started to probe these. However, that has so far proved very difficult because she believes them to be scenes from a life that has yet to begin – a twenty-first-century incarnation!

Somehow it seems harder to accept a future life than one from the past; although if precognition is a reality, future lives may not be as ridiculous as they appear. Unfortunately, it is almost impossible to verify the life of someone not yet born – and Jenny Cockell will probably never be able to confirm it because he or she will be born after she has died. None the less, as she points out, her future children from that future life may be incarnated today, as someone else, and it is these people she wants to trace. Quite how someone will respond to being approached by an apparent stranger who claims they will give birth to them half a century from now is open to considerable speculation.

Children's tales

The way in which Jenny Cockell received spontaneous images from a past life from when she was a young child has provoked an active search for similar cases. Evidence suggests that more children than might be imagined have such memories, but rarely talk about them.

Dr Ian Stevenson's work from countries which accept reincarnation indicates that between perhaps three and eight years of age children, when encouraged to do so, not infrequently describe having anomalous images in their memory that relate to a time before their birth. Occasionally, they even identify with an actual person from the past.

A number of cases other than Jenny Cockell's exist from Europe. They include two young girls from Northumberland who had remarkable memories that seemed to match their two sisters, killed before their own birth in a tragic car accident. There was even a birthmark that seemed to coincide with a scar on the body of one previous child, caused by a tumble off her bike. In another case a Manchester lad described his gruesome death in the American West during the nineteenth century as if it were quite normal. And a Yorkshire child offered extraordinary detail about a life as a man killed in an obscure train crash a hundred years before.

In all these cases the children forgot about their 'past life' completely after the age of about eight. Jenny Cockell may simply have resisted this natural amnesia.

It is difficult to face the ethical challenge of asking young children if they recall past life scenes. The concept of reincarnation will not be familiar to them and most parents would be reluctant to introduce it at that age. They may also not be sufficiently strong in their recall to 'know' that the puzzling images in their head come from another lifetime. Those cases that we know about only occur when a child is motivated to talk for themselves, and when the adults around them do not immediately write off their stories as imagination or plain silliness. Scolding of this innocent yet destructive nature is rife within our society and may well have killed off many past life memories.

Of course, the fact that children describe such memories does not prove that they had genuine past lives. However, the very young are far less likely than adults to have encountered enough material to develop cryptomnesia stories. They also tend to lack the motivation for either conscious or unconscious deception. But what we have here may still simply be a complex process of the human mind – perhaps an ability to tap into a kind of universal store of knowledge, which comes more naturally to children when they are developing their imaginative skills than it does to an adult who has been indoctrinated to reject mental images as both inferior and unimportant.

SOURCES

ORGANISATIONS AND PERIODICALS

Although many paranormal organisations such as the *SPR* and *ASPR* investigate past life stories on an ad hoc basis, the most systematic research is conducted by *ASSAP*, who have operated a ten-year programme of study into spontaneous cases. However, the best source of information is a new journal launched in 1993 by noted researcher Roy Stemman under the clever slogan 'Reincarnation is making a comeback'. This is the only journal that updates new cases and research findings. It also sells a catalogue listing therapists and practitioners who offer to explore past life images.

Reincarnation International   *PO Box 26, London WC2H 9LP, UK.*

More in-depth scientific results such as those of Dr Ian Stevenson, together with debates on the issues raised, are published from time to time in:

The Journal of Scientific Exploration   *ERL 306, Stanford University, Stanford, CA 94305, USA.*

A list of British past life therapists is published by:.

Atlantis   *37 Bromley Road, St Anne's on Sea, Lancashire, FY8 1PQ, UK.*

In the USA a similar service is provided by:

The Association for Past Life Research and Therapies   *PO Box 20151, Riverside, CA 92516-0151, USA.*

BOOKS

Many books exist, and the following have been selected to provide a good grounding. Bernstein tells the story of the first notable case (later editions discuss the controversy over the evidence). Stevenson's first paper has been followed by material published by the University of Virginia, particularly his 1987 and 1990 collections of data on spontaneous child memories. The first Keeton book contains many transcripts from his hypnosis sessions, and the original edition was even accompanied by a record to let you hear the past life stories unfold 'live'! His later book explores some of his therapy work and more recent theories after twenty-five years of research. The book by Wilson is widely considered the most objective sceptical appraisal of the subject, stating the case for cryptomnesia. The paperback contains a new chapter with extra research findings. Hodgkinson is a medical journalist who provides a nicely balanced review of the evidence which would be a good modern starting point. The Cockell book is her own account of the most remarkable case of all. My own two books are based on the TV series *Strange but True?*, and each includes an investigation of a modern case. The first is an American one in which various residents of a town during the Civil War have allegedly found one another in modern California and are exploring their interlocking memories. The casebook reports on what is one of the best hypnosis cases – a man whose past life as a soldier in the Crimean War has been traced through obscure records and verified in considerable detail.

The Search for Bridey Murphy by Morey Bernstein (Doubleday, New York, 1956).

Twenty Cases Suggestive of Reincarnation by Ian Stevenson (American Society for Psychical Research, Riverside, CA, 1966).

Encounters with the Past by Joe Keeton and Peter Moss (Sidgwick & Jackson, 1979).

Powers of the Mind by Joe Keeton and Simon Petherick (Robert Hale, 1987).

Mind out of Time by Ian Wilson (Gollancz, 1981; republished in paperback as **Reincarnation?**, 1983).

Reincarnation: The Evidence by Liz Hodgkinson (Piatkus, 1991).

Yesterday's Children by Jenny Cockell (Piatkus, 1993).

Strange but True? by Jenny Randles and Peter Hough (Piatkus, 1994).

Strange but True? Casebook by Jenny Randles (Piatkus, 1995).

Spontaneous human combustion

Definition

Often abbreviated simply to SHC, this is one of the most controversial phenomena to be considered by serious researchers. Most people, including many paranormal experts, remain unconvinced about its reality. Those who do accept it as a genuine phenomenon struggle to find a working explanation. But it has generated numerous horror stories in fact and fiction for more than a century and study of it seems to be gaining in popularity, despite – or because of – its gruesome nature.

The term spontaneous human combustion refers to the way in which a human body can reputedly burst into flames without any apparent external ignition source. One moment there is no sign of a problem, the next the person is ablaze. The burning is rarely witnessed and usually fatal; consequently, little is known from direct observation. But in the few cases where there are survivors or eye witnesses to an incident, reports sometimes tell of a bluish flame from within the abdominal area which is said to be the seat of the blaze.

More commonly, SHC is only suspected after the remains of a body are discovered. An obviously intense, yet mysteriously localised, fire has occurred inside a room. It has destroyed most of the person in that room – leaving untouched, in many cases, an extremity such as a foot or leg which may even be covered in unsinged clothing. All other parts of the body are reduced to ash – even the bones. This makes a post-mortem almost impossible.

Aside from the extent of the devastation to the body, which has shocked hardened firemen and police officers called to the scene, there is another reason why a less than natural fire becomes suspected. The immediate surroundings, even when they include highly flammable materials such as sofas or curtains, tend to escape without so much as a scorch mark. This baffles experts who have witnessed countless other deaths by fire where the surroundings have been totally destroyed. The spectre of SHC is therefore often invoked by them in an attempt to comprehend the nature of such fires.

Thankfully, SHC appears to be a very rare phenomenon. Few fire and police forensic officers come across a case during their entire working lives. This rarity has contributed to general disbelief, but should not preclude investigation altogether. Given its horrific nature and the potentially incredible forces, it is a subject worthy of both human concern and scientific interest.

HISTORICAL REVIEW

Although earlier cases almost certainly exist within historical records, the first known example of what may be SHC dates from June 1613 at Christchurch in Dorset. A woman awoke during a fierce electrical storm to find her son-in-law and young granddaughter burnt to death in their bed. Speculation might have been that they had been struck by lightning, or today we could suggest ball lightning (see page 30). However, the man's body continued to burn even after it had been removed from the room, and continued to do so for three days until it was no more than ash.

A more typical example occurred at Cesina in Italy in 1731, when a noblewoman went to bed feeling 'dull and heavy'. Next morning her remains were found beside the bed: they comprised just her feet up to the knee, three fingers and part of the skull. The remainder was ash. A thick, smelly soot covered windows and other parts of the room, and an oily yellow substance was running down the panes. But there was almost no fire damage beyond the body. The bedclothes immediately adjacent were untouched, suggesting that she had just got out of bed and stood up when disaster struck.

More recent cases have also included the yellow oil and black soot, which forensic tests have revealed to be residues from the combustion of the body. The yellow oil is in fact melted body fat which resolidifies on cooler surfaces such as window glass.

Victorian investigators

Although most cases of SHC occur inside rooms, examples are known from outdoors. The first well-attested case was reported in the *Boston Medical and Surgical Journal* by the attending physician, Dr B.H. Hartwell. The place was Ayer, Massachusetts and the date 12 May 1890. Called to an open field by a young boy screaming that his mother had started burning, he found a woman blazing from her abdomen and back. Her bones were exposed and alight and it was too late to save her. The fire was only put out by covering the torso with earth to cut off the oxygen supply. Despite the enormous heat a hat, leaves and other objects on the ground nearby were unaffected. No cause was apparent.

Cases such as these led to a growing belief in SHC during the Victorian era. The Christian fundamentalists seized on the theory that excess levels of highly combustible alcohol within the body might be the cause. It was argued that this 'fire from heaven' could strike without warning as God's punishment for drunkards.

Several novels, such as Herman Melville's *Redburn* of 1849, were based on this theme. However, the most famous fictional death by SHC came from the pen of Charles Dickens, whose character Krook in *Bleak House* was fated in this manner. Dickens was the first serious SHC researcher. He had come across a case when he was a court reporter and been so intrigued that he later collected thirty examples that were on record. From this he isolated patterns such as the oily deposit, blue flame and leaving of the body extremities. SHC was apparently a strangely consistent phenomenon, even if by this time most scientists regarded it as mere superstition. Dickens strenuously defended this episode in his novel against its critics by pointing out that he had studied the evidence and it seemed that something strange was definitely taking place.

The Florida enigma

Throughout the next fifty years SHC remained an uninvestigated mystery that, given its nature, few people wanted to debate. There was also an unspoken conspiracy among coroners, doctors, fire officers and forensic scientists to ignore puzzling cases that might have been examples, simply because the idea was regarded as impossible.

Then, on 1 July 1951, sixty-seven-year-old Mary Reeser died at St Petersburg, Florida, in the first SHC case to attract popular media attention as it happened. She was seen alive the night before and found hours later with just a few pieces of bone and one undamaged foot to attest to her presence. The rest of her was burnt to ash, yet minimal damage had been done to her apartment.

Her son was a doctor, and police investigations failed to find any reason for her demise. After this blank had been drawn the FBI were called in. They painstakingly procured data at the scene, yet they too failed to find any natural explanation. The photographs of the aftermath of the tragedy were the first to be made public and the case became a celebrated example, frequently alluded to by paranormal writers over the coming years.

Several investigations of the case followed. One, undertaken by sceptics Joe Nickell and John Fischer in the 1980s suggested she had dropped a cigarette and then suffered a slow, lingering burning after catching fire. In the 1990s Peter Hough and I accessed much of the original FBI data and did a reappraisal which suggested why this theory might not work. The case remains an enigma.

Since 1951 occasional stories about SHC have surfaced in the media, but it remains an issue that most people choose to avoid. A collection of stories revisiting the old cases but with little new material was published in the seventies and until 1993 remained the only book on the subject, but no major systematic study had ever been published.

The wick or candle effect

Following on from Nickell and Fischer's ideas about the Mary Reeser case came the first working sceptical theory. It was proposed by various doctors including combustion expert Dr Dougal Drysdale from Edinburgh University, and was known as the wick or candle effect. The human body can be thought of as akin to a candle. The bones are the wick and these are surrounded by body fat just as tallow encircles the wick in a candle. If there is a source of ignition – for instance, if the person has a heart attack and falls into the fire or a cigarette is dropped down their clothing – then burning can begin. If for some reason the victim does not put it out (they may be drunk or dead) the fire will escalate. Should they be alone in a room for many hours the gradual combustion process will slowly cook the bones to ash as the body fat melts and consumes itself. The body is in effect baked in an oven of its own making; as there is no great source of outward radiated heat, the focus of damage is the body.

This theory is well designed and looks plausible. After April 1989, when BBC television screened a documentary which supported this rational solution, SHC as a paranormal mystery seemed to be a thing of the past. However, as recent events have come to suggest, it may not be quite as straightforward as that.

EXPERIENCING SHC

If there is such a phenomenon as real SHC, recent estimates suggest that you are extremely unlikely to come across it directly, or even indirectly, via family or friends. A country the size of Britain probably experiences at most between two and five cases per year which are even potential examples. Perhaps fifty per annum may occur globally. The odds of it happening to anyone that you know are rather less than having a relative get struck by lightning. By its very nature, even if it does occur in your neighbourhood you are unlikely to witness it taking place. Your only contact is almost certain to be after the event.

However, supposing that you did see a person spontaneously burst into flames, what could you do about it? Speed is clearly important, the few eye witness cases on record imply that the flames can be extinguished, but often only with difficulty. Cutting off the oxygen supply is the most effective method – smothering the area of flame, which is likely to be quite small and probably emerging from the midriff.

You might imagine that the best solution would be to throw water on to the flames, but this is thought to be less successful. Some researchers argue that SHC functions by breaking down the body into its constituent gases through some unknown electrical method. As 70 per cent of a human body comprises water anyway this clearly does not inhibit the flames; and if the trigger force is electrolysing body water into hydrogen and oxygen, adding more may only increase the fuel source.

If you come upon the aftermath of an SHC incident and nothing can be done for the victim, taking photographs or samples of residue will appear both callous and an unjustifiable intrusion into the grief of relatives. However, it may well be the only way to establish whether SHC has occurred. Until some evidence of this kind is gathered outside the normally restrictive methods of official investigators we may never know the truth. Sadly, the police may even consider action of this sort to be tampering with a potential crime scene.

RESEARCHING SHC

The candle theory is an excellent example of a hypothesis built out of observed patterns within the data, and whether you accept or reject this theory it ought to be a model for all future work. Police and fire officers are in the best position to study the evidence as they are likely to be called to the scene. If you are in this situation, familiarise yourself with the characteristics of SHC and be willing to consider the possibility that it might occur. If in doubt, it is worth consulting experts and carefully recording any possible clues.

A common problem reported by the few who have been willing to collect data is that their superior officers or the coroner refuse to allow any hint of SHC in their report; an unexplained death is regarded as preferable. Protection of a victim's family is a more responsible reason, because it is unfair on relatives to encourage tabloid interest in a possible SHC case.

Unfortunately, such problems prevent evidence from being collated. It is very hard to get access to reports after the enquiry is closed, because they are often not considered public property. Indeed, a coroner's judgement as to whether a person has a 'need to know' frequently excludes even close relatives, and hardly ever extends to SHC researchers.

This means that the key responsibility falls on the investigating officers. They should retain their own records even if prevented from making public their suspicion of SHC. Indeed, avoiding the media spotlight is a good idea since so little is yet known about the phenomenon. One day answers will probably be found that place SHC in the realms of known science, but in the meantime it is important to free it from unnecessary supernatural associations which are inspired by the media as well as by many paranormal researchers who ought to know better.

If you are the relative of someone who has died in a fire that you think may have been caused by SHC, try to access these records – you may find a helpful coroner. Without those records old cases become of very limited value.

Useful research can be done by anyone studying cases, seeking patterns and – particularly if you are a scientist – developing theories and testing these with laboratory experiments that duplicate the conditions as far as possible. Without more serious research of this kind SHC is sure to continue as it has for centuries, fodder for silly speculation and lacking any worthwhile evidence.

SHC TODAY

In 1989, at the time of the BBC documentary, Peter Hough and I were in the fourth year of what would be a seven-year study of SHC. It had begun when the police asked us to attend an inquest into a case from Cheshire. A teenage girl had died in January 1985 at Halton College in Widnes: she burst into flames whilst walking down the stairs in full view of several horrified witnesses. Whilst the coroner decided there was a simple, tragic cause – in his view smouldering clothes had ignited due to the updraught from the stairwell – we were less sure. We found significant unanswered questions and fire department evidence which the jury never got to see.

Before deciding to publish any of our research we decided to investigate the basis of the BBC theory. If it checked out, we would drop SHC as a legitimate field of enquiry. Yet one by one scientists, then fire and police officers who had featured on camera, offered us data that seemed to contradict the candle theory. Many expressed doubts about the way the BBC handled the subject.

Unanswered questions

Our strongest evidence came from a case which had happened on 28 December 1987, when a man was found in the kitchen of a flat in Folkestone, Kent. Or rather one foot and a trainer shoe were discovered – the rest of his body had turned to ash, though there was very little damage to the room. The BBC film used photographs of the scene and concluded that it was a classic example of the candle effect. A police officer, who did not later reply to our questions, said they had eliminated all other theories such as murder. This forced them to suggest a different scenario.

The victim was found near a lit cooker ring. It was proposed that he must have had a heart attack, fallen against the cooker, caught fire and then burned slowly. Fifteen hours elapsed between his last being seen alive and the discovery of the remains. This was vital, as laboratory experiment has shown that the candle effect needs many hours to have any chance of working.

Kent police refused to make available to us the photographic evidence – which millions had already seen on TV. Yet the scientists we were consulting needed access if any meaningful conclusions were to be drawn. The police argued that the photographs were 'pornographic' (their choice of word). As we had no 'need to know', we could also not see the report.

Undaunted, we tracked down and spoke to key people involved with the case; some worrying factors emerged. The coroner, for example, told us he could not rule out SHC and had reached an open verdict. A police officer involved in the case said there were baffling questions that were still outstanding. There was some medical evidence that the victim had been alive when the fire was raging. But perhaps most serious was what we discovered when we traced the first person to enter the room – the man who had found the remains and called the police. He had seen the lit cooker ring and there was something else on it – a half-filled kettle of water. As there was no sign of a break-in and the victim lived alone, he must have placed the kettle on the stove himself. It was impossible for him to have done so the night before, then slowly combusted over many hours – at least not without the water boiling dry and the gas jet burning a hole right through the bottom of the kettle.

So the victim was probably alive only an hour or so before he was found. The total devastation of his body could not therefore be due to the candle effect, which needs many hours to operate.

Findings such as this demonstrate that SHC is still a viable option in some cases – provided that an acceptable scientific mechanism can be found by which the process might occur. A few scientists are now working on possible theories, which fall into three categories.

Combustible gases

Chemists argue that a lethal cocktail of products from our diet might produce a spontaneous chain reaction inside the digestive system. Perhaps excess combustible gases are produced, or a self-fuelling, heat-making product that burns its way slowly from inside the body. This would explain the difficulty in quenching the fire (if it is internally generated) and might also fit the way in which the fire seems to begin in and around the abdomen. The problem is finding a viable yet natural chemical reaction that would be rare enough to occur only in unique circumstances.

Another group of theories concentrates on electricity as the trigger. Some people have very high levels of electrical charge naturally occurring inside their bodies and can even get shocks when they kiss other people. Studies by Dr Michael Shallis at Oxford University have suggested a link with diet here too. Perhaps, some SHC researchers argue, people living alone in an environment without a lot of metal cannot use the natural method of releasing this pent-up energy. If the charge went unrelieved for days it might start to break up constituent chemicals in the body by way of electrolysis and ionisation. Nobody has shown that such a theory could work, although it might explain the pattern Peter Hough and I found in a statistical analysis of 120 cases of SHC. Many of them involved elderly people who were house-bound.

Coming right up to date, some theories are based on the release of nuclear energy from within the body. A related argument is that ball lightning, which might have a great deal of nuclear energy locked inside a small area, might form inside a human body, or enter it, and then release this incredible power. This might produce an explosive heat reaction that rapidly consumes the body. Whilst this is speculative and depends upon ball lightning, another mystery about which we still know little (see page 30), it does fit one clue – the reference in several cases to electrical storms or small balls of light seen in the vicinity before an SHC victim is found.

In June 1993 two German scientists at the Heligoland Biological Institute, Dieter Glindemann and Gunter Gassmann, reported in the scientific press that they had discovered phosphane gas inside the digestive systems of cattle. This is a highly combustible gas thought to create will-o-the-wisps – floating pockets of burning gas that have for centuries been misinterpreted as fairies, spirits and more recently UFOs.

From this work the Germans suspected that even higher levels would occur inside human beings, which they proved. However, in vegetarians the levels were much lower. Using this data, SHC researchers suggest that a chemical reaction involving excess phosphane gas within the gut might trigger combustion in the digestive system. If this could be demonstrated it might explain why there are more reports of SHC in Western cultures and few in regions of the world where phosphane would rarely enter the food chain.

Another important clue might have emerged in February 1994 when a woman was taken into Riverside, a Californian hospital, in the latter stages of terminal cancer, with her cell structure degenerating. Before she died, all the members of the medical team attending her collapsed with symptoms ranging from mild nausea and dizziness to incapacitation that left them in hospital for many weeks. A strong, ammonia-like smell was said to have emanated from the dying woman's body and her blood had reputedly begun to semi-crystallise.

So serious was the outbreak that extraordinary precautions were taken, including evacuating the hospital and constructing a special sealed location for the autopsy, which was performed by doctors wearing radiation suits. Radiation posioning was suspected, but ruled out. No medical solution was found, and the official conclusion was that the medical team had suffered a form of mass hysteria with psychosomatic symptoms. This is a view which they utterly reject and which indeed seems hard to equate with the facts.

As part of the fight against this theory, which were it proven might infer that they did not provide full care to the dying woman, they have worked with chemical researchers to find an alternative answer. They are seeking to prove that a combination of natural products and human blood could have led to a freak chain reaction. This complex event inside the system of the dying woman might then have produced a toxic chemical that escaped from her body when blood samples were extracted by the emergency team.

Such a contentious theory is unproven, but if established might leave the way open for a similar process to trigger cases of SHC. At least it will make such a possibility seem more feasible to the many sceptical scientists who still dismiss these baffling fire deaths as a myth.

SOURCES

ORGANISATIONS AND PERIODICALS

No research organisation exists simply to investigate SHC. However, *Naro Minded* have followed through some examples and the magazine *Fortean Times* publishes updates (see, in particular issues 24, 25, 35, 39 and 74); some US cases such as the *Riverside* affair appear in *Strange*. The US journal *The Anomalist* is also interested in serious theories and scientific reports on case investigations. Candle effect research has been published by the *Skeptical Inquirer* (for instance in the summer 1987 issue).

The Anomalist *PO Box 12434, San Antonio, TX 78212, USA.*

Fortean Times *Box 2409, London NW5 4NP, UK.*

Naro Minded *6 Silsden Avenue, Lowton, Warrington, WA3 1EN, UK.*

Skeptical Inquirer *PO Box 229, Buffalo, NY 14215, USA.*

Strange *PO Box 2246, Rockville, MD 20847, USA.*

BOOKS

Gaddis is probably the first author to discuss SHC at any length, but in a wider supernatural context. Harrison devotes an entire volume to pre-1970s' cases. Some of Nickell and Fischer's SHC work is in their book, which takes a more general sceptical approach to the paranormal. The first book by Hough and me contains a detailed examination of the Halton College affair, after which we became the first SHC researchers invited to attend an inquest on a suspect case. The second book is our report on seven years' research into the outstanding questions regarding SHC and our reasons for questioning the candle effect theory.

Mysterious Fires and Lights by Vincent Gaddis (McKay, New York, 1967).

Fire from Heaven by Michael Harrison (Sidgwick & Jackson, 1976).

Secrets of the Supernatural by Joe Nickell and John Fischer (Prometheus Books, New York, 1988).

Death by Supernatural Causes? by Peter Hough and Jenny Randles (Grafton, 1987).

Spontaneous Human Combustion by Jenny Randles and Peter Hough (Robert Hale, 1993, and Berkley, New York, 1994).

SYNCHRONICITY

DEFINITION

This peculiar word was coined by a unique team in the field of paranormal research, leading quantum physicist Dr Wolfgang Pauli and famed psychologist Dr Carl Jung. Technically it means the coming together of events to form what many might simply refer to as a coincidence.

However, Jung and Pauli had something more than just coincidence in mind when they decided upon the concept. It is not meant to describe two events that just happen side by side according to the laws of chance. Synchronicity infers a *meaningful* coincidence – one that is intimately part of the fabric of the universe, an invisible, subtle, guiding principle.

Put simply, if you have a birthday on 30 October and some new neighbours move in and one of them also has a birthday on that date, this is a coincidence. There are only 366 possible birthdays, and the odds of two being shared amongst four or five people are not startlingly high. Fantastic odds of millions to one against do sometimes come up trumps, so many of us love to enter lotteries. We know that the chance of our winning is probably minute, but also that someone, somewhere is going to win – so these odds are great enough to let us keep hoping it will be our turn next.

Given these facts, why should any coincidence be more than just coincidence? That is where synchronicity comes into force, suggesting that when a coincidence works in some seemingly controlled way that an extra factor may be at work.

To take the lottery example, if six numbers come up and they chance to be the six that you have chosen at random, it's just your lucky day. But what if you are travelling to fill out your coupon and six numbers impress themselves upon you in some forceful and bizarre way – say a car nearly runs into you and you note its number plate, someone stops you in the street and asks directions to a certain numbered house, and so on. If the chain of events strikes you as odd and you enter all six numbers and they subsequently come up, that is a meaningful coincidence – or a synchronicity.

Unfortunately, it is not always as straightforward or obvious as that. You may have to work hard to find synchronicities and let them benefit your life.

HISTORICAL REVIEW

Games of chance have existed for centuries, certainly as far back as the Greeks and Romans, so our preoccupation with coincidence is a long-standing matter. However, it is less apparent when what we might now call a meaningful occurrence was first recognised.

The ancient Chinese discovered the *I Ching*, still popular today even amongst new age communities in the West. In effect this uses synchronicity to offer guidance on your day-to-day problems. Yarrow sticks or, in the West, coins are tossed and a pattern is read from the way they land. This directs you to a verse in the *I Ching* book filled with fairly general psychobabble. The idea is that you will throw, through meaningful coincidence, the right pattern to allow you to read the text and answer your question. On face value this concept is absurd, but for thousands of years people have sworn by its efficacy. It may simply be a way to tap that mysterious inner force that generates synchronicities.

Sheep and goats

Astrology in its purest form may work in a similar way. Rather than non-existent magnetic influences from distant planets ruling our lives, the patterns in the heavens may simply synchronise with inner patterns that manifest in the fabric of the universe. So we can use the very visible planetary motions to try to obtain a sense of the more ethereal inner workings that operate deep and unseen through our consciousness. Once attuned in this way, we may goad ourselves into synchronistic happenings – which make it look as if the planets rule our lives.

This may well explain the long-recognised fact that if you believe in something, or develop a positive mental attitude towards it, you are far more likely to find it working for you. Indeed, sceptics of the para-normal in general may take this attitude largely because their intense disbelief creates a disharmony with the workings of the universe. This then effectively blocks synchronicity, ESP, precognition and the like from occurring within their lives. Since they never experience it they naturally disbelieve it even more, and the wave of disbelief emitted by their consciousness reinforces their lack of potential for paranormal experience.

Researchers have given this well-known effect a name – the sheep and goat problem. People called sheep facilitate the paranormal because they accept it readily and allow things to happen without challenge. Goats butt in with endless objections that effectively prevent these things from flowing all around them. It is like swimming with the current and being carried off to strange adventures, or struggling against it and effectively standing still.

Cosmic jokes

The strangest coincidences slowly became recognised as having a paranormal association. The problem is that a mystical interpretation was often placed upon them – they were assumed to be gifts from the gods and so became portrayed in this way. Certainly they were frequently encountered in the nineteenth century. The astronomer Camille Flammarion told of one delightful episode.

The scientist was writing a book when some of his manuscript was whisked out through the window by a sudden blast of wind. Because it was wet outside he decided not to chase after the papers, but some days later he unexpectedly received them from the printers. One of their employees had found the pages scattered in the street outside the print shop, where they had been carried by the billowing winds. He assumed they had been dropped by the author on his way to deliver the manuscript and so thought nothing of it, merely collating them for printing. The chapter recovered in this synchronistic manner was, believe it or not, about the wind.

It is this seemingly intelligent – almost comical – aspect to synchronicity that is its most endearing quality, and the term 'cosmic joker' has been applied to it. However, it seems to serve a beneficial purpose more often than a malicious one.

Jung and Pauli

Various attempts to collect synchronicities have been made since as long ago as 1899, when the SPR first expressed an interest. An excellent, more recent grouping into patterns was published by the philosopher Arthur Koestler in 1972.

Jung approached the matter from his concept of the collective unconscious – the idea that at some deep inner point all minds might share a set of imagery independent of space and time. He saw this as the wellspring for dreams, premonitions and much of the paranormal. Coincidence was to him a very basic demonstration of how things link together at this intimate level.

Pauli, on the other hand, belonged to a new breed of quantum mechanics experts who had penetrated the atom and found that what we perceived as reality was a baffling product of statistical collisions, waves of energy and chance events that were inexplicably ordering themselves into a structured universe. Something was needed to bridge the gap between the large world of tables and chairs that was readily predictable and the micro-world of ghost-like particles and flowing energy out of which what to us appeared so solid and stable was inescapably built. It seemed as if mind and consciousness might hold the key, and that synchronicities might show how consciousness and matter could somehow interact at the most basic, sub-atomic level of the universe to bring about the very different world that we knew.

This was how the possibility that coincidentally occurring events might be shaped from within first emerged. At the very least it seemed that events might resonate with mental processes going on deep inside our collective unconscious. Nothing that either psychology or quantum physics has learnt in the fifty years since this idea was dreamt up has put much of a dent in its apparent validity. If anything, more and more physicists, entranced by the magical world they see through their electron microscopes and cyclotrons, are willing to acknowledge that Jung and Pauli might have been on to something.

EXPERIENCING SYNCHRONICITY

We all experience coincidences. The trick is to be alert to the moment when a coincidence oversteps the boundary and becomes a synchronicity. This can only come from careful observation of both your own life and those of people all around you.

Stay tuned this way and coincidences will fall into your lap. Once you have documented a number of them (keep a diary) you will be in a better position to judge their importance. For example, if you say, 'I wish so-and-so would call', and five minutes later the telephone rings and that person is on the line, this may seem exciting. But put it alongside a dozen other possible synchronicities from your records and you will see it as the weak throw-out it is.

Such an incident is probably just a coincidence. Even if it is supernatural, it is more likely that ESP was at work and you tuned in to your friend's intention to phone. That type of experience only becomes meaningful with added details. Not having heard from them in ten years might seem strong enough to qualify, but even then telepathy would be a better contender than synchronicity.

On the other hand, you might be walking down an unfamiliar street, pass a call box where the phone is ringing, pick it up and find your friend on the other end of the line (having misdialled the number they had intended to call and so been connected to the empty booth in error). Suddenly synchronicity has entered your life.

Learning to make distinctions such as these is important. The next step is to train yourself to respond to the occurrence of synchronicity, which may be working away in the background of your life attempting to get some sort of reaction. It does appear to be motivational and beneficial much of the time, so meaningful coincidence may indeed have a positive purpose.

A wonderfully simple example concerns actor Anthony Hopkins when he was asked to star in the movie *The Girl from Petrovka*. Try as he might, he could not find a copy of the novel to prepare for the role, but synchronicity took a hand. Wandering into a London tube station, he found a discarded copy of the book on a bench. Who knows what complicated processes of mind-scanning, decision-making and so on led him to be in the right place at the right time to find the book just when he needed it. Had he tried to rationalise this process as it was occurring the magic would probably have disappeared like a puff of smoke, for these things go on at a subconscious level and cannot be forced into taking place.

Even this coincidence has a fascinating ending, because when Hopkins flew abroad to make the movie he met the author of the novel who bemoaned his loss of a prized copy in which he had made some notes. He had lent it to someone in London. It was, of course, the very copy that the actor had found by way of serendipity.

Trusting your inner feelings

Sometimes you can get a sense of recognition when synchronicity is working beneath the surface. It is like a tickle inside the subconscious mind. A positive, near-elational feeling may accompany it. You simply ride a wave, like a surfer being carried along towards an unseen destination which he knows will bring pleasure and amusement. If you can avoid the temptation to question, it just might work. Once your rational mind intrudes, the pattern falls apart like a mirage. This may be because synchronicity is a right-hemisphere function of your brain and so operates through instinct and emotion. If too much cross-over from the left brain occurs, the rational, logical, mathematical thinking processes stop synchronicity in its tracks.

Learning to trust this inner feeling is difficult, but if you can harness it you should do so. One man told me that he was desperate for a certain type of hammer but no shop he visited had one. Mulling it over, letting his mind get carried away, he suddenly entered this synchronistic state in which forces conspire to help you out. As he wandered aimlessly down an alley, a hammer of exactly the right kind fell from the sky right beside him. He suspects that someone working on a window high above dropped it by accident. Of course, 'accident' is probably the wrong word here. Something conspired to let this man be where he was and to impose butterfingers on an unsuspecting workman.

RESEARCHING SYNCHRONICITY

Once you have grasped the peculiarities of this subject, usually by assessing events that unfold within your life, there is ample opportunity to scour the world for new data. Coincidences are out there just waiting to be uncovered.

This is one of those areas of the paranormal which you do not need laboratory facilities or university degrees in order to study. All you need to do is compile detailed records from as many sources as possible. One way is to compose a letter and ask your local newspaper to print it, or go on local radio and explain that you have launched a study programme into the level of coincidence in your town. The subject is of interest to so many people that you will probably get ready help from these sources in exchange for a progress report later on.

Simply collecting stories is the first step, but verifying them is just as important. Often this will not be possible because of the very nature of what is reported, but whenever there are independent witnesses who might verify an event get them on record.

Categorise your coincidences as well. There will, for instance, be some that are evidently more likely to be examples of telepathy (the ringing telephone variety) or precognition (when someone describes a dream which seemed to match later events). Siphon off the pure synchronicities and you will find that they break down into at least two broad groups – clusters and motivational incidents.

Clusters are of the type denoted by the old saying 'Accidents come in threes' – a piece of folk wisdom based on centuries of observation of clustering coincidences. Here a name, or phenomenon, seems to crop up in someone's life far too often for it to be just coincidence. Motivational stories, on the other hand – such as those concerning the discarded book or the falling hammer – lead a person into a situation that seems designed to bring them an advantage. It may be that clusters are really motivational events, but that the point of the motivation that was being impressed on the subconscious by the clustering events is simply never spotted. Or perhaps they are different processes altogether. It is too early to be sure – there is a lot of fascinating data collection for you to do first.

SYNCHRONICITY TODAY

The most fantastic coincidence that I have yet experienced occurred in 1983 when I had my weekly radio show. It was a synchronicity about synchronicity, and I am still astonished by it. It shows that when you take synchronicity seriously – for instance by writing or talking about the matter – these things start to happen all around you.

It began with a sequence of events that linked me with helping the police over the course of a few days when some thieves dumped their getaway car outside my front door. Then, on my way to the studios to record a trailer for a show about coincidence, I had a phone call from a man who wanted to report a star that had fallen out of the sky over Liverpool. At the radio station I heard that two youths had been killed by a goods train during the night when they inexplicably dumped their motorcycles and fled across the track into its path. From the incoming telex reports it was obvious that it had occurred in the same area and at the same time as the star fall. Was this falling star what had scared them? Should I call the police, who were baffled? What about the confidentiality of the witness who had called me?

As I mulled it over I was also debating my producer's request not to use the word 'synchronicity' on air. He told me that the mostly young, record-buying audience would not have heard of it. I pondered this and between records debated with a DJ whether I should tell the police about my phone call. Then, almost on cue, in walked two uniformed officers. They had come for a completely unrelated reason, but it felt like I was being kicked into action. The synchronistic mood was taking hold.

I did tell the police, but there is no neat outcome. To my knowledge they never solved the mystery of why the two youths ran across the track. A detective later told me that my hesitant theory about the star fall was as valid as any other.

But the most fantastic aspect to this story came on my way home that day. I was handed a free newspaper that advertised soon-to-be-released records. There in black and white was a predicted hot seller from the group Police. That album, based on the Jung and Pauli theory, was entitled *Synchronicity*. Within weeks the teenage record-buying audience of Radio City certainly knew the word that had so worried my producer, as the title track was being played time and again. More than that, this track, written by Sting obviously long before these synchronous events took place in my life, contained the incredibly appropriate line. 'A star fall, a phone call, it joins all, synchronicity.'

What can you say when something like that happens? You can see why coincidence is inadequate and why the idea of a meaningful process such as synchronicity had to be created.

Collecting evidence

After this amazing experience I was impelled to launch through ASSAP a project entitled 'The Incidence of Coincidence'. It brought together over a hundred examples and defined patterns like the cluster and motivational event. The research to record synchronicities in this way goes on.

In 1993 Jane Henry of the SPR reported on a more structured collection of evidence which she, Ruth West and the late Brian Inglis had put together. It began in December 1989 as an article in the *Sunday Observer* accompanied by a questionnaire which asked readers to describe their synchronicities; 991 people took the time to submit evidence, from a readership of perhaps 500,000. This major response infers that coincidence is a strong force in many people's lives. Some fascinating statistical analysis was undertaken with this material, and as a result we have learnt much about synchronicity. The reports seemed evenly spread across the sexes and social groups and most people were very open-minded about what was taking place, willing to consider chance coincidence as well as deeper ideas about the mind or ESP. Belief in the supernatural was not obviously a factor in whether co-incidences were reported.

By far the most common reports (74 per cent) were of the type where a phone rings and you know who is calling – which, if not simple co-incidence, is more likely to be explained by ESP. The next most common group was what the researchers term 'small world' coincidences, some of which may be motivational and others of which are probably pure coincidence. Typical here would be going on holiday and finding yourself unexpectedly sitting on the plane next to someone you know. Clusters accounted for 51 per cent of the reported coincidences, although these were of varying strangeness. Motivational events covered about 40 per cent of the data. These were the two most obvious and powerful sets of evidence, which certainly matches my ASSAP study.

SOURCES

ORGANISATIONS

If you have any reports of coincidences or intend to set up any studies for yourself, please contact me at the following address so that everybody's efforts can be coordinated.

The Incidence of Coincidence *11 Pike Court, Fleetwood, Lancashire, FY7 8QF, UK.*

PERIODICALS

Articles on coincidence appear from time to time in the *SPR Journal* and ASSAP's *Anomaly* magazine (see pages 100 and 28 for addresses). The following also sometimes carry reports.

Annals *4G Preston Manor, Wick Hollow, Glastonbury, Somerset, BA6 8JQ, UK.*

Folklore Frontiers *5 Egton Drive, Seaton Carew, Hartlepool, Cleveland, TS25 2AT, UK.*

BOOKS

In the following list, Jung outlines the concept of synchronicity, Vaughan and Anderson present a collection of cases, Koestler tries to address philosophical questions arising, and the Inglis book comes closest to a scientific assessment of the problem. My own book suggests a new category of 'super coincidence'. These chain reactions, as I call them, appear to warn of major events (the two examples I cite are of a nuclear power plant leak and the space shuttle disaster). This comes by way of an incredible chain of individually trivial, yet seemingly linked, synchronicities forming on a global scale.

Synchronicity by Carl Jung (in association with Wolfgang Pauli) (Routledge & Kegan Paul, 1972).

Incredible Coincidences by Alan Vaughan (Lippincott, New York, 1979).

Coincidences: Chance or Fate? by Ken Anderson (Cassell, 1995).

The Roots of Coincidence by Arthur Koestler (Heinemann, 1972).

Coincidence by Brian Inglis (Hutchinson, 1990).

Time Travel by Jenny Randles (Cassell, 1994).

UFOs

DEFINITION

As most people will know, UFO stands for 'unidentified flying object'. The term describes anything seen in the air with a capacity for flight and which the witness cannot immediately identify.

It is not, as many people assume, the same thing as an *unidentifiable* flying object. Most UFOs, in fact, turn out to be perfectly identifiable and are then given the name IFO (identified flying object). Between 90 and 95 per cent of all reported UFOs are acknowledged by researchers as eventually becoming IFOs after serious investigation. Nor is a UFO synonymous with an alien spacecraft.

Genuine UFOs are simply objects that are not explicable after proper investigation. The alien spacecraft hypothesis which has such popular appeal is one that might apply to some cases – although there are plenty of UFO researchers (or *UFOlogists* as they are known) who accept the reality of unexplained phenomena but deny that any of these are alien spacecraft.

The term UAP – 'unidentified atmospheric phenomenon' – is often now applied by UFOlogists to cover a range of UFO reports for which there is no mundane solution, but which they believe probably relate to some as yet undetermined natural process or processes. This may be linked with atmospheric physics, meteorology, geophysics, electrical phenomena or several other possibilities. It is believed that the understanding of such UAP will help to develop our scientific knowledge, and that one day they will become accepted as a natural part of our environment. Both UAP and IFOs are strongly supported by hard, scientific evidence, and both certainly exist.

UAP were so termed to distinguish them from those cases where witnesses describe apparently structured craft, reputedly of artificial origin and piloted by some kind of intelligence. Whether such cases do describe what they appear to is contentious, but many UFOlogists think that perhaps 1 per cent of total sightings could relate to some kind of constructed vehicle.

HISTORICAL REVIEW

There are records of UFO sightings in many ancient texts, but they were evaluated according to the culture of the day. The Romans, for example, described blazing shields crossing the sky. In medieval times records tell of sailing ships passing through the heavens. And in 1896, when there was a wave of UFO reports across the western USA, witnesses described a gigantic airship along the lines of those in contemporary novels by Jules Verne and others.

Cultural tracking

This phenomenon is known as *cultural tracking.* Throughout the ages UFOs have always seemed to track the level at which a society has reached with its own technology, and to sit just at the edge of what is possible. That in the space age our UFOs should manifest as alien starships is therefore predictable.

It is possible that there have always been UFOs. Indeed, if we think in terms of UAP we know that is so – a number of atmospheric processes for which we now have rational solutions were once given supernatural explanations. Meteors (or shooting stars), for instance, were not understood until the early eighteenth century – but they had whizzed across the heavens for millions of years before that and were given all manner of interpretations, usually as omens or portents.

Foo fighters and flying saucers

During the Second World War two Allied pilots reported seeing strange glowing lights that pursued their aircraft. They gave them the name *foo fighters* after an American cartoon ('foo' probably derived from *feu*, the French for fire). The Americans and British assumed them to be enemy weapons, but after the war it was learnt that German and Japanese air crew had seen them as well. These were the first true examples of UFO sightings in the modern sense. Despite government investigation the mystery was never solved. To this day, despite speculation about atmospheric electrical phenomena, nobody actually knows what they were. Modern aircraft meet them too.

It was on 24 June 1947 that strange things in the sky were first given a popular label. A pilot flying over the Cascade Mountains in Washington State, USA, saw a formation of reflecting objects in the sky. He thought they were secret aircraft, though sceptics suggested they were mirages or reflections off his aircraft canopy. They were probably none of these things. What makes his sighting so significant is that a journalist invented a phrase, *'flying saucers'*, to describe what the pilot had seen. This was not, incidentally, because Arnold's UFOs were saucer-shaped – in fact they were crescents. The 'flying saucer' image came from the curious description that Arnold gave about their *motion* – 'like a saucer skipping across water' or, we might say, a flat stone bouncing across a lake.

Millions looked to the skies in search of these saucers, and the press had a field day writing up their stories. The movie industry perpetuated the myth of saucer-shaped craft. Whilst some people did claim to see saucer-shaped objects, this was never a major factor in the evidence. Fewer than 2 per cent of all sightings can be described as looking like the flying saucers which filled early 1950s' B movies and cemented this illusion into the human subconscious.

The great cover-up

An official investigation programme was launched by the US government in early 1948. It was put in the hands of the military because airmen were making worrying reports of encounters over secret installations. The authorities presumed that the saucers had to be controlled devices. As they knew they were not American, they next had to eliminate the possibility that they were Russian. The only source left (according to the viewpoint of the day) was outer space. The cover-up of UFO evidence was founded on both its military roots (to which confidentiality is a way of life) and this extreme belief about the origin of the mystery, which was evidently taken seriously by senior military personnel during 1948–52.

In July 1947 some wreckage was found by New Mexico rancher William Brazel. It was light and peculiar, yet remarkably strong. He took it to the nearby Roswell air base who promptly told the world that a flying saucer had been captured. Hours later, on orders from the Pentagon, pieces of a weather balloon were put on display (see photograph opposite page 26) and it was announced that it had all been a ghastly mistake. Yet, even as this was happening, the debris was being flown to Wright Patterson air force base in Ohio where the foreign technology division were to attempt to find the real answers. Many feel this was the starting point of the government cover-up to hide the truth. Nearly 50 years later the Roswell debate still rages and in 1995 alleged footage surfaced supposedly showing top secret autopsies on aliens captured from the wreckage. UFOlogists are unconvinced.

In fact, by 1952 the US government investigation, known as Project Blue Book, was radically reviewing its work. The idea of alien spacecraft could not be entirely eliminated, but was looking less and less likely. It was also becoming understood that most UFOs were really IFOs, and theories about some naturally occurring UAP were starting to gain ground. Given the inadequacy of the 'flying saucer' description and the popular myths now associated with that phrase, the term UFO was conjured up as a piece of US air force jargon that better related to what was being reported.

Governments around the world followed the American lead, monitoring the UFO situation and keeping files. Most nations, including Britain, still do so. Specialist intelligence staff and scientific agencies evaluate the thousands of sightings reported every year. Vociferous UFOlogists constantly complain of a cover-up, alleging that the authorities know the truth (that UFOs are alien spaceships visiting the earth) but are too scared to speak out. In fact, it is more likely that such a huge secret could never be withheld from the world. Surely one country would break the stranglehold, or a group of politicians or scientists 'in the know' would leak the truth?

More probably the cover-up results from ignorance rather than knowledge. The unsolved UFO cases largely remain a mystery even to defence chiefs, and they are watched just in case they reveal material that might prove of value. As one senior defence spokesman in Britain told me when he asked for a briefing about UFOs: 'Our job at the Ministry of Defence is not to find out what UFOs are but to see what we can do with any data that emerges. For example, can we understand the science behind them and build a weapon out of it?' This is a far more likely justification for the cover-up.

Meanwhile a four-way split in attitudes towards the phenomenon has developed which has left meaningful research at a standstill for many years. The media sensationalise and trivialise UFOlogy, reporting only the fantastic theories and way-out cases. UFOlogists who support these views get the most attention, selling lots of books, given the most air-time and seeming to reflect 'the truth'. The minority of UFOlogists who take a more serious approach and eschew conspiracy theories find it hard to be heard. They have no funding and only modest support, so can do little real research. The authorities who may have the funding and do the work that such serious UFOlogists would back dare not cooperate with such people, for fear of sending false signals to the public that they 'believe in spaceships'. And they still need to maintain their own discretion. Outside government circles science tends to see UFOlogy via its tabloid image and considers it a waste of time. Consequently few scientists would investigate the matter for themselves to a point at which they might identify some interesting scientific questions.

Finding a way out of this stalemate is essential before any real progress is possible.

EXPERIENCING *UFO*s

If you see something strange in the sky, what should you do about it? The first step ought to be to stop and think. Do not rush off to tell the world. The chances are extremely high that you will only have seen an IFO. There are references that you can consult in your local library (see page 232) to help you judge whether your UFO is worth reporting. But even more important is to try to find another witness as the sighting unfolds. Since most encounters last only a few moments, you need to think fast. If others are present – even strangers passing by – their observation of the UFO will be a great bonus to your testimony. Do not let them walk away without swapping names and addresses – treat the matter as if it were a car accident.

Furthermore, if there is any chance of using a camera, especially a camcorder, do so. Photographic evidence is invaluable. It is tempting to try to zoom in and 'see' the UFO up close. Sadly the vast majority of video images produced in that way result from the camera failing to focus on a light source, and so creating an illusion that looks like a structured object but is in fact a worthless, out-of-focus mess. Keep the camera on wide angle most of the time, to include foreground that will prove invaluable during analysis. Also record a commentary describing the UFO and what it may be doing. Trying to remember and describe such things at a later date will be more difficult than you expect, and your judgement will probably be affected by what you see on the film.

If you have had a sighting – or better still you have filmed something or have other evidence such as your car engine or lights being affected – the next step is to make a report. Obvious places to go are a university, astronomical observatory, airport or police station. Few of these are likely to take your story too seriously, no matter how credible you sound. They may decide to pass your report on to official channels, but the chances are you will never know since they may just fill out a form and file it on some government computer.

Unfortunately, finding a UFO group is not as simple as looking in the Yellow Pages – although astrologers may be listed there, UFOlogists are not. In any case, UFO groups vary greatly in quality. Some are excellent and will work with you to record your sighting or find an answer, but you may end up with a bunch of schoolchildren who have founded a society in their spare time or a body that thinks it is in telepathic contact with Martians.

Some guidelines are offered on page 231, together with a list of a few of the more responsible groups, but if a group is not included that should not imply that they are not reliable. You may need to trust your own judgement and shop around.

RESEARCHING *UFOs*

There are two ways to study the UFO mystery, in the field or in front of a computer screen. Investigating sightings is probably the way most people first come into contact with UFO research. It is an excellent training ground, and UFO sightings are the basis of all research.

In a sense, UFO investigation is like playing detective, doing a jigsaw puzzle and solving a logic problem all at the same time. You need to collect the pieces and try to assemble them, look for clues of possible misidentification and chase them far and wide, and then apply logic to the results. If you have physical or photographic evidence many more problems have to be faced.

Most of the time, whether a case is well investigated or not will be completely down to you. Years later people may consult your evidence on computer files or via a book and form their own conclusions about the mystery, so your responsibility is considerable. Thankfully there is a postal training course in basic investigation skills.

After honing their skills on investigation for a while some people prefer to tackle pure research. This may involve developing a theory to explain some UFO cases and seeking evidence to support it from the files. Computer databases can be a valuable place to start looking for patterns, and statistical trends may provide insights. Those with experience in psychology and sociology may also find profitable ways forward by posing questions about perception, misidentification or other more obscure features of the UFO phenomenon that could be explored through experimentation.

One question UFOlogists are often asked is how a person can become a full-time UFOlogist and what the pay is like! Unfortunately, nobody is paid to be a professional UFO researcher, but you might get a grant to study related questions at a university.

Sadly, getting a grant for physical research, for instance into some type of UAP, is far more difficult. The only possibility is to persuade university departments to help in their spare time or to use your own research facilities to devise and test experiments. The only UFO-related PhD so far awarded by a British university (York) went to a sociologist asking questions about what people believed about UFOs and why.

UFOs TODAY

It is important never to say never: a case that may seem unresolved may finally crack many years after most people have given up the chase. This was what occurred when Irwin Weider decided to reinvestigate a classic photograph, taken by a microbiologist of undoubted sincerity as he crossed the Williamette Pass in Oregon, that had baffled UFOlogists since 1966. The lens-shaped object climbing skyward from a snow-clad tree line seemed to be sucking a plume of powdered snow upward in its wake. Yet, instead of the one blurred image that the eyes of the witness had seen, the film recorded three separate images – suggesting that the UFO had somehow defied physics, dematerialising and then re-materialising several times during the fraction of a second that the camera's shutter was open.

The UFOlogist found that an old signpost on the mountain road gave an image extraordinarily like the triple UFO shot if it was filmed as one passed it at speed in a car. His re-creation of what the old sign was probably like in 1966, using similar speeds and camera lenses, repro-duced a shot so like that of the famed UFO photograph that there was little room for doubt. Nobody imagined that this very promising case would be explained as something as commonplace as a road sign. Weider's work perfectly illustrates the need for lateral thinking and perseverance during research.

Recent terrifying encounters

However, for each case resolved in this way new ones come along to test the investigator. UAP encounters are still continuing. Clas Svahn and Jortgen Granlie investigated such a case in Sweden on 10 February 1994. A woman was driving her Volvo 245 home to Grillby, south of Enkoping, late one night when a bright rectangular light with jagged spokes com-ing out of it appeared over a forest near the Hara turn-off. The big glow illuminated the road around the car and immediately the Volvo started to falter. It lost power and finally coasted to a halt. The fascia lights faded to pale yellow and then went out. Something had drained energy from the vehicle.

The woman got out and summoned help. When her husband finally reached the scene the car started normally. The UFO had long since vanished.

The UFOlogists paid for a thorough investigation of the car's ignition and electrical system, but there were no faults. They could see no reason to doubt the woman's view that the UFO had caused the loss of power. Of course, in this case, as in most others of its type (known as car stops), the UFO was more properly a UAP – and presumably some as yet unidentified natural atmospheric phenomenon.

Strange things like foo fighters have also been pursuing aircraft in greater numbers during recent years. Since the summer of 1991 at least ten cases have been reported in the UK. In January 1995, for example, a British Airways jet heading for Manchester Airport over the Pennines was approached almost head-on by a bright light. The crew even momentarily ducked, fearing a collision. Luckily nothing untoward took place. The Civil Aviation Authority report, released in January 1996, determined that the object was a UFO of unknown origin!

On 1 August 1995, a Boeing 737 of Aerolineas Argentinas had an even more frightening mid-air encounter. As the plane came to land at San Carlos de Bariloche the airport lost all power and was plunged into darkness. The crew had to abort the landing and then, as they climbed upward, observed a dish-shaped object pulsating orange, with green flashes coming from its edges. It seemed to be escorting the jet towards the airport, which was confirmed by a military aircraft flying nearby which saw both the UFO and the Boeing.

After ten minutes the airport regained power, thanks to its own generator. But as the aircraft attempted to land once again, with the UFO still in close attendance, all power across a wide area disappeared, including that supplying houses around the airport. Radio contact was also lost with the ground. The aircraft had to pull up sharply to avoid crash landing in the darkness. As the startled pilots looked on, the UFO now performed some extraordinary movements, flashing beneath them, executing right-angled turns that would be impossible for any airliner, and shooting away into the distance within just a couple of seconds. Power returned to the airport and the 737 landed safely.

It scarcely matters what these UFOs are – and they may again be some strange type of UAP. Terrifying encounters such as these are occurring on an alarming basis and putting air traffic at risk. Science surely cannot continue to ignore them, or a disaster may follow.

SOURCES

There are more local and national groups in existence, and a larger number of books available, on UFOs than on any other topic covered in this volume. It is impossible even to recommend most of these, so the notes that follow simply offer a good place to start.

ORGANISATIONS AND PERIODICALS

Some of the organisations and publications mentioned in other sections are well worth considering. The *J. Allen Hynek Center for UFO Studies* and *MUFON* (for addresses see page 19) are probably the leading American groups. Associations and journals such as *New UFOlogist*, *Enigmas* (Scotland), *Clas Svahn* in Sweden and the *Australian Centre* featured in the Abduction, Crop Circle and Ghost sections (see pages 20, 111 and 67) all spend a large percentage of their time effectively investing UFO reports. There are others. As with all sections of this book, the annotated index will help in this regard.

Northern UFO News lists active regional groups in much of Britain and will forward sightings to a reliable group in all parts of the UK. If you send a stamped addressed envelope to the *Northern UFO News* address it will provide details of its six-month course which assists students to develop their investigation skills and ends with an examination and certificate. It has been sub-let to associations covering Scotland and Wales and is otherwise available throughout the UK for a small fee (£10 in 1995).

An asterisk below indicates that either an English language edition or summary of the major issue content of a magazine is published. Other journals are in English. The excellent new venture *Trans-UFO* translates non-English material and provides a great source of new case histories, notably from Europe.

Just Cause is a good specialist review of the latest sober research into the alleged UFO cover-up.

UFO Afrinews   *PO Box MP49, Mount Pleasant, Harare, Zimbabwe.*

AFU (Scandinavia)*   *Box 11027, 600 11 Norrkoping, Sweden.*

UFO Nyt*   *SUFOI Postbox 6, DK 2820, Gentofte, Denmark.*

CENAP*   *Postbox 520231, D-68246, Mannheim, Germany.*

NUFOC*   *Tien Esteenweg 78/401, 3800 Sint-Truiden, Belgium.*

Phenomena* *SOS Ovni, BP 324, 13611 Aix-en-Provence, Cedex 1, France.*

Northern UFO News *11 Pike Court, Fleetwood, Lancashire, FY7 8QF, UK.*

Trans-UFO *Derwent Cottage, Derwent Dam, Bamford, Sheffield, S30 2AQ, UK.*

Just Cause *PO Box 176, Stoneham, MA 02180, USA.*

Finally, *BUFORA* has a news and information line, updated at weekends, which offers the latest on UFO sightings, research activity, lectures, conferences, books and so on. It can be called anywhere from the UK at premium line rates (36p per minute off peak in 1995) via *UFO CALL 0891 – 12 18 86*.

BOOKS

Of the following books, that by Hough and me gives a general historical overview, Jacobs provides a detailed look at the social response to UFOs in the USA from 1947 for the first three decades, and Ruppelt offers very good first-hand insight on the government investigation over the first ten years. Hynek looks at the cases and assesses them from a positive scientific aspect, whereas the Condon report is negative in conclusion but provides the most in-depth scientific appraisal of the subject available. It was funded by a US government grant and run by a team of scientists at Colorado University over a two-year period. The Page and Sagan book is in debate format and offers a wealth of study of individual cases by several scientists. My more recent book is a colourful guide to witnesses to help you evaluate your own sighting and determine whether it might be a UFO or IFO. Hendry's book is aimed more at investigators and is an excellent field manual for those wishing to become UFOlogists. The alleged cover-up is featured by Good in an exhaustive but forceful tone and by Fawcett and Greenwood via a sober reflection on documents released by Freedom of Information laws in the USA. For more unusual theories the books by Keel and Vallée are worth a look. Finally, for a look at UAP you should also study the books by Devereux and Project Hessdalen (see Earth Mysteries) and Randles and Fuller (see Crop Circles).

The Complete book of UFOs by Peter Hough and Jenny Randles (Piatkus, 1994).

The UFO Controversy in America by David Jacobs (Indiana University Press, Bloomington, IN, 1975).

The Report on UFOs by Edward Ruppelt (Doubleday, New York, 1956).

The UFO Experience by J. Allen Hynek (Corgi, 1973).

Scientific study of UFOs edited by Edward Condon (Bantam, New York, 1969).

UFOs: A Scientific Debate edited by Thornton Page and Carl Sagan (Cornell University, Ithaca, NY, 1972).

UFOs and How to See Them by Jenny Randles (Anaya, 1992).

The UFO Handbook by Allan Hendry (Doubleday, New York, 1979).

Above Top Secret by Tim Good (Sidgwick & Jackson, 1987; updated as **Beyond Top Secret**, 1996).

Clear Intent by Larry Fawcett and Barry Greenwood (Prentice-Hall, New York, 1984).

Operation Trojan Horse by John Keel (Putnam, New York, 1970).

Passport to Magonia by Jacques Vallée (C. W. Daniel, 1970).

ZOOLOGICAL MYSTERIES

DEFINITION

There are hundreds of thousands of species of animal on the planet today, of which mankind is just a single example. Because of changing ecological conditions species are dying out at the rate of at least a hundred a year.

From time to time we lose a major group of creatures. One of the most famous examples is the giant flightless bird called the dodo, which was hunted to death when humans first began serious exploration of the East. But just how extinct are some of these long-gone creatures? The quite similar-looking moa followed the dodo to the evolutionary graveyard in the mid-nineteenth century, yet reports of occasional sightings continue.

Part of the search for zoological anomalies is to tackle that very question – researching legends and rumours that in some remote location survivors may live on. They are often creatures only recently thought to be extinct, like the moa, in which case they are less of an anomaly and more a scientific birthday present should they be found. But when the animals concerned were believed to have died out millions of years ago, the position changes dramatically. Claims of their continued existence are often rejected by all mainstream zoologists and find their way into the hands of a branch of research known as cryptozoology – literally *puzzle animals*. Cryptozoologists battle like other paranormal researchers for the truth as they see it.

'Puzzle animals' even better describes the second major aspect of the field – creatures that are utterly unknown. Stories about entities such as the bigfoot or yeti represent a species that is talked of in legend and reputedly witnessed in reality, but which science unilaterally claims does not exist and never has existed beyond imagination. We then enter a much more obviously paranormal universe where the quest for physical evidence struggles to convince and some researchers openly propose more exotic, supernatural theories to account for these mysterious creatures.

HISTORICAL REVIEW

Until European travellers started to explore new continents in the sixteenth century many of the animals now familiar in zoos were totally

234

unknown to most humans. Indeed, when explorers first brought back giraffes and rhinos these were openly laughed at as freaks. Gradually, as more people made the journey, scientists drew on-the-spot sketches and more specimens were captured, doubts slowly dissipated.

Treasures from the deep

The sea, which is still mostly unexplored, is a rich area for these discoveries. In December 1995, the fourth brand-new group of animals this century was found lurking here, when a minute blood-sucking creature like a two-headed monster from a horror movie was revealed to live inside the mouth of a Norwegian lobster (more familiarly known as scampi). The fact that something unique can turn up in the late twentieth century indicates that there may well be other things out there still undiscovered. However, there is a great difference between a creature a few millimetres long living deep in the ocean and one as large as a man supposedly wandering about on dry land.

Abominable snowmen

The frozen heights of the Himalayas and the impenetrable African jungles are two regions where there is a good chance of cryptozoological finds of major proportions. It is indeed these two locations where the strongest modern legends persist.

Tales of the yeti (or abominable snowman, as it is sometimes known) surfaced when serious mountaineers began their attempts to conquer Everest and the surrounding peaks in the 1920s. They heard many stories from local people about the white-furred hairy human-like creature of great strength that lived in the snows. Alleged examples of yeti scalps are still preserved at monasteries in the area, but considered to be religious artefacts held for show and not true specimens. There have been sightings of the yeti by explorers and mountaineers, and close calls where camps have been disturbed by some nocturnal intruder or photographs taken of the large tracks that climb the slopes through virgin snow. But no probative film of the creature itself is in existence.

This suggests that the yeti is either very rare or the stories about it are misperceptions of other animals. Indeed, the fact that no bodies have ever been found on the mountainsides remains a real problem for zoologists, although it might be argued that the creature would bury its dead, as many ape-like creatures were known to do millions of years ago.

Moreover, the yeti legend does not stand alone: astoundingly similar creatures feature in the folklore of most remote, hilly areas. In Europe they are known as almas and their skin is brown. In Australia aboriginal legends tell of the yowie, with its foul stench and dark, matted hair – another common characteristic reported worldwide. And, of course, native Americans in the west of both the USA and Canada have long known of the sasquatch – now more commonly known by the name coined by settlers, bigfoot, from huge footprints sometimes observed in the mud.

The consistency of accounts such as these suggests that there may be truth behind the stories. However, aside from a controversial piece of ciné film taken in October 1967 in the Six Rivers Forest area of California there is little solid evidence. This film clearly shows a creature of the bigfoot type and is undoubtedly either genuine proof of the creature or a hoax created by a man wearing a gorilla suit, as sceptics unsurprisingly allege. But the overall lack of physical evidence bedevils those researching these so-called man-beasts, despite frequent attempts to track them down in countries, notably the USA, where that ought not to be impossible given mass communication.

The Loch Ness monster and its relatives

The African Congo is said to house an even more remarkable creature, according to stories that first surfaced at the start of the twentieth century from missionaries who had probed the deepest jungle to face headhunting tribes, deadly snakes and killer insects. They had heard about the *mkoele mbembe*, a thirty-foot-high, long-necked animal that lived in the water systems around Lake Tele and appeared to be a living dinosaur.

The most famed example of such a creature is the Loch Ness monster – a long-necked, water-living animal of quite similar proportions that has figured in legend since the sixth century but was not seen in real numbers until the early 1930s, when a new road beside this beautiful Scottish waterway made more of its shoreline visible to passers by. A photograph of the neck of the monster was taken by a London surgeon in 1934 and published by the *Daily Mail*, to global acclaim. This led to monster-hunting expeditions, further sightings, more photographs and the creation of a big local tourist industry, which has become such an important part of the rural economy that it may need to self-perpetuate regardless of the evidence.

Loch Ness is a deep, peat-ridden watercourse that fills a geological rift. It was formed millions of years ago when dinosaurs did live in the area, and cut off from the sea after the last ice age. The idea that a colony might have become trapped and somehow survived in this small ecosystem gave a semblance of credibility to the stories – which, frankly, rarely deserved it on the strength of their evidence alone. Numerous scientific expeditions have used ever more sophisticated methods to find the elusive proof that Nessie is real. Every summer the boats come out, bristling with radar, sonar and underwater cameras. Every autumn they go home disappointed.

However, what probably establishes the credibility of the Loch Ness story more than anything else is that, like the yeti, it is not an isolated example. The bridge between a Scottish loch and the African Congo, each with its own closely similar water-dwelling dinosaurs, includes reports from almost every major lake system in the world.

But once again the question arises: if there are so many cousins of Nessie, where are the bodies? There is not one shred of physical evidence to support the existence of these creatures.

What has made the Congo so attractive to cryptozoologists – and several expeditions by French, American and British scientists have been there in the last twenty years – is that there are strong claims about natives capturing one of the animals in 1959. Because the creatures reportedly leave the water to eat the flowering liana plants on the tops of high trees, they are readily visible. They appear to be fairly gentle creatures and have not been granted the status of some ferocious beast which heroes from the tribe could hunt and kill. If the stories are just myth this would be surprising. It matches what we know about the real creature that is potentially involved, if the stories have a basis in reality. Unlike the familiar images of science fiction, this type of dinosaur was probably no threat to man.

Some of the Congo expeditions have had close encounters, but none has brought home proof. One French scientist even claims to have seen the creature at close quarters in May 1983, but filmed it on a macro setting of his camera by mistake – the result was a blurred mess. The accounts recorded from local people all match and imply that the animal might be an atlantasaurus, a herbivorous dinosaur that lived in this region during the Cretaceous period, over sixty million years ago. The Congo has altered remarkably little during that time, so it is more than possible that a small group could have survived. The race is on to find them.

EXPERIENCING ZOOLOGICAL MYSTERIES
—

The chances that you will see a dinosaur in the African rainforest or encounter a yeti whilst climbing K2 are remote. If you do happen upon such things, you are unlikely to be alone or without some kind of camera. Both will be vital.

Witnessing something on Loch Ness during a weekend break, or seeing a strange animal such as a jungle cat in a place where no big cats should exist (see page 239), is rather more feasible. Again, you may well be in a position to obtain other witnesses and photographs. If you are, do not pass up this once-in-a-lifetime opportunity.

There are many sources for possible misidentification. Often, for example, lake monsters are nothing more than small creatures such as otters swimming near the surface. If you assume that the animal is larger and further away than it really is, strange perceptions can follow. Being in a place like Loch Ness with its legendary associations is sure to enhance your expectations.

Locals also know that boat wakes can be seen on the water surface many minutes after the vessel that has made them has completely disappeared. Quite a few reports of the monster, including some of the best photographic evidence, simply show anomalous ripples like these. Alternative explanations must therefore always be considered.

It is probably a very good idea to discuss your sighting with someone who lives in the area and has local knowledge. They may well offer a perfectly reasonable solution which you as a visitor had simply never considered. For instance, it is believed that methane gas from rotting vegetation on the floor of a lake can cause rafts of leaves or dead tree trunks to float to the surface and then sink deep down again. It is easy to imagine what this would look like from a distant shoreline.

Thankfully, it is not essential these days to rush to the media to report what you have seen. There are now reputable cryptozoological organisations which will be interested in your evidence and do all they can to study the case. As they are usually formed by professional zoologists they should be your first stop – although, failing that, you could consult a zoologist at a local university or wildlife park.

RESEARCHING ZOOLOGICAL MYSTERIES

Perhaps the simplest opportunity to get involved is to research another aspect of cryptozoology not yet discussed: out-of-place animals, or alien animals as they are sometimes known. Unfortunately, this term is easily misunderstood by the public. When researcher Peter Hough used it naturally enough during an interview, discussing an investigation he was mounting into the sighting of a big cat in Lancashire in the spring of

1995, the story gathered momentum and arrived on television as a cat from outer space! Alien, in this context means not local to the environment in question. That is certainly how one would have to describe these big cats, which are said to resemble lynx or pumas.

Britain has had a whole spate of reports since the mid-1960s when the so-called Surrey Puma was alleged to have killed sheep and the police launched an investigation. A fuzzy photograph of a large, cat-like animal was taken by one policeman at Worplesden, but the creature was never caught. Periodically since then big cats have been reported from many parts of Britain, with the most famous being frequently described by farmers and other local people on Exmoor and in Devon and Cornwall. There have been several attempts to hunt down 'the beast', as it is known, involving the police and army as well as hordes of worried farmers anxious to protect their livestock. These have always ended in failure, although paw prints, a number of photographs and, more recently, some video film have been obtained.

An investigator can certainly join the quest by tracking down reports and accumulating evidence on such alien big cats – sometimes known as ABCs. Most of the sightings do not reach the media and doorstepping in rural communities can produce new evidence of potential value.

ZOOLOGICAL MYSTERIES TODAY

The Loch Ness story suffered two big blows in 1994. First, Adrian Shine, a leading cryptozoologist who has spent considerable time at the loch, speculated that the animal which he believes to be there may only be a giant fish. There have been reports of freak sturgeon up to twenty feet long in some parts of the world, and sturgeon are known to live in the loch. But he still feels that, whatever the answer, there is something of zoological interest down there.

Hoaxes and misidentifications

Then zoologist David Martin and Loch Ness researcher Alastair Boyd reported that they had tracked down the truth behind the famous 'surgeon's photograph' from 1934 – the case that had initiated modern interest in the monster. By interviewing people who claimed to have been involved at the time, they extracted a confession that it was just a hoax. Researchers had long argued that computer studies of the photo suggested from the ripples that this was not a large object, as it would be if it were a monster's neck, but something only inches long. Indeed, if the confession is to be believed, the monster was fabricated out of a toy submarine and some plastic wood by a skilled model-maker whose joke went further than expected and became too hard to explain.

Phantom creatures?

In September 1995 more depressing news came with the results of a Ministry of Agriculture investigation into the beast of Bodmin in Cornwall. No big cat, alien or otherwise, was found. There were no bodies, no physical evidence and nothing that the experts considered positive.

It is believed that some ABCs may be animals that have escaped from wildlife collections, or even from country houses where they were being illegally kept as pets. However, they are thought unlikely to be able to survive in the wild for long, and certainly not to breed. So this is probably not the answer to the lengthy catalogue of cases – or what researcher Andy Roberts delightfully terms the many ongoing 'cat flaps'.

Some of the photographic evidence in Bodmin was thought to be of dogs such as alsatians, which could resemble big cats from a distance. Other shots were too fuzzy to identify. Not all witnesses find this conclusion believable, and there remains a strong body of opinion that there are ABCs out there.

However just as with bigfoot and the yeti, there are no ABC carcasses, or even bones, found in the wild. Cryptozoologist Dr Karl Shuker made a detailed study of those few alleged bodies which have been discovered for a December 1995 report. He found that some were wild cats (a slightly larger cousin of the domestic cat), others were ordinary cats that had gone feral, one or two were even a hybrid between the wild cat and prowling domestic moggies. But there was no sign of a genuine lynx or puma, despite countless reports which suggested that they should be out there by the score. This elusiveness is an increasingly intriguing aspect of the evidence. It is almost as if the animals appear and disappear like phantoms.

Windows on other worlds

More free-thinking cryptozoologists speculate about parallel worlds, other dimensions or window areas which allow such creatures briefly to enter our reality and then to disappear. It is certainly true that in some locations around the planet far greater numbers of strange occurrences have taken place than chance should dictate. These are the locations where UFO close encounters, alien spacenappings, timeslips and weird apparitions all seem to congregate. They also happen to be the places where alien animals roam. For example, the quarries of the Pennines in northern England are home to the best UFO evidence in the UK, as well as to more alien abductions than anywhere else in Europe. There have also been several outbreaks of big cat sightings here. In Texas there are the famous Marfa lights that have puzzled local citizens for years, as well as seemingly reliable accounts of winged creatures that resemble the pteranadon – a long-extinct aerial dinosaur.

What does it mean? As you will see elsewhere in this book (Earth Mysteries, page 79; Crop Circles, page 52; UFOs, page 223) much investigation is taking place into the idea that atmospheric energies can be generated at such hyperactive locations as a result of geological processes going on there. Other evidence implies that these energies may cause interference in the brain wave patterns of some people who pass through or live there, triggering hallucinations. Perhaps alien animals are just another example of these intrusions from the nether world, and emerge not from zoos but from out of our collective unconscious?

Of course, the few photographs and limited physical evidence are difficult to square with this – and even the geological activity that has undoubtedly occurred around Loch Ness may not be enough to convince a monster hunter that Nessie should be regarded as a hallucination. That is why some people believe that these creatures do somehow take on temporary (but none the less real) residence in our world, only to vanish back through the window whence they came. Some cryptozoologists propose that this means stepping back into a parallel dimension. Others wonder if the force of the collective mind might not be so strong as to allow our belief to become extraordinarily powerful after many years of legend and mythology. Is that somehow enough to shape a monster out of whole cloth?

These zoological enigmas seem to defy simple resolution; they do not appear to be ordinary animals hiding from mankind. It is surely forgivable that more revolutionary ideas are sometimes sought by researchers to try to understand their seemingly magical nature.

SOURCES

ORGANISATIONS AND PERIODICALS

The International Society of Cryptozoology publishes learned reports via their journal *Cryptozoology*, available via *Professor Bernard Heuvelmans, Box 43070, Tucson, AZ 85733, USA.*

For the Loch Ness monster there is good irregular coverage in *Enigmas* (for address see page 111).

Articles on cryptozoology, particularly the latest sightings, appear in most issues of *Fortean Times* (for address see page 151). An annual book-length digest, *Fortean Studies*, is often packed with relevant material – the 1996 edition, for instance, contains the in-depth report into big cat carcasses by Dr Karl Shuker.

Fortean Studies (edited by Steve Moore)　*20 Paul Street, Frome, Somerset, BA11 1DX, UK.*

Strange magazine also features regular reports and has an unequalled facility to offer old and new books on cryptozoology from around the world.

Strange Books　*PO Box 2246, Rockville, MD 20847, USA.*

The following organisations and journals also cover the field either regularly or infrequently. *Annals* offers news updates on stories including cryptozoology. *Animals and Man* is the journal of the Centre for Fortean Zoology.

Animals and Man　*15 Holne Court, Exwick, Exeter, Devon, EX4 2NA, UK.*

Annals　*Apt 4G, Preston Manor, Wick Hollow, Glastonbury, Somerset, BA6 8JQ, UK.*

Bigfoot Info Research Center　*21 Benham Street, Apt F, Bristol, CT 06010, USA.*

Borderland Sciences Research Foundation　*PO Box 429, Garberville, CA 95440, USA.*

Dead of Night　*156 Bolton Road East, New Ferry, Merseyside, L62 4RY, UK.*

International Fortean Organisation　*PO Box 367, Arlington, VA 22210–0367, USA.*

Nessletter　*Huntshieldford, St John's Chapel, Bishop Auckland, Co. Durham, DL13 1RQ, UK.*

BOOKS

Some very good general reviews of the subject have appeared. Bord (1980) is a good place to start. The titles by Heuvelmans, Mackal (1980) and Shuker (1991) are written by scientists and cryptozoologists and together reflect thirty-three years of progress. The book by Healy and Cropper is a rare but worthy look at Australian cryptozoology, which is as rich as you might expect. Specific research into bigfoot, ABCs, dinosaurs and Nessie are evident from the book titles. Francis tells more of the hunts to trap the cats, Shuker of the possible science behind them. Campbell's book is a well-argued critique of Nessie, although his idiosyncratic writing might be a little frustrating to some. Mackal (1976) offers the best scientific report, while TV newsreader (and long-time monster hunter) Witchell tells the human story well. Meurger offers a folklore and mythological perspective. Shiels, an allegedly real-life wizard who has invoked and then filmed monsters, provides a unique and bizarre angle on cryptozoology. Clark and Coleman argue the more esoteric side of encounters well. Keel and Holliday step into those parallel dimensions more than anyone; although my book tries to set up a more current working hypothesis along these lines (Keel's is a 1994 update of a twenty-five-year-old book originally called *Strange Creatures from Time and Space*). Barker and Wilson wrote the official report into the Bodmin beast as conducted for the British government.

Alien Animals by Janet and Colin Bord (Grafton, 1980).

On the Track of Unknown Animals by Bernard Heuvelmans (Hart Davis, 1958).

Searching for Hidden Animals by Roy Mackal (Doubleday, New York, 1980).

Extraordinary Animals Worldwide by Karl Shuker (Robert Hale, 1991).

Out of the Shadows by Tony Healy and Paul Cropper (Ironbark, Australia, 1994).

Cat Country: The Quest for the British Big Cat by Di Francis (David & Charles, 1983).

The Loch Ness Monster: The Evidence by Steuart Campbell (Aquarian Press, 1986).

The Monsters of Loch Ness by Roy Mackal (MacDonald, 1976).

The Loch Ness Story by Nicholas Witchell (Corgi, 1990).

Lake Monster Traditions by Michael Meurger (Fortean Tomes, 1988).

Monstrum by Doc Shiels (Fortean Tomes, 1990).

Creatures of the Outer Edge by Jerome Clark and Loren Coleman (Warner, 1978).

The Complete Guide to Mysterious Beings by John Keel (Strange Books, Rockville, MD, 1994).

The Goblin Universe by F.W. Holliday (Llewellyn Books, 1986).

The Dragon and the Disk by F.W. Holliday (Sidgwick & Jackson, 1973).

The Evidence for the Presence of Large Exotic Cats in the Bodmin Area and Their Possible Impact on Livestock by Simon Barker and Charles Wilson (Ministry of Agriculture, Food and Fisheries, 1995).

Mind Monsters by Jenny Randles (Aquarian Press, 1991).

Bigfoot, Yeti and Sasquatch in Myth and Reality by John Napier (E.P. Dutton, 1973).

The Evidence for Bigfoot and Other Man-beasts by Janet and Colin Bord (Aquarian Press, 1984).

A Living Dinosaur? by Roy Mackal (E.J. Brill, 1987).

Mystery Cats of the World by Karl Shuker (Robert Hale, 1989).

SPECIALIST SOURCES

It is often difficult to obtain books and publications about the paranormal, as only a few of the most current titles are carried in all but the largest bookshops. The purpose of this final section of the book is to assist you in locating specialist material.

Most of the leading organisations referenced throughout this book (see section headings in the index for particular subject areas) produce their own journals and, if you send them a stamped self-addressed envelope or an international reply coupon, will advise on the availability of back issues or the possibility of gaining access for research.

A number of the societies have case files that are accessible to bona fide researchers, usually with some restrictions to protect the identities of witnesses. Research via organisations such as ASSAP, BUFORA and the SPR is possible through such means. There are probably many other opportunities, and it is always worth asking.

Some associations retain computerised data that can be searched. Others such as NARO in north-west England, have hard copy case files in central Manchester which can be consulted. The internet and world wide web are a rapidly expanding area of data available to researchers – mostly consisting of news and discussion of current topics, but also with some access to case files. Sites are many and varied and quite a number of magazines such as *Fortean Times* and *The Skeptic* now put material from their magazines on-line.

Some of the organisations also have excellent reference libraries of books that cover their specialist areas. These can either be consulted or are sometimes available on loan following payment of a refundable deposit. In most countries the library system also collects material, and at least one regional library will have a specialist collection. This is often not on display but can be perused on request. In the UK, for example, Newcastle-on-Tyne central library has an extensive collection of UFO files, books and specialist magazines from the field.

A library of hundreds of audio (and many video) recordings of lectures in Britain and the USA, mostly UFO-related and dating back over thirty years, is available from:

Robin Lindsey   *87 Station Road, Whittlesey, Peterborough, PE7 1UE, UK.*

Another useful source of video archive material across a wide range of paranormal topics is:

Rodney Haworth   *37 Sandyway Drive, Harle Syke, Burnley, Lancashire, BB10 2JS, UK.*

A large SAE should be sent to either source for a listing of what is currently available. Rodney Haworth may well be able to initiate customised searches.

A free (no obligation to purchase) search for rare titles in the field is offered by:

Booktrace International   *Dept F, PO Box 45, Totnes, Devon, TQ9 5XP, UK.*

There are also a number of specialist booksellers who offer mail order on a wide range of titles. This is often the only way for people living outside cities to get hold of even current titles, let alone older or out-of-print books that are still important. The list which follows is certainly not complete (although if anyone wishes to advise me of further examples for inclusion in any future edition I would be pleased to hear from them at the address given on page 5). All sources offer the latest and major in-print titles across a range of paranormal subjects. The addition of a letter (C) indicates that they will supply a catalogue if you send postage and an (S) that they also sell second-hand, out-of-print titles. These latter sources may also be able to search for rarer titles upon request.

Altered States (C)   *4 Gundry St, Newton, Auckland, New Zealand.* Also titles on lucid dreaming and technology.

Aquarian Book Centre   *Shop 3, The Galleria, Cradock Avenue, Rosebank, Johannesburg, South Africa.*

Arcturus Books (C)   *1443 SE Port St, Lucie Boulevard, Port St Lucie, FL 34952, USA.*

Atlantis Bookshop (S)   *49a Museum St, London WC1A 1LY, UK.*

Australian Skeptics   *PO Box A2324, Sydney, NSW 2000, Australia.*

Excalibur Books (C)   *1 Hillside Gardens, Bangor, Co. Down, BT19 6SJ, Ireland.*

Midnight Books (C) (S)   *The Mount, Ascerton Road, Sidmouth, Devon, EX10 2BT, UK.*

Nexus (C)   *PO Box 30, Mapleton, Queensland 4560, Australia.*

Phenomenal Books (C) (S)   *14 Gresham Road, Thornton-Cleveleys, Lancs, FY5 3EE, UK.*

Prometheus Books (C) (Skeptical Fortean)   *700 East Amherst St, Buffalo, NY 14215, USA.*

Psychic Press (C)   *Clock Cottage, Stansted Hall, Stansted Mountfitchet, Essex, CM24 8UD, UK.*

Quest UFO Publications (C)   *PO Box XG60, Leeds, LS15 9XD, UK.*

Spacelink Books (C)   *115 Hollybush Lane, Hampton, Middlesex, TW12 2QY, UK.*

Specialist Knowledge (C)   *20 Paul Street, Frome, Somerset, BA11 1DX, UK.* Specify subject areas.

Strange Books (C)   *PO Box 2246, Rockville, MD 20847, USA.*

Sydney Esoteric Books (C)   *408 Elizabeth St, Surry Hills, NSW 2010, Australia.*

UFO Library (C)   *11684 Ventura Boulevard, Suite 708, Studio City, CA 91604, USA.*

GENERAL INDEX

SOURCES INDEX

This listing by subject refers you to active contact points that study each of these areas. The page reference in brackets will lead you to the address.

ALIEN ABDUCTION & UFOS ACUFOS (p. 19), UFORA (p. 19), BUFORA (p. 19), NARO (p. 19) UFORIC (p. 19), Becassine (p. 19), CUFOS (p. 19), UFO Witness Group (p. 19), Intruders' Foundation (p. 19), New UFOlogist (p. 20), MUFON (p. 20), UFO Sweden (p. 67), SPI Enigmas (p. 111), Fortean Times (p. 151), Journal of Scientific Exploration (p. 202), The Anomalist (p. 213), UFO Afrinews (p. 231), AFU (p. 231), UFO Nyt (p. 231), CENEP (p. 231), NUFOC (p. 231), Phenomena (p. 232), Northern UFO News (p. 232)

ANGELS ASSAP (p. 28), Strange (p. 28), Angels & Fairies (p. 28), AURA Z (p. 122), IUFOPRA (p. 141), Promises & Disappointments (p. 141), Fate (p. 187)

BALL LIGHTNING ASSAP (p. 28), TORRO (p. 39), Information Centre (p. 39), Journal of Meteorology (p. 39), AURA Z (p. 122), INFO (p. 129), Sourcebook Project (p. 129)

COSMIC MESSAGES New Light (p. 50), Concept Synergy (p. 50), The Voice (p. 50), Mind, Body & Soul (p. 50), Nexus (p. 50), Promises & Disappointments (p. 141)

CROP CIRCLES Journal of Meteorology (p. 39), Crop Watcher (p. 66), Circular (p. 66), North American Institute (p. 66), Australian Ground Effects (p. 66), UFO Sweden (p. 66), GEM (p. 90), IUFOPRA (p. 141), Fortean Times (p. 151)

DREAMS ASSAP (p. 28), London College (p. 78), Institute for Psychophysical Research (p. 78), Lucidity Project (p. 78), ELF (p. 78), SPR (p. 100), Psychic News (p. 121), ASPR (p. 141), Fate (p. 187), Theta (p. 187)

EARTH MYSTERIES Ley Hunter (p. 90), GEM (p. 90), London Earth Mysteries (p. 90), Northern Earth (p. 90), RILKO (p. 90), Stonehenge Viewpoint (p. 90), Stonewatch (p. 90)

ESP NARO (p. 19), ASSAP (p. 28), SPR (p. 100), SPI Enigmas (p. 111), Psychic News (p. 121), ASPR (p. 141), IUFOPRA (p. 141), Fate (p. 187), Theta (p. 187), Journal of Scientific Exploration (p. 202)

GHOSTS NARO (p. 19), ASSAP (p. 28), Strange (p. 28), Institute for Psychophysical Research (p. 78), Parapsychology Foundation (p. 111), SPI Enigmas (p. 111), Ghosttrackers (p. 111), Ghostwatch (p. 111), Psychic News (p. 121), ASPR (p. 141), IUFOPRA (p. 141), Fortean Times (p. 151), Fate (p. 187), Annals (p. 222), Dead of Night (p. 242)

HEALING Mind, Body & Soul (p. 50), Nexus (p. 50), Matthew Manning Centre (p. 121), Federation of Spiritual Healers (p. 121), Healing Centre (p. 121), Psychic News (p. 121), AURA Z (p. 122), Australian Spiritualist Association (p. 141)

ICE BOMBS NARO (p. 19), Strange (p. 28), Journal of Meteorology (p. 39), INFO (p. 129), Sourcebook Project (p. 129), Fortean Times (p. 151)

LIFE AFTER DEATH NARO (p. 19), ASSAP (p. 28), SPR (p. 100), SPI Enigmas (p. 111), Psychic News (p. 121), ASPR (p. 141), Australian Spiritualist Association (p. 141), IUFOPRA (p. 141), Metascience (p. 141), Noah's Ark Society (p. 141), Promises & Disappointments (p. 141), Spiritualist Church of Canada (p. 141), Two Worlds (p. 141), Fate (p. 187), PSI Researcher (p. 187)

MIRACLE IMAGES NARO (p. 19), ASSAP (p. 28), AURA Z (p. 122), INFO (p. 129), FUFOR (p. 151), Mars Mission (p. 151), Fortean Times (p. 151), The Anomalist (p. 213)

NDEs NARO (p. 19), SPR (p. 100), Psychic News (p. 121), ASPR (p. 141), University of the West of England (p. 160), University of Connecticut (p. 160), IANDS (p. 160), Journal of Scientific Exploration (p. 202)

OUT-OF-BODY EXPERIENCES NARO (p. 19), Mind, Body & Soul (p. 50), Nexus (p. 50), London College (p. 78), SPR (p. 100), SPI Enigmas (p. 111), Psychic News (p. 121), ASPR (p. 141), University of the West of England (p. 160), University of Connecticut (p. 160), PSI Researcher (p. 187)

POLTERGEISTS NARO (p. 19), ASSAP (p. 28), SPR (p. 100), SPI Enigmas (p. 111), Psychic News (p. 121), ASPR (p. 141), Fate (p. 187), PSI Researcher (p. 187), Theta (p. 187)

PRECOGNITION NARO (p. 19), ASSAP (p. 28), SPR (p. 100), SPI Enigmas (p. 111), Psychic News (p. 121), ASPR (p. 141), Fate (p. 187), PSI Researcher (p. 187), Theta (p. 187)

REINCARNATION ASSAP (p. 28), Nexus (p. 50), Psychic News (p. 121), Reincarnation International (p. 202), Atlantis (p. 202), Journal of Scientific Exploration (p. 202), Association for Past Life Research (p. 202)

SKEPTICISM The Skeptic (p. 141), Skeptical Inquirer (p. 151)

SPONTANEOUS HUMAN COMBUSTION NARO (p. 19), Strange (p. 28), AURA Z (p. 122), INFO (p. 129), Fortean Times (p. 151), The Anomalist (p. 213)

SYNCHRONICITY NARO (p. 19), ASSAP (p. 28), SPR (p. 100), Fortean Times (p. 151), Fate (p. 187), PSI Researcher (p. 187), The Anomalist (p. 213), Incidence of Coincidence (p. 222), Annals (p. 222), Folklore Frontiers (p. 222)

ZOOLOGICAL MYSTERIES Strange (p. 28), SPI Enigmas (p. 111), AURA Z (p. 122), INFO (p. 129), Fortean Times (p. 151), Journal of Scientific Exploration (p. 202), The Anomalist (p. 213), Annals (p. 222), Cryptozoology (p. 241), Animals and Man (p. 242), Bigfoot Info (p. 242), Borderland Science (p. 242), Nessletter (p. 242)

LEICESTERSHIRE LIBRARIES AND INFORMATION SERVICE — REFERENCE & INFORMATION LIBRARY HUMANITIES